Improve
and
Modify
MGB

Lindsay Porter

Foulis

Haynes

A FOULIS Motoring Book

First published 1988
Reprinted 1992

© Porter Publishing & Haynes Publishing Group 1988

Published by:
Haynes Publishing Group,
    Sparkford, Nr Yeovil,
    Somerset BA22 7JJ, England

Haynes Publications Inc.,
    861 Lawrence Drive,
    Newbury Park,
    California 91320 USA

Produced by:
Porter Publishing,
The Storehouse, Little Hereford Street,
Bromyard, Herefordshire HR7 4DE, England

British Library Cataloguing in Publication Data
Porter, Lindsay, 1949-
Improve & Modify: MGB.
1. Cars, Maintenance & repair - Amateur's manuals
I. Title
6.29.28 '722
ISBN 0-85429-668-9
Library of Congress Catalog Card No: 88-80840
US softback edition ISBN 0 85429 749 9

Editor: Lindsay Porter

Design, typesetting and artwork:
    Typestyle, Sea King Road, Lynx Trading Estate, Yeovil,
    Somerset BA20 2NZ, England

Printed in England by: J. H. Haynes & Co. Ltd.,

Contents

Contents

Foreword

By Roche Bentley

Roche Bentley had the idea in 1973 of introducing a Club for MG owners which concentrated mainly on the MGB, MGB GT, Midget, MGC and other post-war MG classics. Few imagined then that the Club would grow to become the largest one-make car club in the world and that the Club's motto, 'Enjoying MG', would echo the sentiments of hundreds of thousands of MG owners everywhere. Through the Club magazine, also styled 'Enjoying MG', members could learn how to repair and restore their MGs and how to improve them. In concentrating on developing a range of club products and accessories, members could obtain practically everything they needed for their cars and at special prices.

In 1979, the MG Owners' Club became internationally famous with its campaign to 'Save MG Abingdon'. Partially successful in that the MG name was retained, thousands of MG enthusiasts, spurred on by the Club's campaign, persuaded British Leyland that MG was worth saving and should not go the way of other famous British marques. The Club now caters for fifty thousand Club members and has many affiliations with MG clubs throughout the world.

Roche writes ...

"I welcomed Lindsay Porter's previous books on 'MGB: Guide to Purchase and DIY Restoration' and 'Midget: Guide to Purchase and DIY Restoration'. These books helped members and enthusiasts alike to choose their MGs carefully and to restore them properly. I was delighted to learn that Lindsay had produced a book on improving the MGB as this is something which every MGB owner likes to do. MGBs are super and yet highly personal cars. Each one seems to have its own style and personality. Owners are faced with a choice of products and benefit from careful guidance and can tastefully and safely improve their cars without spending a fortune. MG to the historian means Morris Garages, to some owners it can jokingly mean 'Money Gobbler'."

With the help of Lindsay's book and the dedication of the Club and recommended suppliers, there's absolutely no excuse for spending too much money or buying the wrong parts.

This book deserves to be as successful as Lindsay's other books on the MG and on other marques and I wish him and this latest publication, my best wishes.

Roche Bentley
Club Secretary, MG Owners' Club

Introduction

by Lindsay Porter

At the start of its production life in 1962, the MGB was considered by road testers to be a 'lively performer' and 'a pleasure to drive' with 'every saloon car amenity'. It was said that the MGB was 'a car with a lot of performance; verve has been blended with refinement'. In its day, all of that was true, and even by today's standards, a car which is capable of around 108 mph is no slouch! However, it has to be said that the new, cheeky generation of 'hot hatches', pioneered by Volkswagen with the Golf GTi and since copied successfully by others, have set fresh standards in roadholding, acceleration and comfort. What they have singularly failed to achieve, however, is the incredible sense of **character** that MGB owners have enjoyed in their cars ever since their launch.

The idea behind this book is to help owners continue to enjoy the character and individuality that sets the MGB apart while showing how to stir some better performance, road manners, comfort and modern in-car entertainment into the MGB brew. Between ourselves, Porter Publishing and TypeStyle, we have come up with a style of presentation which has been designed to be attractive and satisfying to look at in its own right, while giving the information required by the MGB owner.

We felt that there was no reason at all why step-by-step information has to be presented in the manner of that indispensable workshop tool, the Haynes manual. Incidentally, the Haynes MGB Owners Workshop Manual makes an ideal companion to this book, describing in detail all of the stripdown procedures referred to here, while my book, 'MGB: Guide to Purchase & DIY Restoration' has guided many tens of thousands of MGB owners through the repair and restoration of their cars.

1
Back in the early 1960s, the MGB gave respectable, even exciting performance, in comparison with other cars of the day. In the intervening years, the appeal of the MGB has grown rather than diminished but at the same time, owners have come to expect more of their transport.

The range of improvements you can make to your MGB is vast! Among the simplest are styling stripes for the bodywork, mats for the interior and performance-boosting air filter and exhaust pipe swaps for the engine. In addition, this book shows you how to add simple styling accessories - mainly of the bolt-on, bolt-off variety - or even how to completely restyle the car as a 'Sebring' MGC replica, if that's how far you want to go. Still at the easy-to-fit stage is a wide range of cosmetic 'goodies' such as stainless steel oversills and wheel trims. Then there are modifications which are capable of uprating the MGB's mechanical specification in small but worthwhile ways. You could fit telescopic shock absorbers and a stiffer front anti-roll bar to improve handling; more efficient brake pads to improve stopping; modern tyres to improve grip; better lights to improve visibility and safety. Inside the car, there is whole range of improvements waiting to be tried out in order to quieten the interior, add comfort and add to your driving pleasure through the aesthetic appeal of a leather steering wheel, a wooden dash or a top-flight stereo system.

2
A relatively small number of the 6-cylinder MGCs were modified and improved in their day in a manner which makes you wonder why BMC didn't turn the car into the high performer it could have been without so many of the drawbacks. This, one of the MGC's owned by super-enthusiast Pearl McGlen, had a Downton Stage 3 conversion from new, which endowed the car with 175 bhp and acceleration from 0-60 in 7.2 secs. So you see, improving and modifying 'our' cars is **not** new!

3
Typical of the sort of cosmetic improvements that owners may be keen to make, this MGB has been fitted with chrome wheel trims, stainless steel oversills, hardtop, side stripes and rear fog lamps. All are described in this book. The luggage rack is a simple bolt-on item.

The production of this book has required the investigation of an amazingly wide range of skills and information. As with 'MGB: Guide to Purchase & DIY Restoration', published by Haynes, it has been essential to enlist the help of a large number of specialist companies. Some, such as MG specialists Murray Scott-Nelson of Scarborough, Moto-Build of Hounslow and Blaupunkt gave their assistance throughout a whole Chapter or Chapters, while others, too numerous to mention here, lent their weight to an individual part of the book. In each case, we went to the best we could find in any particular area, and we are proud to list, from page 238-on, all of the companies who have helped with this book.

In addition, my thanks are gladly given to Dave Pollard who provided an enormous amount of assistance with the writing of Chapters 2, 3 and 4 of this book and to Giles Photographic for their darkroom skills. Clive Murray, John Scott-Nelson, Rae and Daryl Davis, my assistant Miranda Horobin and the Staff at TypeStyle have all made their crucial in-depth contributions while Roche Bentley has provided the foreword, a section on 'Going Racing' and kindly proffered advice and photographs on behalf of the MGOC. Thanks also to Zoe Heritage for allowing us the use of her photographic skills. My thanks are due to them all.

Lindsay Porter
County of Hereford & Worcester

Chapter One
Bodywork modifications

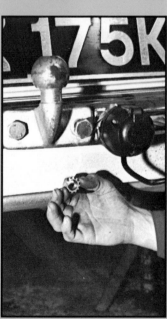

Fitting door and sports mirrors

DM1 ▶
Shown here is the standard Unipart mirror fitted to all MGBs from the 1975 model year-on, and right is a high quality 'bullet' mirror alternative, both available from Murray Scott-Nelson.

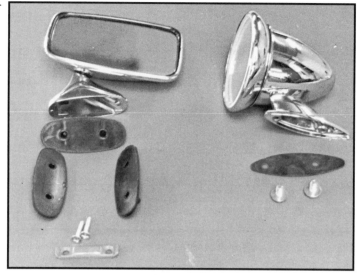

It is impossible to say which MGBs should and which should not be fitted with door mirrors. From the advent of 'rubber bumper' cars in the 1975 model year, all 'Bs' were fitted with door mirrors as standard, but it is impossible to say at what stage door mirrors became available as a BL accessory. It thus becomes largely a matter of taste as to which mirror you choose to fit to your MGB. You may even feel that on earlier cars, the 'racing' style door mirrors shown here and available from Murray Scott-Nelson look best. Door mirrors are infinitely more practical and less likely to cause rusting than wing mirrors which are rarely fitted to MGBs these days.

◀ DM2
When deciding upon the position for fitting the mirror, it is clearly of paramount importance that the mirror can clearly be seen! For that reason, don't fit the mirror so low that the passenger side glass disappears below the door top, nor so far towards the front of the car that the quarter light gets in the way.

DM3 ▶
Here, Clive Murray sits in his MGB and holds the driver's door mirror in what seems to be the best position. A helper must do the same on the other side of the car, making sure that the two mirrors are fitted the same distance from the front of the door and from the door top. Final glass adjustment can later be made when the mirror is fitted. Note that the door paintwork has been protected by placing several overlapping strips of masking tape on the door prior to fitting the door mirror.

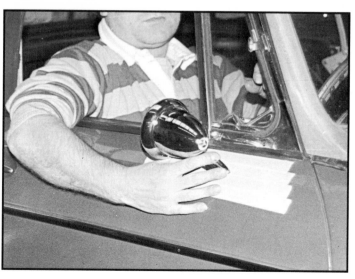

Fitting door and sports mirrors

Wise MGB owners tend to ensure that their cars are properly rustproofed. Don't spoil it when drilling holes in the car's bodywork! Turn to page 228 where you'll see an ideal anti-rust primer for touching in the drilled holes and page 224 where Corroless aerosol cavity wax is shown. It is perfect for covering the back of the mirror mounting rubber and the inside of the door where you have drilled through.

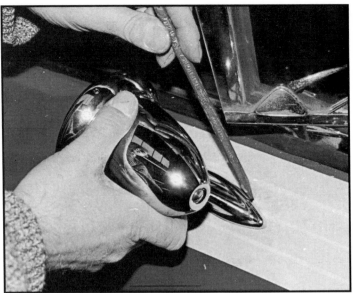

◄DM4
The mirror should now be held firmly in place in the position established in the previous shot. Draw around the mirror base and on the masking tape with a pencil or felt pen, as shown.

DM5►
Locate the rubber gasket that fits between mirror base and door accurately onto this marked out area and precisely indicate the positions for the holes to be drilled.

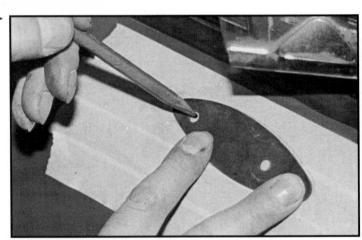

◄DM6
Note that the MS-N mechanic has emphasized the hole positions by drawing two accurate crosses before marking the centres of the crosses lightly with a centre punch. This is the only way of accurately starting off a drill bit so that it is both accurately positioned and so that it does not wander across your nice, shiny paintwork.

DM7 ▶
The bullet-type door mirror looks particularly good with the early type of MGB shown here, fitted with pull-out door handles. It looks the part with chrome bumpers, wire wheels and wind in the hair ...

DM8
The later type door mirror fits in a somewhat different way. The method already shown for marking out the position of the mirror can broadly be followed and it is always useful to place masking tape over the area to be drilled, just in case the drill **does** wander, in spite of all your efforts. With this type of mirror, the gasket also acts as a special kind of captive nut which holds the mounting plate in position. As the fixing screw, being held here twixt thumb and forefinger, is screwed into the gasket (the gasket having already been pushed down into place with its protusions through pre-drilled holes in the door), it causes the gasket protusion to expand and grip on the back of the door.▶

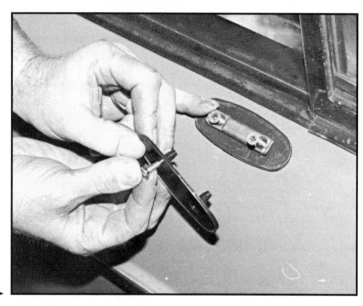

One of the hidden benefits of door mirrors is that, correctly positioned, they can help to prevent the inevitable door splits that take place in a line with the rear quarterlight support. Eventually, this support presses on the door skin in such a way that a split occurs. The area can be strengthened by placing the door mirror base across the imaginary line that runs down from the quarterlight support pillar. Do make sure, depending upon the type of mirror that you are using, that you can still see the mirror glass when it is fitted!

◀DM9
Before fitting the mirror in place, the mounting plate is securely tightened to the door.

Fitting door and sports mirrors

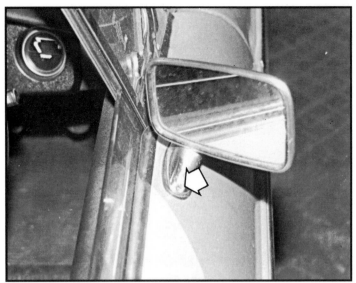

◀ **DM10**
The door mirror is then slotted onto the mounting plate and held tightly in place with a small grub screw (arrowed), at the rear of the mirror base. For all later MGBs, these are most certainly the only 'correct' type mirrors. Ensure that the lip around the base gasket is not trapped beneath the mirror base, preventing it from sealing correctly.

Fitting stainless kickplates

Stainless steel kickplates are functional in that they stop the sill top from gathering its inevitable paint scuffs. In addition, they make an attractive visual feature in themselves.

◀ **SKP1**
Murray Scott-Nelson sell a range of kickplates with either a plain finish, a textured finish or with an MG logo.

SKP2 ▶
Fitting is a doddle! Hold in place, measuring back from the door pillar to ensure uniformity, drill a small pilot hole through the pre-drilled holes provided in the kickplate, and tighten down with the self-tapping screws provided.

MF1 ▶

As can be seen, the shape of these Link-Sedan mudflaps fits that of the wing curvature quite nicely and protects the lower side of the wing, too.

There are several styles of MG mudflap on the market besides a number of 'universal' ones. These Link-Sedan mudflaps, as supplied by Murray Scott-Nelson, are probably best because of their octagonal MG logo and the fact that they are made to fit accurately.

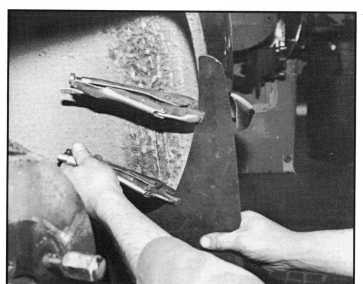

◀ MF2

Start by clamping the mudflap into place using a couple of self-grip wrenches.

◀ MF3

Always measure the amount the mudflap protudes downwards and sideways so that it can be compared with the position of the mudflap on the other side.

MF4 ▶

Drill a pilot hole at the top and bottom, fit the self-tapping screws and washers required and then, after removing the clamp, drill holes for the other fixing screws. Note that wheel removal is a must. Support the car soundly on axle stands, **never** on a jack, and securely chock the front wheels.

Fitting mudflaps

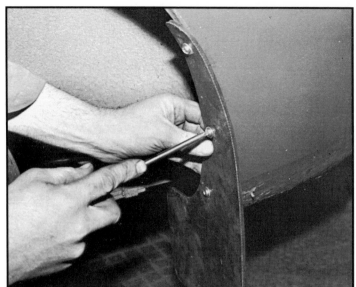

◄MF5
The holes should be painted before inserting the screws to discourage rust, or you could spray on Corroless rustproofing fluid once the screws are inserted.

Fitting exhaust pipe extensions

A Sedan exhaust pipe extension gives an attractive sparkle of chrome where the old, and possibly rusty, exhaust pipe end used to be. As Clive Murray points out, the end of the extension must never protude beyond the bumper line for safety reasons.

◄EP1
Sedan produce a range of high quality exhaust pipe extensions with plain, chamfered and even double endings in various sizes. Made of solid brass they will never rust.

◄EP2
Nothing could be simpler to fit! The exhaust pipe extension is held firmly in place with a clip which is an integral part of the component. All that is needed is a screwdriver to tighten it up.

EP3 ►
MS-N took advantage of the Sykes-Pickavant hacksaw which they had on site to reduce the length of the existing exhaust pipe, allowing the fitting of this extension.

Fitting a sunroof

SR1 ▶
Darryl Davies uses a template on the GT's roof to mark out where the sunroof will go.

Murray Scott-Nelson much prefer, when asked, to fit a folding fabric sunroof to an MGB because this, rather than the ubiquitious glass-hatch, is the correct ware for an MBG GT. In addition, it gives you the next best thing to open-top motoring, since it can be fully opened, exposing a vast amount of blue sky above your head, while the built-in wind deflector keeps your coiffure in place!

SR2 ▶
The paintwork had been stripped back from this car, so there was no need to do what he would have done if the car had been fully painted ... place a strip of wide masking tape over the paintwork to protect it from the foot of the jig-saw.

SR3
The brave bit completed, Darryl lifts the redundant piece of steel away from the roof. He would most ▶ certainly have already cut out the headlining from inside the car before starting work with the jig-saw.

▲
SR4
Darryl lifts the new sunroof in as a complete unit and fits it into place.

Fitting a sunroof

It would be silly to pretend that fitting a sunroof was a DIY operation. You need to work accurately and with experience to know that the hole is going to be correctly positioned and you also require the skill to ensure that the trim inside looks as good after you have finished as it did beforehand. It is highly advisable to take your car to the experts mentioned here, such as Murray Scott-Nelson, if you live in the North of England, or Moto-Build if you live in the South.

◄ SR5
After the car had been finished and painted, the sunroof was finally fitted, giving an attractive fabric look to the GT's roof line.

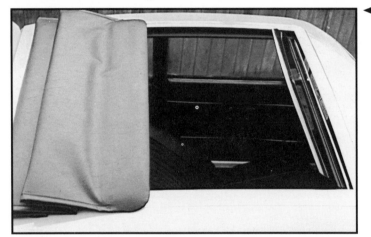

SR6
Many GT owners feel that a folding fabric sunroof gives them the best of both worlds because, although a sunroof gives far less fresh air than an open-topped sportscar, the folding fabric sunroof opens up far more of the
◄ outside world than any glass hatch.

SR7
Inside the car, everything looks perfectly professional and standard, as well it should with a sunroof that is similar to those fitted as an optional extra when the car was new.
▼

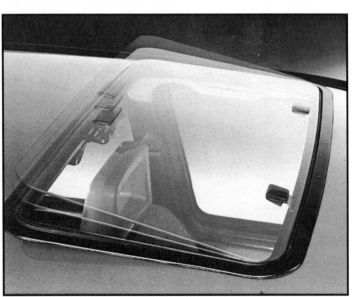

◄ SR8
It must be said that the glass hatch does have one or two advantages: one is that it is probably less easy to break into, and the other is that it lets more light into the car. Only go for a good quality hatch; cheaper ones can allow water to leak into the car.

H1 ►
First job involves unhooking the rear of the soft top from the snap fastener slotted brackets at the rear of the soft-top, then removing the folding mechanism fitted to the vast majority of cars. The whole soft-top can then be lifted away and should be stored, wrapped in a soft cloth, in a clean, dry place ready for use next season. Using the three existing screws per side, refit the tonneau bracket.

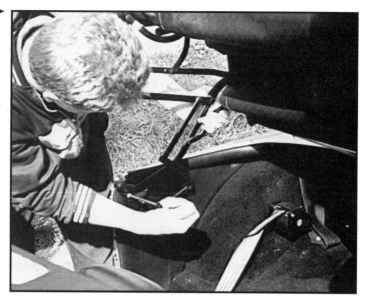

Just as a folding fabric sunroof could be said to give GT owners the best of both worlds, a Lenham hardtop gives roadster owners something of a 'GT' option. Fitting is simple and while the first bit is often carried out by the suppliers, such as Murray Scott-Nelson, the owner is usually more then happy to remove and re-fit the hardtop him or herself on subsequent occasions.

◄**H2**
The new Lenham hardtop is lifted into place and lightly placed onto the car, with doors open.

H3 ►
The very first time the hardtop is fitted, it may require some pushing and shoving to locate the two integral plates, built into the hardtop, into the chrome slots onto which the soft-top is fitted. All that you need to do is press down hard on the rear of the hardtop, compressing the new sealing rubbers sufficiently to let the hardtop slide home. Next season, you will probably be able to accomplish the job single-handed.

Fitting a hardtop

Murray Scott-Nelson are happy to recommend and supply Lenham hardtops, Lenham being probably the best known manufacturers of hardtops, their expertise going back over many years. The quality of Lenham hardtops is known to be superb and their looks complement the appearance of the MGB very well indeed.

H4 ▶
Having fitted the hardtop at the rear, the next job is to clip it down at the front, using the over-centre catches which are removed from the hood and fitted to the hardtop. At this stage, the door glass sealing rubber, which Lenham deliberately leave too long to allow for variations between different cars, must be cut to length at the front of the hardtop, using a pair of tin snips. Time spent making a neat joint will be rewarded later by the absence of leaks!

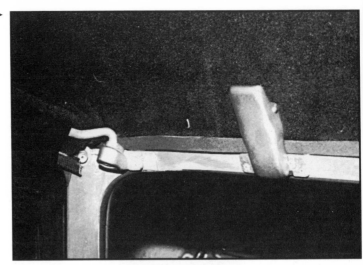

H5 ▶
Tighten down at the B-post using the hook bolt supplied, hooking it into the tonneau bracket. Finally, trim off the rear of the draught excluder to seal off the door shut properly.

H6
The great majority of owners find the black leather-grain finish complements the car's body colour rather well, matching the colour and texture of most soft-tops.
▼

◀TB1
Keith, at Murray Scott-Nelson, starts in the time honoured way by laying all the components out alongside the car, 'exploded diagram' style and studies the instructions before commencing work.

TB2
After removing the rear bumper, the first job is to offer up the Witter tow bracket's main cross-bar so that the position for each hole can be established and clearly marked.
▼

Surprising though it may seem, the MGB makes an excellent tow vehicle for medium weight trailers and caravans. Because it is so solidly built, the MGB is relatively heavy for its size and copes with a twelve foot caravan with surprising ease! In addition, the renowned torque and gutsy pulling power of the 1800 engine means that the slog of towing is no trouble to this car. In practice, most MGB owners these days may want to tow nothing more demanding than a camping trailer and that, for the MGB, is a piece of cake!

TB3
Keith carefully and lightly centre-punched each hole, and then used a Black and Decker drill with a speed control in the grip. This enabled him to start each hole slowly, thus reducing the risk of the drill bit slipping across the MGB's paintwork, and then, once the hole had started, he increased the pressure on the trigger and hence the speed of the drill.
▼

TB4 ▶
Large holes had to be drilled in the rear of the bumper to accommodate the main mounting bolts. After drilling a pair of pilot holes, Keith opened them out by using the Sykes-Pickavant Varicut, which is a conically-shaped drill. It just keeps on opening up the hole until you tell it to stop!

Fitting a towbar and electrics

Witter towbars are the best selling towbars in Britain with over two and a half million sold. Witter say that, no matter what the make or model, one of their towbars will not affect a new car's warranty, which gives some indication of their reputation. Witter towbars are built to British (BS) and International (ISO) standards, but are sold at a competitive price. All fittings, bolts and parts are included as part of each kit.

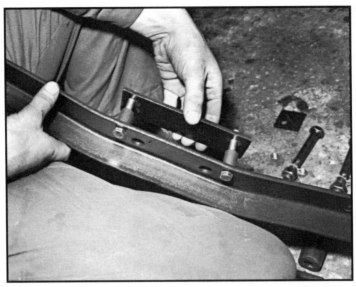

◀TB5
Next, the small diameter long bolts, specified in the instructions, were pushed into the tow bracket followed by spacers and the additional support bracket held here in Keith's left hand.

TB6
Keith then offered the sub-assembly back up to the car, pushing the threaded ends of these long bolts through the drilled holes in the rear apron. Murray Scott-Nelson point out that holes such as this should be protected with paint before fitting the bolts.
▼

TB7
In the interior of the car's boot, the two large black load-spreading washers were first pushed over the bolts, followed by the spring washers and nuts supplied in the kit. The fixings can then be tightened up with a ring spanner.
▼

TB8 ▶
Now, the towball and Hella wiring socket bracket (both purchased separately), large cast-iron spacer, designed to fit the shape of the MGB bumper, are held in place, while the two large high-tensile steel bolts are passed through the mounting holes drilled through the bumper.

◀ TB9
Shaped cast-iron spacers also fit inside the bumper, followed by round spacers with flats on them. Keith found that these flats had to be turned so that the round spacers slid easily over the tow bracket.

TB10
The complete bumper and towball assembly can now be manoeuvred into place. It's best to have a helper here, or at least to tape protective cloths to the rear body of the MGB. It's all too easy for the ends of the bumper to dig into the bodywork as the bumper is offered up.
▼

Witter also produce a number of towing accessories. One is the drop plate, used if your trailer has a particularly low tow bracket height and is designed to fit between the towball and the cast-iron spacer shown in TB8. This should never be used as a raising plate because the tow bracket just isn't designed that way. There's also a special Witter towball available with a rubber mounting to absorb some of the load shocks, similar in principle to those of your MGB's engine mountings. Trailer or caravan owners whose set-up suffers from snaking can purchase the bolt-on Mongoose Major Stabiliser, which bolts to the car and trailer tow bracket and cuts down dramatically any propensity to snaking.

TB11
Hold on tight to stop anything dropping away again and place the spring washers and large nuts onto the high-tensile bolts, holding the towball in place. Before you do so, ensure that the wiring for the rear number plate light has not become trapped or lost in the maze, and pass the wiring through the grommeted holes already in place in the rear apron.
▼

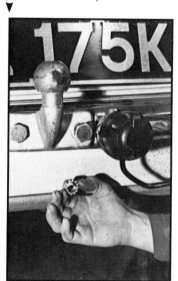

TB12 ▶
After tightening all the bumper and mounting bolts, the job is complete and here Keith fits the Witter protective towball cover, intended to stop grease on the towball getting onto your clothes as you pass by or load the boot.

Fitting a towbar and electrics

Murray Scott-Nelson recommend the use of high quality electrics, such as those produced by Hella. Efficient electrics are taken very much for granted; poor ones are, at best, irritating when they fail, or at worst, downright dangerous. The Hella kit includes the obligatory-by-law internal warning light, telling you whether the trailer lights are flashing or not. Hella produce either a single seven-pin socket for normal use or double sockets where you may be using a caravan with lots of electrical accessories.

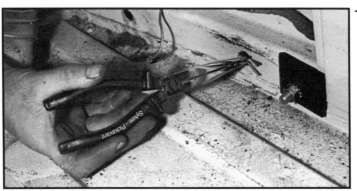

◄TB13
Working the socket wiring through the hole in the rear valance is quite a tricky operation but was made easier by the Sykes-Pickavant long-nosed pliers which were used to grasp the wires as soon as they became visible through the hole.

TB14 ►
The electronic control box for handling the indicator lights wiring can be fitted to any suitable place. Murray Scott-Nelson tend to prefer the top of the footwell panel beneath the dash. The warning light can be fitted to any easily visible position. Murray Scott-Nelson use a Sedan bracket, screwed to the underside of the dash, to avoid drilling any unnecessary holes in the dash panel itself.

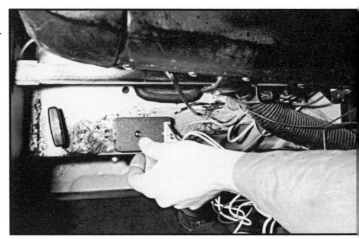

Add-on electrics
Fitting driving and spot lamps

◄SL1
These Hella spotlamps throw out a remarkably powerful beam - compare them to the brightness of the MGB's standard headlamps!

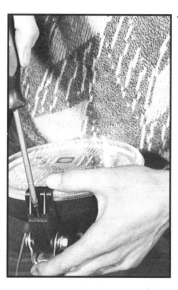

◄ SL2
In order to fit Rallye 1000 lamps to the MGB, MS-N's Keith began by taking out the screw that holds the body clamp in place.

SL3 ►
The Halogen 55W bulb has to be fitted to the bulb holder. It's essential that your fingers don't touch the glass envelope around the bulb. Keith uses a clean cloth to grip the bulb.

Murray Scott-Nelson chose to fit Hella fog and spot lamps here because of their high quality and excellent reputation. Hella Rallye 2000 lamps offer a choice of patterns to suit the speed, road, terrain, the traffic and the weather. Where mounting space could be a problem, you could fit Rallye 1000 lamps with an aperture of 155mm as opposed to the aperture of 190mm for the Rallye 2000. Ther are also other Hella lamps known as the 500 and 550 Comet series.

◄ SL4
The bulb, complete with bulb holder, is clipped into the back of the lamp reflector with the spring clip provided.

SL5 ►
The Hella kit comes complete with wiring and a relay which has to be located in a convenient place, preferably on the right-hand flitch panel somewhere near the fuse box. Keith removes an existing mounting screw and fixes the relay to that.

Fitting driving and spot lamps

It is a legal requirement in the UK that driving lamps are mounted in such a way that they are at exactly the same height from the ground and the same distance apart from the centre of the vehicle. Also make absolutely certain that the lamps do not prevent sufficient air from reaching the radiator.

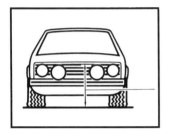

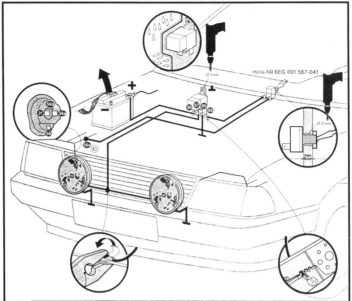

◄ SL6
This excerpt from the Hella instructions, provided with the kit, shows exactly how to wire up the spotlamps if they are to be used with a switch independently of the headlamps. (They should only be switched on to complement the headlamp main beams.) They can also be wired so that they only illuminate with the headlamps on main beam and Hella supply another wiring diagram to show how this can be done.

SL7 ►
Here MS-N's Keith has already wired in the earth connection and now pushes the feed wire through the grommet in the back of the Hella spotlamp body.

◄ SL8
Next, Keith strips off a few millimetres of the wire sheath.

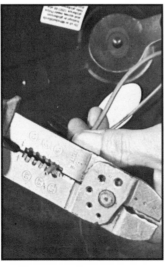

SL9 ►
The connector supplied in the kit is simply crimped onto the end of the wire as shown.

SL10▶
Keith then simply pushed the connectors onto the terminals on the back of the bulb, following which the whole lamp assembly was simply clamped back together again.

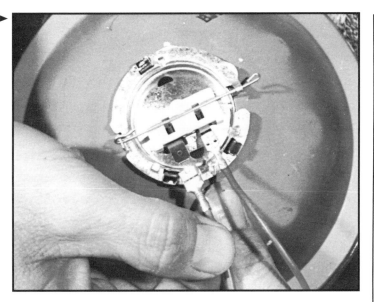

Hella Rallye 1000 lamps can be fitted with bulbs giving either of the two beam patterns shown here. Rallye 2000 lamps can be fitted with a number of alternative beam patterns and 100W bulbs although, legally speaking, these are intended for off-road use only in the UK.

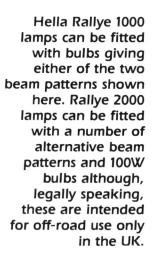

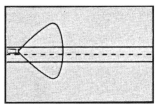

Fog lamp beam pattern

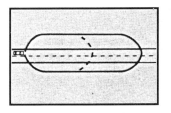

Driving lamp beam pattern

◀SL11
Murray Scott-Nelson would not normally dream of drilling an MGB bumper for mounting lamps although, to be fair, it is the most rigid way of fitting them. On this car, small holes were already present, so it was simply a matter of opening them out a little further using a Black & Decker drill.

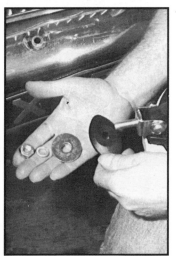

◀SL12
The oval mounting plate goes above the bumper while the large washer, spring washer and nut fit beneath. It makes sense to do all of this work with the lamp cover fitted in case of accidents.

SL13▶
After bolting the unit down, lamp height adjustment was made by means of the pinch bolt passing through the base of the body.

Fitting driving and spot lamps

Before using these lights on the road, it is essential that the car is taken to a testing centre so that the beam height and angle can be checked accurately. Misaligned driving lamps, of any sort, are not only illegal but could be a major road hazard.

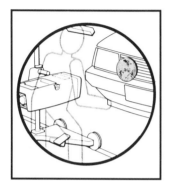

▲ SL14
Fitted to the MGB, the Hella Rallye 1000 spot lamps give a dramatic improvement to the MGB's front-end appearance during the day as well as considerably improving visibility at night. Rallye 2000 lamps can be fitted with a Hella protective grille set (part no. 9HG 124 320-801), available in a set of two.

SL15▶
The protective cover supplied could protect your lamps from being broken by stone chips.

◀SL16
Here's how to fit driving lamp brackets to rubber-bumpered MGBs. With the front bumper removed (see **Fitting a front spoiler**), the two towing eye mounting points are clearly visible and ideally placed. Murray Scott-Nelson tackle this job first, taking off the existing towing eye ...

SL17▶
... and then clamping it in a vice along with the new lamp bracket they are making up so that the tow eye acts as a template. The mounting holes then line up perfectly.

◄SL18
Murray Scott-Nelson recommend that if you haven't done this job before, you should now fit the complete bracket to the bumper and offer up the driving lamp, so that the position of the mounting hole can be determined, allowing you to fit the lamp an appropriate distance away from the bumper.

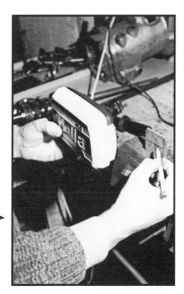

SL19►
Mark the position of the hole, centre punch it, drill through with a clearance size and paint the bracket for protection.

These Hella Scout, Model 155 Halogen fog and driving lamps, are ultra thin and ideal for fitting to sports cars. They're also available with a chrome body, which would probably be more appropriate to the MGB. Like the circular models, all Hella rectangular lamps are reversible, allowing upright or pendant mounting.

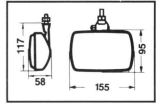

SL20 ►
Wiring is similar to that shown earlier (there is a full set of instructions with every Hella kit), and attachment is simply a matter of bolting to the new bracket.

SL21
These rectangular or driving lamps suit rubber-bumpered models particularly well. Fog lamps are generally best mounted as low down as possible.
▼

AKY 141T

Fitting halogen headlamps

Changing over to Hella Halogen headlamps is one of the most sensible modifications which you can make to your MGB. It will bring a tremendous improvement in headlamp output and there's the additional bonus that it's one of the simplest modifications to carry out, too!

◄HH1
Take out the retaining screw from the bottom of the bezel (where fitted), and lever off the bezel from the bottom. It sometimes helps to press down at the top at the same time. Murray Scott-Nelson tip: place a piece of stiff card or a filler spreader behind the back of the screwdriver while levering off to avoid damaging paintwork.

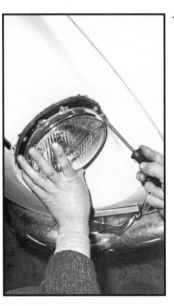

◄HH2
This reveals the chrome plated retaining ring which is held in place with three self-tapping screws.

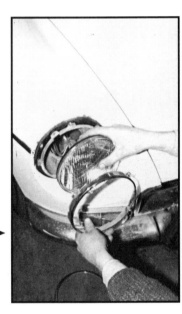

HH3►
Carefully take off the ring and take hold of the existing sealed beam unit so that it does not slip down and break or damage paintwork.

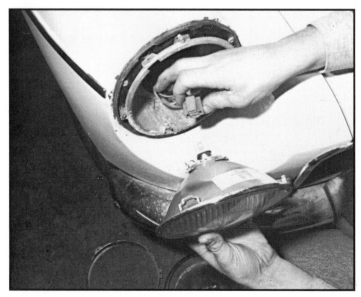

◄HH4
On the back of the sealed beam unit, the wiring connection can be simply pulled away.

HH5 ▶
In typical Hella fashion, Hella halogen headlamp units have a rubber sealing shroud which fits over the back of the headlamp. It is an excellent seal and has to be pushed very firmly with the thumbs over the bulb holder to get it to seat correctly.

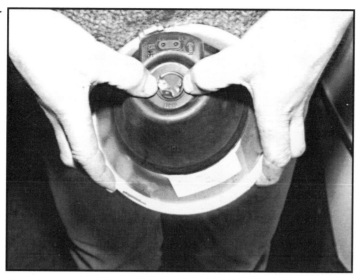

◀ HH6
Until you have done so, the wiring connector cannot be pushed over the new headlamp terminals.

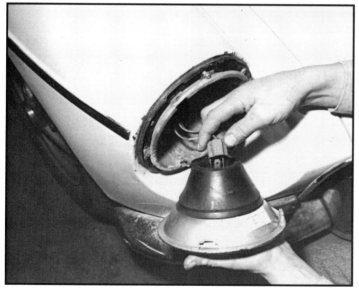

Very early MGBs are not fitted with the standard sealed beam connecting plug shown in HH4. In this case, it will be necessary to have the correct plug wired in and to change the headlamp mounting to the one which is suitable for sealed beam units. The mounting is a screw-in replacement. Murray Scott-Nelson also point out that most headlamp units lose a significant amount of their power because of a deterioration in the wiring system. Make absolutely certain that all wiring connections are soundly made, that all terminals are clean, and that none are hanging off the end of the wire by a thread! In terms of safety and lighting performance, it will pay you to go through your wiring with a fine toothcomb, replacing any faulty connections or having them replaced by a professional electrician if necessary.

HH7 ▶
The new Hella halogen headlamps look scarcely any different from the old; until you turn them on, that is! Naturally enough, they come with a full set of instructions should you require them.

Fitting a rear fog lamp

When fitting this or any other of the lamps shown on these pages, always start off by disconnecting the battery earth cable to avoid the risk of a short circuit causing an accident or fire. When fitting a single lamp to a vehicle driven in the UK, ie, where cars are driven on the left-hand side of the road, the lamp must be fitted on the right-hand side of the car. In countries where vehicles are driven on the other side of the road, the lamp must be fitted on the left-hand side of the car. It may be that some countries demand the fitting of these lamps only in pairs. Check your local regulations.

Fitting the lamp was a case of carefully measuring the proposed location of the mounting, after which a pilot hole was first drilled and then the hole was opened out with a larger drill, but still nowhere near large enough. To open the hole out to its full size the ingenious Sykes-Pickavant Varicut drill was used. This conically-shaped drill will produce any one of a series of hole sizes.

◄ RFL1
You could fit a switch with a separate bracket, mounted beneath the dash, but whatever you do, it is essential that there is a warning light visible to the driver, which illuminates when the rear fog lamp(s) is/are turned on. Hella recommend one of their switches with a integral warning lamp.

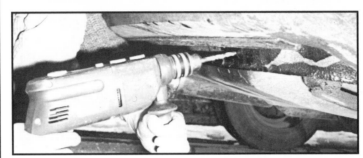

◄ RFL2
Murray Scott-Nelson find that the best place to fit these lamps is on the rear apron. They recommend protecting the specially drilled 10mm hole by painting it and allowing the paint to dry before fitting the lamp.

◄ RFL3
Murray Scott-Nelson's Keith offers up the new Hella lamp before tightening the mounting nut at the rear of the apron.

RFL4
Note the regulations for maximum and minimum height when mounting either one or two rear foglamps. In particular, note that each lamp must be at least 10cms away from the edge of existing stop lamps.
▼

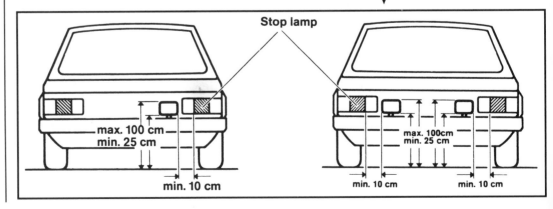

Stop lamp

max. 100 cm
min. 25 cm

min. 10 cm

max. 100cm
min. 25 cm

min. 10 cm   min. 10 cm

Fitting rear window brake lights

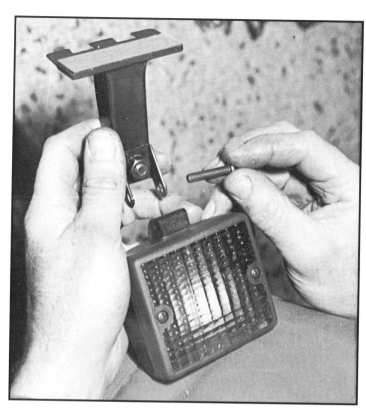

◄ RWB1
Supplied by Link-Sedan, these rear window brake lights come complete with brackets which allow them to be fitted to the rear window glass, or to the rear parcel shelf on some cars. The base of the bracket has a self-adhesive pad, covered by protective paper. The angle of the lamp can be adjusted in one direction by slackening the screw shown here.

RWB2
Ease back the rubber surround on the inside of the window, taking very great care not to damage the heated rear window elements, if fitted, and slot in the three lugs on the mounting bracket. On the outside of the glass, draw around the outline of the mounting bracket with a felt tip pen.
▼

It is important that rear window brake lights conform to road vehicle lighting regulations which, in the UK, state that they must be at least 400mm and no more than 1500mm, from the road, with no less than 600mm between each lamp. The lamps are to be used for brake light use only and "E" approved for that use. Murray Scott-Nelson recommend that you check regulations at your local police station if you are in any doubt.

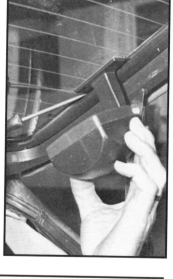

▲
RWB3
Next, Link-Sedan recommend the inside of the glass be cleaned carefully with spirit wipe. Then, the self-adhesive pad's backing paper can be removed and the bracket pressed into place very firmly. As you can see, the brake lights give a highly visible warning to those several cars behind when you are braking.

RWB4
Wiring is simple. The brake light leads are Scotchloked into the existing brake wiring circuit, while the other leads (supplied with the kit), are taken to earth. Feed any wires through the existing cable grommets at the top of the door.
▼

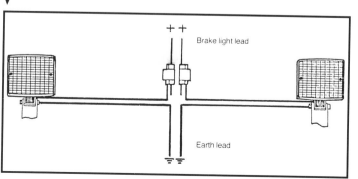

++

Brake light lead

Earth lead

Fitting a rear window wash/wiper

Fitting a rear window wash/wiper is not such an easy job but the results are certainly impressive in terms of enhanced rear visibility. Murray Scott-Nelson have found that the high quality Hella kit featured here has all the attributes that one could require. For one thing, it actually fits the MGB GT rear door layout rather well, while, for another, it comes complete with all the components produced to original equipment standards.

WW1 ▶
The parts laid out in the boot of this GT show just how extensive the kit is. All the components you require are supplied with the kit, even down to a sealing grommet for the hole you'll have to cut in the rear door's inner panel.

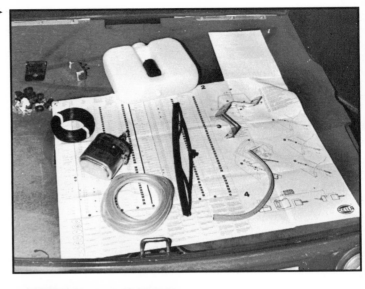

WW2
A template with a self-adhesive backing, supplied as part of the Hella kit, is attached to the rear door in the position shown.
▼

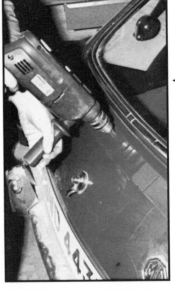

◀ **WW3**
After drilling a hole for the spindle, from the inside of the rear door, Murray Scott-Nelson opened out the spindle hole in the outer panel to the size stipulated. The inner panel then had to be cut to take the body of the windscreen wiper motor. The template shown in WW2 actually shows the centres for the holes to be drilled around the periphery of this cut-out and the sizes to be drilled.

◀ **WW4**
After drilling the holes, you could use a small, sharp chisel to remove the metal, followed by a file, as shown here, to clean up the edges of the hole.

WW5

The hole in the inside of the rear door panel has to be made so that the motor is a snug fit. The easiest way is to file it out to the line shown on the template described in WW2.

▼

WW6 ►

The components of the rear wash/wipe system are installed as described here.

WW7

Before inserting the wiper motor, connect the earth cable to the body of the motor having first fitted the correct electrical connector to the end of the wire from the kit supplied. MS-N ensure that all electrical terminals are covered with the sheaths supplied with the kit.

▼

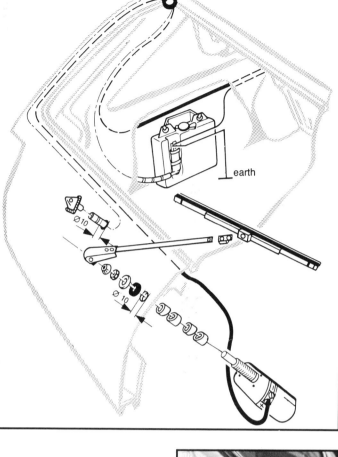

earth

The Hella wiring diagram shows clearly how to connect up the rear washer/wiper. At the bottom of this diagram is the existing windscreen wiper set-up. Always disconnect the battery before commencing work on the wiring.
(Diagram courtesy of Hella)

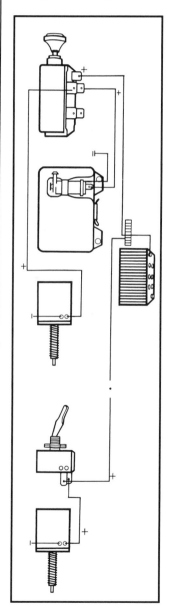

WW8 ►

Once the spindle is bolted down, the wiper arm can be fitted; its position can be finally adjusted when the system is in use.

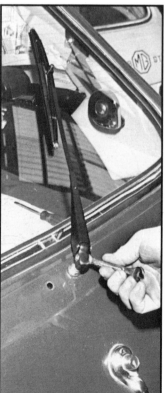

Fitting a rear window wash/wiper

With each kit comes a wide range of washers and spacers which enable you to work out an appropriate combination for the wiper motor spindle on your particular car. Murray Scott-Nelson have got it down to a fine art; you'll have to use trial and error to obtain the right combination.

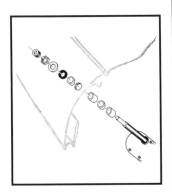

WW9 ▶
The washer reservoir bottle looks as if it was made to fit in this part of the GT's boot. Cut away part of the trim and fix the mounting bracket to the inside of the rear wing with double-sided tape.

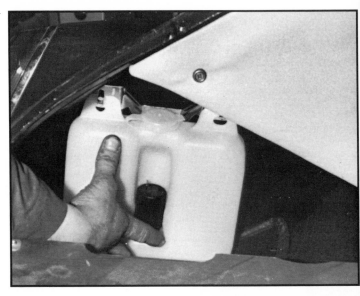

◀ WW10
The washer jet is fitted to the rear door, adjacent to the wiper arm. The jet angle can be adjusted later with a pin inserted into the nozzle.

WW11 ▶
Inserting the washer tubing through the rear door can be very tricky and you'll need to first insert a 'fish' made of stiff wire to which the end of the tube can be taped and pulled through.

◀ WW12
One flick on the Hella operating switch makes the wiper work; a second, against the spring loading, operates the washers. This MGB's dash had an appropriately positioned blanking plug where the switch was mounted. You may prefer to add a separate bracket to the underside of the dash.

Improving the appearance
Fitting a rear window louvre

RL1 ►
The first step is to fit the brackets supplied with the kit to the window louvre. Then, with the window louvre held exactly in place, the positions for the brackets can be marked with a pencil or felt pen

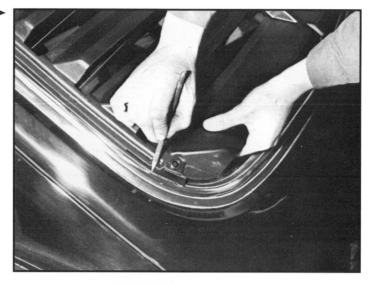

The Autoplas rear window louvre helps to keep the rear window of the car clear and clean as well as giving the rear end a distinctive appearance. For those who want to retain the GT's long-term classic status, there's no problem because the rear window is not a permanent modification. It can be removed almost as easily as it can be fitted, there being no permanent fixings or holes to drill. If it **had** been a permanent fixture, Murray Scott-Nelson, who are very 'originality conscious', wouldn't have wanted to know!

RL2 ►
At the top of the rear screen, the louvre is held into position with these clips, one of which is pushed under the window rubber in each corner of the screen ...

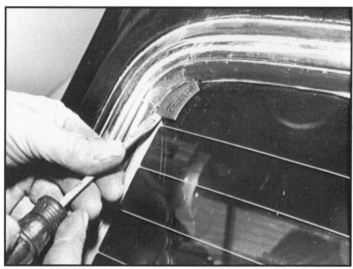

RL3
... while another clip, under which the top of the louvre hooks, is pushed beneath the rubber at the top-centre of the screen.
▼

RL4 ►
The 'catches' which hold the louvre in place in the bottom corners are tucked under the rubber and held to the glass with adhesive pads. After cleaning the glass with a grease remover, the Black & Decker heat gun (used for a range of tasks at MS-N), was gently applied to warm the glass, soften the adhesive and make the pads stick really well. The centre support bar has been fitted in this shot.

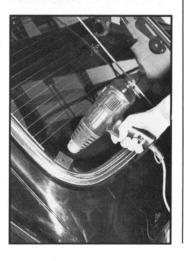

Fitting a rear window louvre

One of the advantages of the rear screen louvre is that it unclips and unhooks in a matter of seconds for cleaning the outside of the rear window glass.

RL5 ▶
With the support bar tucked under the rubber and stuck down to the glass ...

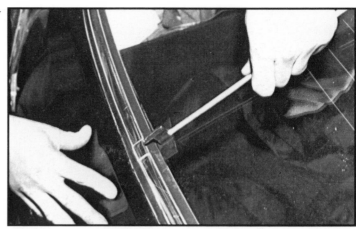

RL6 ▶
... the louvre can simply be slipped over the bar, tucked beneath the clips in the top corners ...

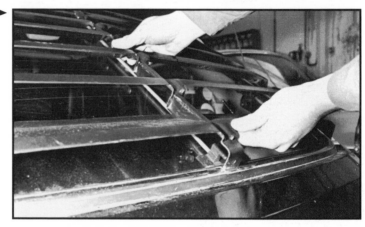

RL7
... and snapped into place in the 'catches' fitted to the two bottom corners of the screen. This is the special tool used to detach the catches.
▼

RL8 ▶
The end result is an eye-catching and practical 'fun' accessory that some will like, but others will, no doubt, loathe! A removal operation can be carried out at any time in the future, of course, and will leave no visible scars.

Fitting a front spoiler to an MGB is relatively inexpensive, gives the car's appearance a touch of 'dash' and makes a noticeable improvement to motorway stability and fuel economy. Rubber bumper MGBs in particular seem to wear a front spoiler to good effect but, even if you have a chrome-bumpered 'B', the consolation will be that a front spoiler stops part of the huge rush of air that normally passes under the car at speed, lifting weight off the front tyres and causing wandering and wind disturbance on motorways. Many MGB specialists, such as Murray Scott-Nelson, sell their own 'favourite' brand of front spoiler, but Richard Grant spoilers, in a flexible, shatter-proof plastic, are available nationally. Glass fibre is much more prone to breakage.

▲
FS1
When Lindsay Porter owned this V8, he fitted a front spoiler to it and found that motorway stability was vastly improved. The matt black of the spoiler complimented that of the front bumper perfectly.

◄**FS2**
Before fitting a front spoiler, the front bumper must be removed which, in the case of rubber-bumpered cars, means disconnecting wiring to the front flasher lamps first.

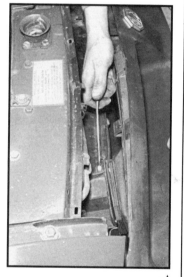

▲
FS3
After unclipping the grille behind the top of the bumper, the bumper mounting nuts and washers can simply be removed.

◄**FS4**
Murray Scott-Nelson have found that some MGBs have additional mountings holding the bumpers in place, but these are self-evident even if they are not always easy to get at in order to undo! Take care when lifting the rubber bumper away; it's heavy!

Fitting a front spoiler

Murray Scott-Nelson point out that one of the few disadvantages of fitting a front spoiler is that you have to be careful when driving up to a curb or other low obstructions, because it's all too easy to catch the spoiler on such a projection and damage it.

▲ FS5
This flexible plastic front spoiler was fitted after first making the cutouts for the bumper mountings that can be seen here, and then 'hanging' the bumper on a couple of bolts which hold the front apron in place. Other holes are drilled through the spoiler to align with these mounting holes.

FS6 ▶
The original mounting bolt washers are large enough to support the front spoiler as well. Note that the hole positions have been marked in felt pen on the visible part of the car's bodywork so that the hole positions can easily be found. It's quite possible that some of these bolts may have seized solid, in which case you will have to drill out and re-tap. Allow time for this; don't plan to use the car in a hurry!

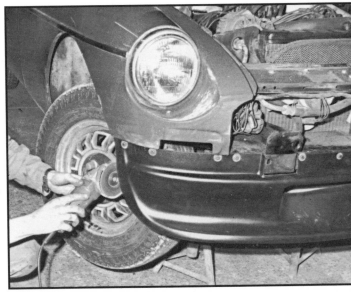

FS7 ▶
In this particular position, the rear edge of the front spoiler didn't quite match the contour of the wing. It was dressed back with a sanding disc. At Murray Scott-Nelson, a mask is always worn when sanding plastics, for safety reasons.

FS8 ▶
Murray Scott-Nelson can supply different types of front spoiler although this one may be no longer available. It is a particularly deep spoiler and could actually protude too far for everyday road use.

FS9 ▶
For this particular job, Murray Scott-Nelson decided to remove the existing front apron. This probably makes particularly good sense on cars where overheating can be a problem, and on rubber-bumpered cars where the oil cooler is fitted beneath the radiator panel. This method should increase cooling air circulation.

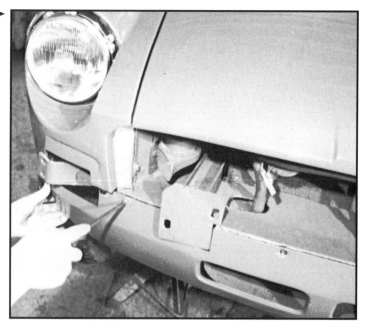

When painting a plastic spoiler such as those supplied by Richard Grant, you must remember that ordinary paint simply flakes away from most types of plastic. Plastic must always be primed with an appropriate primer before attempting to put on a colour coat. If the panel is being professionally sprayed, recommend Glasurit's top-quality plastic primer to your spray shop or alternatively, if you're doing the job yourself, turn to page 223 where Spectra's aerosol plastic primer is described.

◀ FS10
After unscrewing all of the fixing screws (in this case they were of cross-head type, not hex head), the panel is lifted away.

◀ FS11
This glass fibre spoiler was clamped into place first and then all of the cutouts for the bumper mountings and screw holes were marked out in situ.

FS12 ▶
The long-reach Sykes Pickavant clamps were removed and then one of their hacksaws used to cut away surplus material.

Fitting a front spoiler

The MGB front spoiler made by Richard Grant appears to be inherently superior to glass fibre spoilers in that it has a flexible quality and will not necessarily break upon first impact. Glass fibre can shatter quite badly. When drilling or sanding glass fibre, it is essential, for health reasons, to always wear an efficient particle mask. See pages 207 to 210 for more safety notes when working with glass fibre.

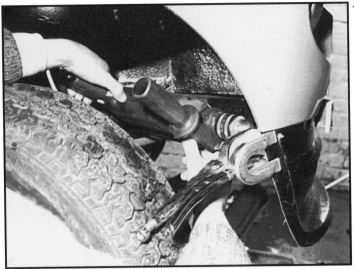

◄ FS13
After all the appropriate cutouts had been made, the spoiler was clamped back on using the Sykes Pickavant body clamps and those holes which could be reached from the reverse side were drilled through, thus aligning them perfectly.

◄ FS14
The last one or two holes were, however, drilled from the front of the spoiler ...

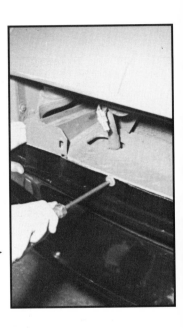

FS15 ►
... and the remaining screws and washers driven home with a screwdriver, similar to those shown in FS6.

◄ FS16
The finished result, still on it's axle stands in the Murray Scott-Nelson workshop, shows how the MGB's appearance is actually enhanced in most people's eyes by the addition of a front spoiler. After all, the last few MGB's had one as standard ...

Fitting a rear spoiler

RS1 ▶
The first job was to wipe the entire spoiler down with Valentine spirit wipe, just to ensure that no silicones were left on the surface of the glass fibre. With glass fibre this is particularly important, because silicone release wax is used to stop the glass fibre sticking into its mould.

◀ RS2
Valentine cellulose primer and then colour paint was sprayed onto the spoiler after flatting it thoroughly all over with P600 grit wet-and-dry.

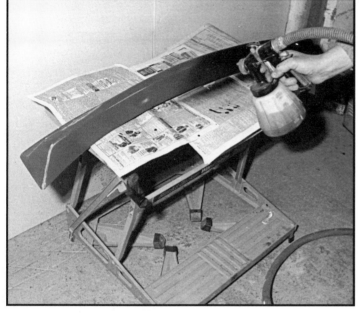

While his wife hovered patiently around taking the photographs, Lindsay Porter fitted this rear spoiler to his V8. The idea of a rear spoiler is to add downward thrust from the air passing over the car, further improving the car's stability. First time out, road dirt was found to be accumulating beneath the spoiler while none was in existence above it, indicating that there was a good flow of air over the top of, and pushing down, on the spoiler, having the desired effect.

◀ RS3
Before doing anything else, the trim panels on the inside of the tailgate were removed so that no damage was caused when ...

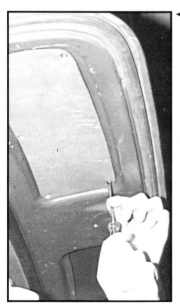

RS4 ▶
... drilling through from the outside for the rear spoiler retaining bolts.

Fitting a rear spoiler

Murray Scott-Nelson find that people are becoming increasingly reluctant even to drill two small holes in the rear of their MGB bodywork. In one sense, however, they shouldn't worry too much! If they really do feel like changing their minds later, small holes of this sort can be MIG welded up again (see page 196-on) with no distortion to the panel work, sprayed over and everything will be original again.

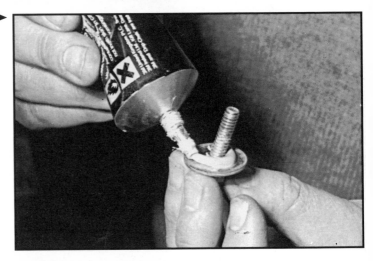

◄ RS5
The next job was to fit the edging strip supplied with the rear spoiler around the raw edge of the glass fibre. This just pushed on over the edge of the spoiler although small cut-outs had to be made around the mounting brackets and small 'Vees' cut, where it passed around the corners, to prevent it from kinking.

RS6 ►
Before inserting the mounting bolts, the large washers which sit on the inside of the panel were given a coating of drip-check sealer ...

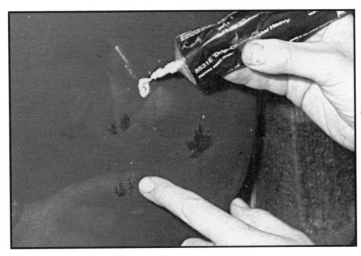

◄ RS7
... while more sealer was applied to the same area on the outside of the tailgate panel. The idea was to make absolutely certain that no water could penetrate through these mounting holes. The holes had been painted and the paint allowed to dry.

◄ **RS8**
The spoiler was held in position, the mounting bolts pushed through and then tightened up from the inside of the tailgate.

RS9 ►
Naturally enough, the whole thing looked better with the original badging in place. The 'MGB GT' badge fits into these three plastic retainers.

Although glass fibre front spoilers were shown to have some limitations in the previous section, Murray Scott-Nelson have advised that, of course, glass fibre rear spoilers fitted in this position can come to no harm, making glass fibre the perfect material.

◄ **RS10**
After drilling three holes in the glass fibre in appropriate positions, the retainers were pushed in, followed by the original badge. The 'V8' on the other side is held on with double-sided tape.

RS11
Having been painted in semi-matt black paint, the appearance of the rear spoiler matched that of the rear rubber bumper when it was valeted (see page 59-on).
▼

MWP 527P

Fun accessories

Fitting side sills

Purists throw their arms up in horror at these accessories, and it has to be said that Murray Scott-Nelson were among them. However, these are fun accessories and in many ways, MGBs are fun cars. So, if you like them, fit them ... if you don't; don't fit them, it's as simple as that!

◄ **SS1**
The Sykes Pickavant clamp was used to grip one end of the Richard Grant side sill while the other was marked for length.

SS2 ►
Tin snips cut easily through the flexible plastic material.

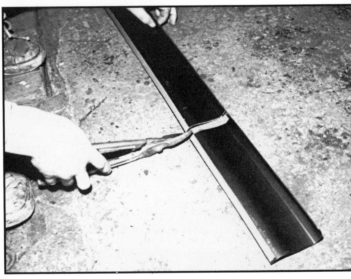

◄ **SS3**
Hold the end piece to the wheel arch, mark it and carefully cut it to suit the curvature.

SS4 ►
Remove the protective tape from the surface of the end piece and press the end piece firmly into place, at the end of the side sill.

SS6
The easy-to-fit Richard Grant side sills could be left black or painted in the body colour (see page 223 on painting plastics first).

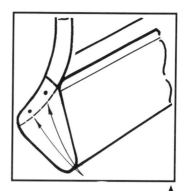

SS5
After removing the protective tape from the strip along the top edge of the side sill and cleaning the bodywork with degreaser, the sill can be firmly stuck into place. The end piece and wheel arch can then be drilled through and pop rivetted into place.

The two sets of fun accessories on these pages have to be the simplest equipment to fit. Richard Grant have even ensured that the side sills come complete with two different sizes of pop rivet and plastic caps. In addition you'll need a degreaser to ensure that the side sills stick into place.

Fitting a turbovane

TV1 ▶
Nothing could be simpler than fitting these Richard Grant cosmetic clip-on, clip off accessories. They may actually improve airflow across the rear window, improving rear visibility in dirty weather.

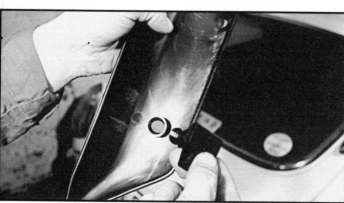

◀ TV2
The clips supplied are pushed into the oval holes in the back of the turbovane, then turned through 90 degrees to lock them into position. The plastic clips are simply hooked over the sides of the tailgate and, tightly held, are impossible to remove with the tailgate closed.

Fitting a Sebring kit

It would be unthinkable to fit a modern-style bodykit to an MGB or MGC, but some owners are interested in building themselves an MGC 'Sebring' replica. Known at Abingdon as the GTS, the lightweight MGC finished tenth overall at Sebring in 1968. The all-aluminium engine would be beyond any of us but here's how to fit a GRP replica bodykit, the work being photographed at Murray Scott-Nelson's premises in Scarborough.

▲
SBK1
The painted, fully fitted Sebring replica has a powerful, efficient look about it. Compare it with the shot of an 'actual' Sebring car on page 51 and, if you can't afford the real thing (you could buy two Jaguars, new, for the money!), you may consider having a go at a Murray Scott-Nelson replica.

▲
SBK2
At Murray Scott-Nelson, the new wing was clamped in place over the existing panel and then a line was drawn so that the new panel could be cut smaller than the existing one along the front, rear and top edges.

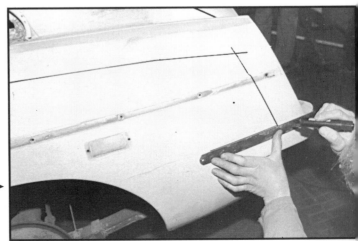

SBK3 ▶
Then the existing rear wing was similarly marked out all the way round with a felt pen ...

SBK4 ▶

... before being cut away with a mini grinder as shown. The old wing and the new were thus allowed to overlap by a couple of inches.

▲ **SBK5**

The outer half of the existing wing was in exceptionally good condition (see page 48), and was cut away for later re-use. MS-N can supply a new panel if necessary.

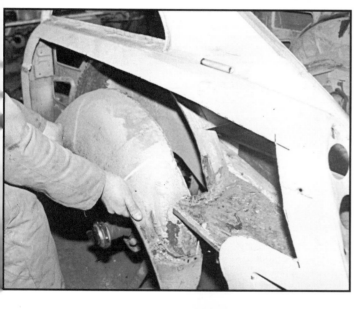

We have talked about the possibility of returning modified cars to standard spec in other parts of this book. In the case of the Sebring replica, it is still possible to return to standard spec at some time in the future. Bolt-on front wings and rear apron are no problem, although replacement of rear wings and inner wings with standard items would certainly necessitiate fairly major surgery. One or two brave souls have fitted a Sebring kit to enclose the extra rear width of a Jaguar rear suspension assembly and a V8 engine up-front to give themselves a very potent and non-standard MG ... but MG what?

SBK6 ▶

With the rear wings partly prepared, attention was turned to the fronts, where a front support panel was carefully detached from the old steel wing.

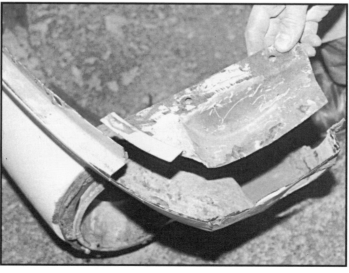

Fitting a Sebring kit

It's worth mentioning here the background to this particular MGC. Most unrestored MGCs are full of rust and would require extensive renovation before the Sebring body kit could be fitted, especially to areas such as the sills, floors and inner wings. This one, however, is one of Murray Scott-Nelson's specialities! Clive Murray and John Scott-Nelson visit the United States on a regular basis and have several contacts there for 'discovering' totally rust-free MGs from the desert areas. This is just one of those cars.

◄ SBK7
The front wing support panel was carefully cleaned up and fitted in place at the front end of the flitch panel.

SBK8 ►
The inner panelling for supporting the rear of the front wing was similarly carefully detached by the MS-N panel beater and fitted in place on the MGC's flitch panel.

◄ SBK9
A layer of glass fibre mat and resin was laid-up on the mating faces of both the support panels, front and rear, and the corresponding areas on the inside of the GRP wing.

SBK10 ►
The new GRP front wing was then offered up into position by the MS-N panel beater and pressed hard into place so that the glass fibre surfaces squeezed into one another. This bonded the mounting panels perfectly in position with the wing on the car, ensuring a perfect fit. Further reinforcing was carried out later, with the wing removed once more.

As Murray Scott-Nelson point out to anyone buying these wings for DIY fit, there are several highly important safety considerations to bear in mind when working with glass fibre. Pages 207-210 of this book show in some detail, **Working with filler and glass fibre**, using Plastic Padding products. In addition, bear in mind that if you use too much hardener in the filler, the peroxide can 'bleed' through the paintwork ruining an otherwise attractive paint job.

◄ SBK11
With the full, composite GRP and steel panel made up, it could then be bolted into place after fitting new wing beading between the scuttle panel and the top of the front wing. Here is one of the vertical line of bolts just in front of the door hinge pillar.

SBK12 ►
The front of the wing is held in place with bolts found just inside the grille opening. Bottoms of the front wings were secured with screws and nuts.

SBK13 ►
The most obvious bolts are those which run down the top of the wing holding it to the top of the flitch panel; the least obvious are those which hold the wing to the scuttle top panel. The front lower part is held with a line of self-tappping screws. Before finally bolting each wing into place, fit its adjoining door and the bonnet to ensure accuracy of fit.

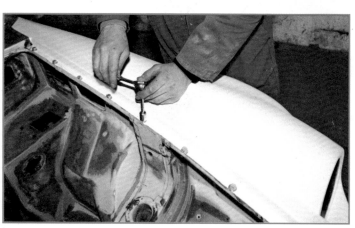

Fitting a Sebring kit

It would not be realistic to expect any GRP panels to fit anywhere near as accurately as their steel equivalents. Murray Scott-Nelson (who don't actually make these panels), found that there was an awful lot of work to do to make the panels fit correctly. It's very important that you don't put too much stress into the panel when pulling it into shape, otherwise cracks will later appear. You will also find that the surface of GRP panels tends to be rippled. You can do two things about this: spend a great deal of time applying stopper and rubbing down with flatting paper on a long, flat backing board until all the ripples are removed and; be sure to only paint the panels in light coloured paint which helps disguise any ripples which may remain.

◄ SBK14
Rather than leave the GRP rear wing hanging free, Mike, Murray Scott-Nelson's ace panel beater, made up an accurate extension piece to fit between the inner and outer halves of each inner wing.

SBK15 ►
This he tack-welded into place, offered up the new rear wing to check for fit and then, when satisfied, he fully welded in the new, extended rear inner wing.

SBK16
It was now time to fit the rear wing permanently into place. It was held onto the body with a series of self-tapping screws inserted every eight inches or so. In addition, a lot more holes were drilled near the edges of the GRP panel.
▼

SBK17 ►
The Sebring rear wing was then removed and a layer of glass fibre and mat laid-up all the way along the joining area where the new wing touched against the existing panels. The insides of the new wing were roughened and resin was also painted onto those surfaces.

▲ SBK18
The new Sebring rear panel was then offered up again and held in position with clamps and self-tapping screws (pop rivets could also have been used), so that it was tightly held all the way around its edge.

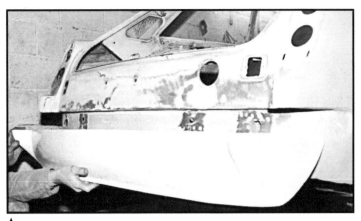

▲ SBK19
With the rear bumper brackets removed, the rear bodywork was to be smoothed out by the addition of this GRP rear apron.

SBK20 ►
It, too, was to be bonded and screwed into place and the joints filled smooth giving a clean, rounded appearance. The exhaust pipe aperture had to be measured and cut out.

◄ SBK21
The almost-complete car in Murray Scott-Nelson's workshop awaiting, in this shot, the rear apron and preparation for paintwork.

Fitting a Sebring glass fibre kit is no easy option for restoring a corroded car as these pages will have indicated, especially when the work is carried out to Murray Scott-Nelson's usual extremely high standards. Even with the addition of steel reinforcements - another testament to MS-N's thoroughness - the Sebring-bodied car cannot conceivably have the same degree of integral strength as a conventional steel-bodied car. In the event of a collision, steel front wings offer additional strength to the already massive strength of the MGB/C body shell. The use of glass fibre in the structure will clearly reduce that advantage.

SBK22 ►
RMO 699F was the second of the actual lightweight MGC GT race cars. How close can a replica get to this, a 'real-life' Sebring MGC?

Painting

Once Murray Scott-Nelson had finished their preparatory work on the Sebring-kitted car, it went away for professional painting. It is very difficult indeed for the DIY painter to match professional standards, but acceptable results can be obtained by following the correct techniques. Here's how Valentine paints suggest that their cellulose paint can best be used. Valentine's top-class cellulose paint is produced, primarily, for the 'professional' market but, being far safer to use than 2-pack paint, is excellent for DIY use, too.

◀ **P1**
First, fill all small minor scratches with stopper, such as Valentine G112.

▲ **P2**
Then, after washing the car with sponge and water, sand to a smooth finish with P600 wet and dry paper.

◀ **P3**
The car can then be primed all over after masking off, using Superspeed Primer Filler or Valentine Wash Etch Primer if priming onto bare metal.

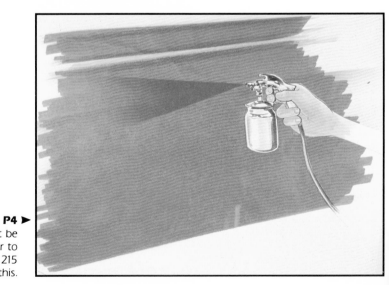

P4 ▶
Next, the spray gun must be set up correctly. Refer to Chapter 5, pages 211 to 215 for details of how to do this.

P5 ▶

Don't forget to mask off the engine bay and the door openings. Paint all the 'fiddly bits' first, such as panel edges and grille and lamp surrounds. Then you don't have to dawdle over them, causing runs, when painting the whole car.

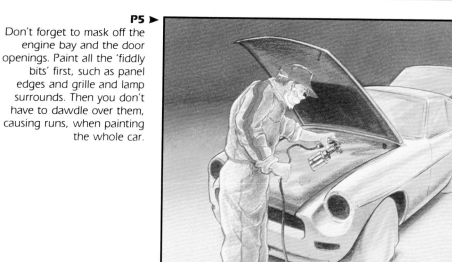

On a GT, spray the roof first, followed by one side, the bonnet, the other side and the back of the car.

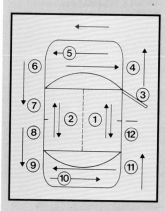

P6 ▶

Each fresh strip of paint should half overlap the previous strip, If the first coat is sprayed on as a deliberately light covering, running and sagging of paint may be less of a problem.

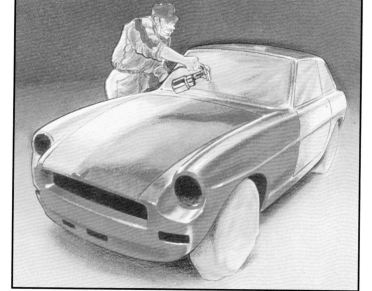

Cellulose paint is a perfectly good, durable, chip-resistant paint which can be polished to give the best shine of any type of paint there is. However, it has to be said that 2-pack paint is probably better! The big disadvantage with 2-pack is that it is nowhere near as simple to use by the DIY painter because its use can present a very significant safety hazard. Glasurit 2-pack paint is shown being used on the next page, but it cannot be over emphasized that 2-pack paints should only be used by those who are familiar with the necessary health and safety regulations (consult your supplier), and who have the safety equipment to enable 2-pack to be safely used.

▲ P7

Apply three full coats of suitably thinned Valentine 178 paint allowing ten minutes between each coat.

P8 ▶

One problem frequently encountered in the home garage is that dirt particles will have fallen onto the paint. If so, polish them out by using P1200 wet and dry paper with plenty of soap and water, then polish to a high gloss with an ammonia-free polishing compound followed by a fine polish such as Comma Top Cut.

Painting

Glasurit paint is shown being used here by a professional bodyshop. Valentine cellulose paint is suitable for use by the DIY enthusiast (as well as the professional body shop), but it is important to carefully read the safety regulations printed on every Valentine can. Follow them at all times. Good ventilation, for example, is essential, as is adequate fire protection, and a face mask or respirator should always be worn when spraying or sanding. Glasurit/Valentine insist that users should obtain all necessary health and safety data and follow it without fail.

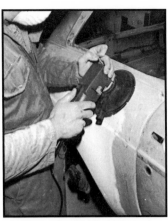

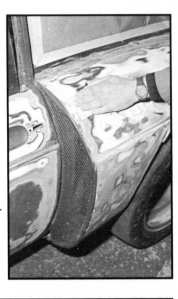

◄ P9
Here a Black & Decker random orbit sander is used on Murray Scott-Nelson's Sebring replica to produce high speed scratch-free sanding before painting.

P10 ►
This hill-climb MGB encountered by Murray Scott-Nelson had previously been painted - dozens of times, by the look of it!

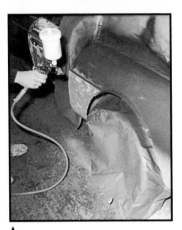

▲ P11
The MS-N painter had to use Glasurit Isolator paint to stop any risk of reaction from the old paint beneath. Glasurit Isolator is water-based and puts an impermeable barrier between the old paint and the new.

▲ P12
This 'solid colour' Glasurit 2-pack paint gives a wonderfully tough and deep shine that will never need polishing in order to retain its lustre.

◄ P13
In the booth, the painter starts to apply the Glasurit finish coat.

Adding styling stripes and decals

◄ SD1

It is essential, if the stripe is to stick down properly without pulling away, that the bodywork where it is to be fitted is wiped down first. We used Valentine spirit wipe, a material which is made for the job.

Branyl produce a very wide range of styling stripes and decals in many different colours, widths and designs. Murray Scott-Nelson say that they are not too happy with the use of some of the more outlandish designs on a car like the MGB, but concede that it's all a matter of taste! For the American market, quite a few MGBs were fitted with pre-sale stripes and decals to add to the car's 'sporting' image ...

SD2 ►

The Branyl styling stripe has a self-adhesive backing which is exposed by removing the protective paper strip. Stick just a few inches down at the front of the car ...

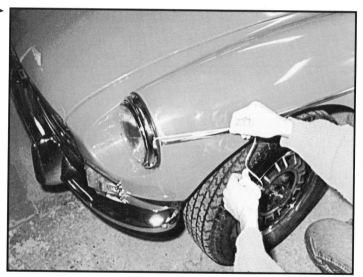

◄ SD3

... then go to the rear of the car and cut the stripe off to length. With doors closed, work it down the length of the car, pulling off the backing strip as you go.

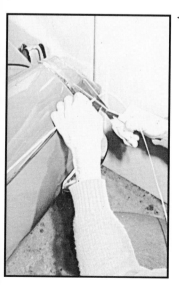

SD4 ►

Use scissors to cut the stripe along the middle of door gaps and then fold the surplus material around the edge. Place a dab of clear nail varnish over each of the ends of the styling stripe to prevent any risk of lifting and peeling off.

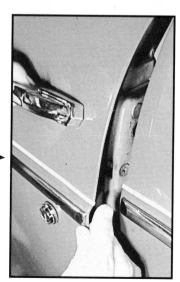

Some kinds of styling stripe, including some of those sold by Branyl, have a top covering strip as well. Then, you have to stick the styling stripe down as shown on the previous page before peeling back the self-adhesive top covering strip, leaving the colour stripe in place.

Always have an assistant help you to align the stripe, looking down the length of the car as you stick it down. Nothing looks worse than a wavy, amateurishly applied styling stripe.

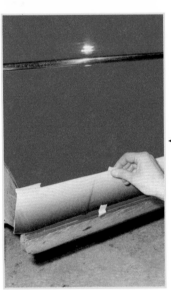

▲ SD5
The finished result is subtle and rather pleasing, emphasizing as it does the chrome moulding strip that runs down the side of the car, rather than creating a new visual reference point all of its own.

◄ SD6
Rather more daring but still by no means outlandish is this Branyl 'shading' stripe. You fit it by cutting to length, sticking down every few inches, top and bottom, with small pieces of masking tape.

SD7 ►
Then, every six inches or so, place more masking tape with its edge butting exactly up against the edge of the styling stripe.

◄ SD8
Remove the styling stripe and the tags of masking tape shown in SD6 (but not those in SD7!) and peel off the styling stripes backing paper.

SD9 ►
Assuming that you have already wiped down with Valentine's spirit wipe, thoroughly wet the surface of the car's bodywork with soapy water and also wet the entire 'sticky' surface of the styling stripe.

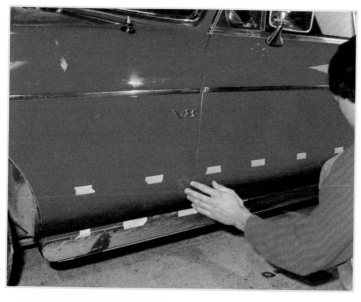

◄ SD10
The soapy water, used as described on the previous page, enables you to slide the styling stripe accurately into place without the glue on its rear surface taking a hold too quickly.

▲ SD11
Once in place, cut down the edge of each panel. We used a Sykes-Pickavant craft knife which is ideal because it has an adjustable blade protrusion.

◄ SD12
Finally, use a filler spreader, or even a clean cloth, to wipe any air bubbles away from between the stripe and the car's bodywork. As the water dries off, more bubbles may become apparent, and will have to be carefully squeezed away. Then, as the water fully evaporates, the stripe will be found to be stuck in place.

SD13
This Branyl shading stripe looks rather effective, especially in conjunction with the stainless steel oversills (see page 58).

▲ SD14
Branyl also produce a wide range of stick-on badges, many of which may not be appropriate to a 'standard' MGB. Of course, you might genuinely have fitted a turbo

If you should ever want to remove a Branyl or any other styling stripe because it is damaged or because you want an inexpensive change of theme, you could follow the Murray Scott-Nelson tip and use a Black & Decker heat gun on a low setting, or even a hair dryer on a higher setting. Start at one end heating the styling stripe and teasing the end free with a kitchen knife, then carefully peel back the redundant stripe, heating as you go.

Finishing touches

After getting as far as fitting your stainless steel oversills as described in FT2, continue by taking the sill off the car and positioning the finishing strip on its own along the marked pen line. Drill 1/8 inch holes and fit this finishing strip with the pop rivets supplied. Clive Murray of MS-N recommends coating the inside of the oversill and the outer surface of the existing sill with Corroless to help prevent rust.

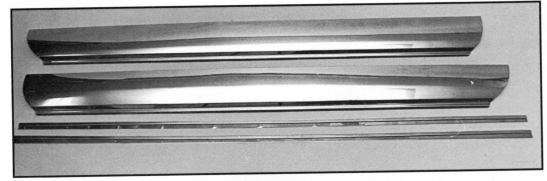

▲
FT1
Stainless steel oversills come complete with finishing strips, pop rivets and self-tapping screws. This particular sill set was purchased through the MGOC.

FT2 ►
This MGOC shot shows the first stage in fitting the sills. Hold them into place against the car while a friend drills through the lower part of the sills and screws them into place with the self-tapping screws available. Press the sill firmly against the car and, using a fine point felt-tipped pen, mark along the top edge of the finishing strip which will have been clipped into place along the top of the sill.

▲
FT3
It is best to seal each end of the sill with a compound such as Richard Grant's Flexi Fix. This highly efficient two-pack adhesive is also excellent for mending broken front spoilers, should you be so unfortunate!

FT4
A lesser way of protecting sills from stonechips is to use Plastic Padding's aerosol Stonechip Protect. It can be sprayed on top of existing paintwork and also be painted over for a standard finish.

▲
FT5
Branyl produce these special 'felt pens', designed to pick out lettering on tyre sidewalls. If you make a mistake, or become fed up with the lettering, wipe it off with a rag dampened in spirit wipe.

Cleaning and protecting bodywork

BV1 ▶
Before starting the valeting process, it's a good idea to clean down the underside of the car. The KEW-Hobby washer, here used at Murray Scott-Nelson, allows you to pressure wash all salt-retaining dirt and mud from underneath the car. It creates quite a mess and fetches out an amazing amount of road dirt so do this job **before** valeting the car.

The Comma valeting range was initially formulated for the trade user and so produces the highest standards of protection and finish available. The Comma valeting range covers interior and engine bay care as well as bodywork - see relevant Chapters. Here we look at the bodywork valeting range.

▲
BV2
If you're unlucky enough to have a windscreen leak, seal it now with Comma Seek'n Seal while the car is still dry. Ease back the rubber with a screwdriver and inject Seek'n Seal between rubber and glass.

BV3 ▶
Comma Tyre Black is simply painted on with a paint brush - wipe any over-paint from the wheels with a rag dipped in spirit wipe.

◀ **BV4**
A really useful feature with Comma 300ml plastic packs is the way in which the instructions and details are contained in a handy booklet, stuck to the back of the bottle. It's sealed down one side and can be opened, read, and then resealed.

One of the reasons for regularly cleaning your car's bodywork will be to preserve it but, as shown on the previous page, rust can attack either side of the car and underbody corrosion can best be tackled by regularly cleaning the underside of the car with a hose pipe, or better still, a power washer such as the KEW-Hobby. KEW also have an accessory available called, lyrically, the 'Guzunder'. Shaped like an upside-down walking stick, it directs a lower pressure jet of water under the car for chassis cleaning while the operator stays dry - theoretically!

Comma Clean Wheels has replaced Mag'n Alloy and is non-acidic, non-alkali, water-based and sprays on and wipes off.

A
BV5
At Murray Scott-Nelson, Ailsa demonstrates the way in which Trim Black brings a depth of finish to an MGB's black rubber bumper without adding an unnatural sheen.

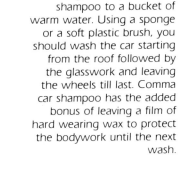

◄ BV7
Ailsa cleans the wheels down last, along with the dirt-encrusted sills, so that no soiling from those areas gets onto the upper part of the car.

BV6 ►
Comma break car valeting down into two stages. Ailsa commences first stage preparation of her MGB by adding two capfuls of car shampoo to a bucket of warm water. Using a sponge or a soft plastic brush, you should wash the car starting from the roof followed by the glasswork and leaving the wheels till last. Comma car shampoo has the added bonus of leaving a film of hard wearing wax to protect the bodywork until the next wash.

BV8 ►
Unfortunately, alloy wheels in particular, such as those fitted to this V8, pick up oil, grease, brake dust and white corrosion like magnets. Comma Mag'n Ally wheel cleaner is sprayed on with the trigger action gun ...

◄ BV9
... then worked around with a small paintbrush where there is deep soiling, before the wheel is washed off, bringing it back to pristine condition.

◄ BV10
Still on 'Stage One', Ailsa uses Comma Tar remover to remove any oily tar deposits that have built up on the paintwork. She has poured a little Tar Remover onto a soft cloth and lightly rubs the affected area. The deposits instantly emulsify and disappear without harming the paintwork at all.

▲ BV11
No mattter how often a car is shampooed, oxidisation of the paint will take place, especially if cellulose paint has been used. In addition numerous small scratches can appear, all helping to dull the finish. An automatic car wash will cause this 'dullness' to develop even quicker. Comma Top Cut can be used to gently remove the 'dead' upper layer of paint exposing the fresh paint underneath. Alternatively, Super Cut'n Wax will remove scratches while leaving a waxed finish as the polish is rubbed off.

Valeting the bodywork of the car you enjoy can be a pleasure rather than a chore if it's done properly. While you're at it, check for any paint chips or stone damage so that you can touch them in before rust takes a hold. Preserving your car's bodywork also helps to preserve its value, see also pages 224 to 228 for further details on body maintenance.

BV12 ►
Once a normal paint surface is clean and dry, Comma Silicone Polish can be applied using a soft cloth or stockinette, rubbed sparingly to small areas at a time with an even, circular motion. **Don't** apply polish in direct sunlight as the polish will dry out too quickly, leaving a 'patchy' finish. After a few minutes, polish back with another soft, clean cloth to leave a shine which Comma say will last many months.

◄ BV13
Pre-1975 MGBs have even more chrome on them than alter rubber-bumpered cars, making Chrome Cleaner an essential part of the valeting kit. Comma say that their Chrome Cleaner is only lightly abrasive, so it does not scratch the softer bright metals, such as the aluminium trim used on some parts of MGB's, but its cleaning powers will still cope with any brightwork.

BV14 ►
Many owners neglect to adequately clean windscreens and door glass, forgetting that these comprise a large percentage of the area of the car.

Comma Window Clean is one of the best glass cleaners around, containing finely ground clays which will clean and absorb the dirt, grime, traffic film, insects and tobacco haze that accumulate on windows. As it dries, it turns white and polishes back to a smear-free surface. The makers are proud of its 'unique' anti-static protection.

Chapter Two
In-car comforts

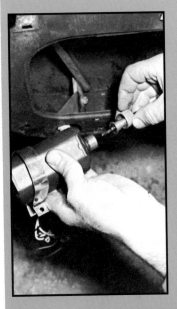

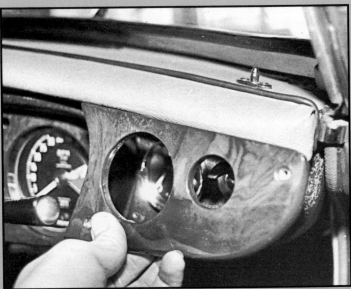

Fitting a replacement steering wheel

ICI.1 ▶
The centre cap from the original MG wheel pulls off revealing the single nut holding the wheel to the steering column.

ICI.2
On this particular car, the wheel nut was 1 1/16 inch and required a socket to suit. Wheel retaining nut size varies from year to year so you'll have to check the size on your particular model. ▼

ICI.3 ▶
As you can see, someone had butchered this one! Fortunately, the Moto-Build engineer found that it came off fairly easily.

ICI.4
The original wheel will probably 'stick' on the splines. The wheel nut should be placed on top of the column as shown and then tapped **lightly** with a soft-faced mallet while a ◀ helper pulls at the wheel. **Problem!** The wheel is prone to springing off and smacking the helper in the face!

ICI.5 ▶
Fit the new boss to the splines, adding a smear of grease to them first. The Moto-Lita wheel is commended by Moto-Build as making a great improvement to the driving aesthetics of the 'B'.

Some caution is urged by Moto-Build when removing a steering wheel from a post '72 MGB. After this date, they were fitted with collapsible steering columns and if you use a hammer and too much force, you are quite likely to break the shear pin which means that the column will come free and slide up and down as you try to fit the wheel. Repair is tricky and likely to be more expensive than your new Moto-Lita steering wheel!

Moto-Lita produce a wide range of very high quality steering wheels and the model shown here is considered to be **the** wheel for the MGB owner, the wooden rim wheel adding beautifully to the Olde English charm of the beast. Before tightening the new Moto-Lita wheel boss in place (order at the same time as the wheel), make sure that the front wheels are aligned in the straight ahead position. Always replace the friction washer under the nut. The wooden rimmed wheel requires only the horn wire connecting and the centre push replacing before it is finished.

Fitting a replacement steering wheel

When choosing your new Moto-Lita wheel, make sure that the correct boss is supplied too; do so by specifying the exact year and model of MGB. Early cars had the horn push in the centre of the wheel, for instance, whereas on later models it migrated to the steering column. Moto-Lita wheel bosses are all available with either a blank centre or the horn push version.

◄IC1.6
The Mark 9 Wood Rim is a 'classic' wheel, finished in a deep, rich mahogany and is an alternative to the attractive and highly popular Mark 3 shown being fitted on the previous page. Mark 9 spokes can have slots, as shown in this picture, or traditional round holes. This is a 15 inch wheel and is available either flat or dished.

IC1.7►
For a complete contrast, how about the Mark 8 model, a modern, four spoke wheel, with a leather rim and available in either black or dark and light tan. If you like the style, but not the leather, Mota-Lita can do it with a wooden rim. Like the Mark 9, it comes either flat or dished but is available only in 14 inch diameter.

Fitting replacement seats

Moto-Build regularly race MGs and find that such motoring activities demand a special seat to hold the driver firmly in place and one which will stand up to the incredible stresses and strains that are part and parcel of racing. Their race prepared cars are fitted with Ridgard competition seats which more than meet these exacting requirements. However, for those with slightly less ambitious plans for their MGBs, Moto-Build can supply a wide range of road going seats from the same manufacturers.

▲
IC2.1
The Ridgard RS6 fully reclining seat. It has a suspension system designed to support kidneys and lumbar regions and has forward tilt facility. It is seen here with the optional headrest in vinyl cloth finish.

IC2.2
The RS7 is built to the same high standard as the previous model, but has a built-in headrest for even better support. Like the RS6, it too has the forward tilt facility.
▼

▲
IC2.3
The GT1 is the MGB GT V8 of competition seats! All competition seats **must** be fitted with a competition sub-frame.

Poor seats make a poor car! If your seats are sagging and lacking in support, the time you spend in your car will be uncomfortable. To a great extent, this will negate any other improvements you have carried out. Don't forget that the driver's seat is usually more worn than that of the passenger.

▲
IC2.5
If your seats look anything like this, it's high time you paid them some attention! This leather seat is typical of those that Moto-Build are given to rebuild.

▲
IC2.6
Hard to believe that it could one day look as good as this. This is just one of the many seats that have received the Moto-Build treatment.

IC2.4
Using a Ridgard seat necessitates the fitting of a special sub-frame. This will raise the height of the seat by around 1½ inches which, to many drivers, will be welcome indeed, as the standard seat can leave all but the tallest owners struggling for visibility over the steering wheel. ▶

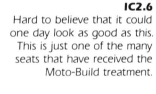

◀**IC2.7**
The first job when tackling a seat rebuild is to remove the seat. A spanner at the rear and ...

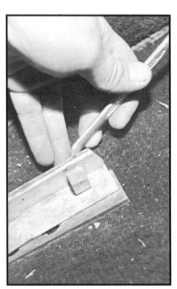

IC2.8▶
... a socket at the front and the task is done. You might have difficulty in sliding the seat to the full extent of its runners in order to reach the mounting bolts.

Fitting replacement seats

When removing the clips from the seat coverings, Moto-Build recommend that great care is taken as they can quite easily spring off and cause injury. Holding your hand over the clip as it is prised away is the best bet.

IC2.9 ▶
There are 16 of these 'C' clips which must be unclipped in order to remove the covering. Note that on this seat, the underside has cross-hatch webbing. The seat backrest cover is held by two 'C' clips and four 'D' clips, in a similar manner.

IC2.10 ▶
With the covering taken off, the squab foam padding can be removed. Note that this seat has a solid diaphragm.

IC2.11
Moto-Build put new diaphragms, like this one shown here, or webbings, into all their rebuilt seats.
▼

IC2.12
The frame, in all its glory. Having got down to basics, the task of rebuilding begins.
▼

IC2.13► A new back rest cover being pulled down onto the frame. As yet, no adhesive has been applied.

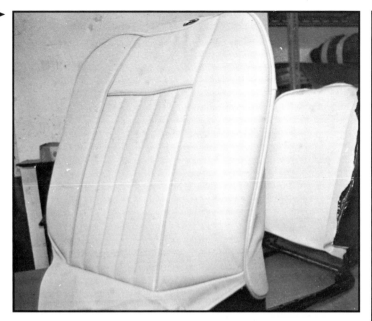

During the seat rebuilding process, Moto-Build use only spray-on adhesive, which reduces the possibility of getting the stuff all over the place and is considerably less messy for the user. Note the safety instructions on the tin, whichever type you use.

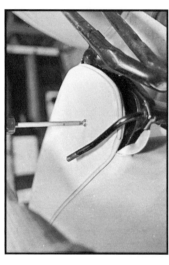

◄IC2.14 This is done when the cover is tight and exactly in position. Glue from a nozzle is considerably less messy than when applied with a spreader.

IC2.15► Here, the two screws (one each side), are being replaced. These hold the cover in position at the lower part of the backrest.

◄IC2.16 Now work can start on the seat squab. Here, the new diaphragm is being tensioned into the correct position. Note the use of a special Moto-Build tool; you could make your own equivalent.

Fitting replacement seats

The Pirelli webbing fitted to post '70s cars is considered by Moto-Build to be vastly inferior to the diaphragm type fitted to earlier models. It is not as strong, does not provide as much support and is prone to ripping where it attaches to the frame. As such it causes many seats to get that 'sinking feeling'!

IC2.17 ►
The new foam for the backrest is sprayed inside, after the cover is fitted over it. Again, a spray adhesive is used.

◄ IC2.18
In order to make sure that the cover sticks to the foam, a heavy weight must be placed on top of it until the glue sets. There's not much danger of this cover coming unstuck! This is left for at least three hours to make sure that the glue is fully set.

IC2.19 ►
Back in position, the edge of the squab cover is pulled down tight ...

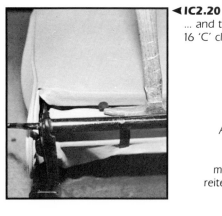

◄ IC2.20
... and then secured with the 16 'C' clips.

IC2.21 ►
At the bottom of the back rest, the cover is held in place by the small clips mentioned earlier. We must reiterate the need for caution when fitting these items.

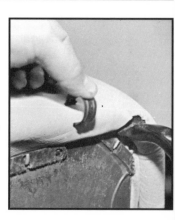

IC2.22 ▶
Headrests too are well catered for by Moto-Build. They can be re-covered as originals or in something totally different. Some owners go for a contrast with the seats ...

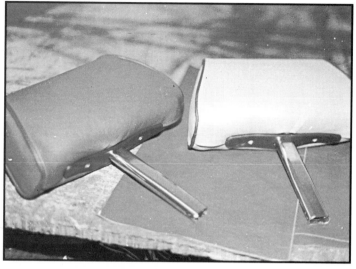

Moto-Build's expertise extends in all directions and, naturally, covers the rebuilding of standard seats for those who wish to retain the authenticity of their car. Covering materials can be whatever the owner wishes, from vinyl and cloth to leather with contrasting piping.

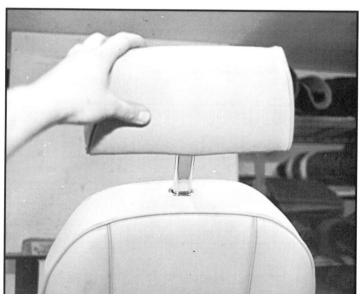

◀**IC2.23**
... whilst others prefer a direct match. No problem, as can be seen here.

IC2.24 ▶
Headrests for MGBs have changed over the years. On the left is seen a later 'flat' type. On the right is the earlier 'sculptured' version.

Fitting replacement seats

Moto-Build take a great deal of care with what some may consider to be minor points. Getting the piping **exactly** lined up is the difference between amateur and professional. Likewise, the flutes should be treated in the same way.

IC2.25 ▶
The finished seats are virtually works of art and are almost too good to sit on! The headrests match the seats, even down to the piping.

IC2.26
Having had your seats rebuilt, why not go the whole way and retrim the door panels as well? These complement the seats perfectly and, being of a lighter colour than 'MGB Black', give the car a light and airy feel to it.
▼

▲
IC2.27
If you have a GT model, Moto-Build can also restore your rear 'seat'. A relatively simple task, this involves removing the old covering and then stretching the new covering tightly around the base and foam. This is then stapled into place, taking great care to avoid those fingers!

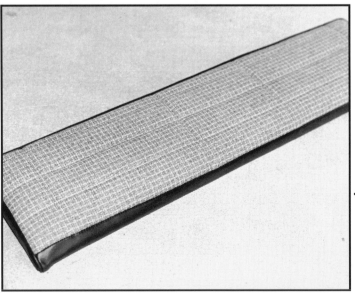

◀**IC2.28**
As good as new! Again, the pattern/design is a matter of choice; you're certainly not restricted to the original design and colour, although those are available if you want them.

IC2.29 ▶
Spot the difference! The driver's seat is the standard late-model item with striped covering. The passenger seat is a Moto-Build special, being a late model frame, with an earlier style covering. The best of both worlds!

All of the parts shown in this Chapter can be supplied by Moto-Build to the DIY enthusiast who wants to build his or her own seats. They will supply individual items or, if required, a whole seat refurbishment kit. It's up to you!

◀IC2.30
These totally non-standard seats were made to order by Moto-Build who start such a task ...

IC2.31
... by marking out the basic shape of the seat and the pattern on the material.

◀IC2.32
Each part of the pattern is then individually sewn. The age of craftsmen is, fortunately, not yet gone.

Fitting a wooden dash

In your English sports car, there is little you can add that is more 'English' than some wooden dash trim. The Rokee kit featured in this section is used by Moto-Build to give a stylish new look to the fairly dull standard dashboard. The holes for the self-tapping screws are pre-drilled in the various pieces of trim. However, it is best to start the screw before fitting the wooden trim to avoid the possibility of the screwdriver slipping and damaging the veneer.

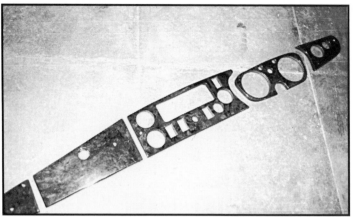

◄ IC3.1
The kit laid out in schematic order. Instructions are minimal, but it doesn't take **that** much effort to work out which bit goes where!

IC3.2 ►
Moto-Build usually start at the driver's side and work across. The facia end piece has to be held in position and the screw holes marked through with a bradawl or similar. Once marked, the screw holes can be drilled.

◄ IC3.3
With the end piece screwed into position, the trim around the dials can be positioned and fixed in the same way. The screws are cross-heads which reduce the risk of the screwdriver slipping, although it is vital that you use the correct size tool.

IC3.4 ▶
This is the middle section in situ. Note how all of the original inhabitants of the dash can carry out their normal function. Neither switches, dials nor air vents need re-siting or modifying in any way.

Care, time and patience should be taken when positioning and fixing the various panels. It would be wise to have a helper to steady them whilst marking out. When not busy helping in a practical way, he can stand back and decide whether the panels are level!

◀ **IC3.5**
To the left of the centre section, the glovebox is first positioned accurately, to ensure that the lid will open without fouling. Then ...

◀ **IC3.6**
... it can be screwed into position as shown.

IC3.7 ▶
The same care has to be taken with the facia end piece that fits onto the dash at the passenger side.

Fitting a wooden dash

Rokee kits are, naturally enough, designed to fit around all of the 'standard' protrusions, such as heater switches, dials, gauges, etc. However, if you have added anything to your dashboard, you may find that the new dash will not fit. It is then a question of deciding whether to modify the dash (which would have to be done extremely carefully), or to remove, if possible, the non-standard item and reposition it elsewhere.

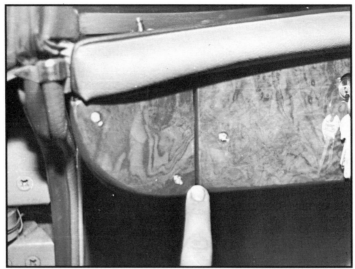

◄IC3.8
Finally, the last piece can be positioned and screwed down. Again, it is important to get it absolutely right so that the glovebox will open.

IC3.9►
There was, by now, a definite air of up-market refinement with this car, the Rokee trim adding a touch more grace to go with that provided by the leather seats and door trim already fitted.

◄IC3.10
The Rokee kit is available for any model or year of MGB, including LHD as can be seen on this car. This model, as enthusiasts will know, is an earlier one which is denoted by the radio in the dash aperture rather than air vents.

Fitting door and footwell pockets

IC4.1▶
This extremely useful footwell pocket was fitted by MG as standard on later model cars, although it is a simple matter to retro-fit one to an earlier model. Also, it maintains a certain degree of originality.

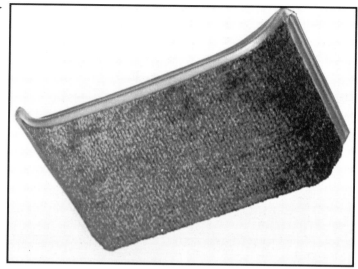

Storage space in the MGB is hardly a strong point. However, when you've cleaned out the rubbish which has collected under and behind the passenger seat for the tenth time in a month, you may well want to give some thought to a better way of storage!

◀IC4.2
It fits, naturally enough, in the footwell, but on the passenger side only, for obvious reasons. With the position marked, holes are drilled to take the self-tapping screws which hold it in place.

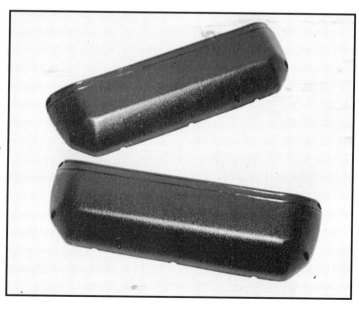

IC4.3▶
As an alternative to the standard item, Moto-Build can also supply these Richard Grant door pockets. They fit to the bottom of both doors and are held in the same way as the above. Those owners with loudspeakers mounted in the doors should check that they do not foul in any way.

Fitting transmission tunnel storage

This worthwhile modification will only fit later model MGBs. Earlier cars, with the three-synchro gearbox, have a different shape to the gearbox tunnel and will not accept the unit shown here. Although supplied through Moto-Build, it is a genuine part, which accounts for the ease with which it blends into the rest of the interior trim.

IC5.1 ▶
The tray is held at the front by two clips which fasten to the lower part of the new centre console.

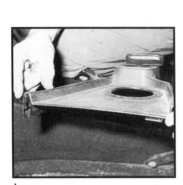

▲
IC5.2
From an end view, the clips are clearly visible.

IC5.3 ▶
With the clips in position, the gearstick gaiter has to be squeezed slightly to allow the tray to be eased down into place.

◀IC5.4
A chrome bezel is self-tapped into place around the gearstick. Note that of the four screws, the shortest goes nearest the front.

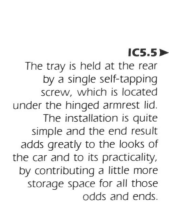

IC5.5 ▶
The tray is held at the rear by a single self-tapping screw, which is located under the hinged armrest lid. The installation is quite simple and the end result adds greatly to the looks of the car and to its practicality, by contributing a little more storage space for all those odds and ends.

Cassette storage

IC6.1►
All Fischer C-Box products are made from shatter-resistant plastic and many have a soft, rubberised outer casing. This is the universal 33 052 model, made to mount vertically and which holds six cassettes. The bracket supplied will fit wherever is convenient by means of the self-adhesive pad supplied or with two self-tapping screws. As can be seen, the drawers are spring-loaded and, once in place, the cassette slots on to spindles which hold the mechanism in position and prevents the tape from unravelling inside the cassette.

The in-car cassette player (more ususally nowadays, the radio/cassette player), is a boon to those of us who regularly have to make long journeys. However, this means that cassettes have to be carried and, as most of us like to have a reasonable selection at hand, it can pose a storage problem. Moto-Build can provide the answer from the wide range of Fischer C-Box storage systems. Apart from making the interior of your car considerably tidier, the use of a C-Box will prevent damage to cassette mechanisms and also protect them from excesses of both heat and cold.

IC6.2►
The Car Carry case, model no 33 048, is extremely useful as it enables cassettes to be transferred easily from car to home. It comes supplied with two brackets which can be fitted on to any flat surface. This means that this portable C-Box can be held securely in position whilst in the car, but still be unclipped and removed - a good security measure!

Carpets and mats

IC7.1►
Laid out in schematic order is the 13 piece kit for an MGB Roadster, which has slightly fewer pieces than the GT. As can be seen, they are all cut exactly to size and where necessary, the edges are hemmed to prevent fraying. Note the reinforced rubber panels on both driver and passenger side front sections, to guard against excessive heel wear.

The best MGB in the world will manage to look tatty if the carpets are dirty and worn. By definition, any original carpet set will have had more than a fair amount of wear and tear by now! Moto-Build have recognised the problem and now produce their own, tailor-made sets which are attractive as well as durable.

Carpets and mats

The Moto-Build carpet sets for the MGB Roadster model, as featured here, are almost the same as the GT version. For the GT the wheel arch pieces are bigger and there are extra sections: behind the lights, by the rear wheel arches and the large rear mat.

◄ IC7.2
Although the car seen here has been completely stripped out, the items which **must** be removed are the seats, the front and rear quarter trim panels and the centre console. And, of course, the original carpet! With a clear deck, Moto-Build find that this is also a good opportunity to apply Corroless rust inhibiting primer to any areas in need, after first vacuuming out.

IC7.3 ►
Starting from the outside and working in, the wheel arch, sills and transmission tunnel sections are fitted first. The car is equipped with a piece of felt on the transmission tunnel and it is best to refit this as it acts as sound deadening and also absorbs some heat. The areas which will have carpet glued to them (sills, wheel arches, etc), should be wiped over with spirit wipe to make sure that there are no traces of grease left.

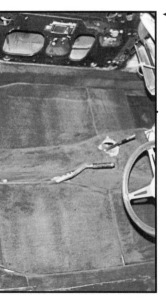

◄ IC7.4
The Moto-Build carpets vastly improved the worn interior of this car. They can provide kits for DIY owners (for any model of MGB), or are prepared to do the whole job for those who require it.

IC7.5 ►
Having fitted beautiful new carpets to your car, it would be a shame to ruin them the first time you get in with mud covered shoes! These Link-Sedan rubber mats will help to protect them, which will pay dividends if you come to sell the car; a clean car is easier to sell than a dirty one!

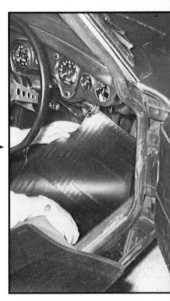

Fitting a sound deadening kit

IC8.1 ▶
As always, the first task is to read the instructions thoroughly. All of the sections are cut to size and have numbers marked on the rear which correspond with the instructional notes.

By their very nature, MGBs are fairly noisy beasts. Whilst an interesting engine and exhaust note can be pleasing to the ear, when combined with other undesirable sounds (tyres, wind noise, etc), especially over long distances, life can get very tedious indeed. Moto-Build have found the Acoustikit sound deadening kits most effective.

◀ IC8.2
Some of the pieces simply lay in position, such as those for the driver and passenger floor area and ...

IC8.3 ▶
... the piece for the boot floor

IC8.4 ▶
The piece which fits on the underside of the bonnet is self-adhesive. It comes as one section, but as the 'B' bonnet is, effectively, in two halves because of the rib, it has to be cut in two. Measuring before cutting has to be accurately carried out.

Fitting a sound deadening kit

Acoustikit panels are fibrous and shed their 'hair' everywhere, so it is wise to keep your carpets away from them as much as possible (especially if you've just replaced them as in Section 7). However, you'll probably still end up having to use the vacuum cleaner again!

◄ IC8.5
Having drawn a nice straight line, it then needs a steady pair of hands and a good eye to make a nice straight cut!

IC8.6 ►
The protective paper backing simply peels off to reveal the self-adhesive glue. An ambient temperature of around 15-20 degrees C is recommended so that the adhesive will stick correctly. It is best to check the piece for size **before** removing the backing.

IC8.7 ►
The underneath of the bonnet has to be cleaned thoroughly with spirit wipe (not petrol!) to remove all traces of oil and grease. Do **not** do this whilst the engine is hot. To do so could possibly result in a fire, or worse, an explosion. Take care in positioning the felt as the glue sticks most tenaciously and you won't get a second chance.

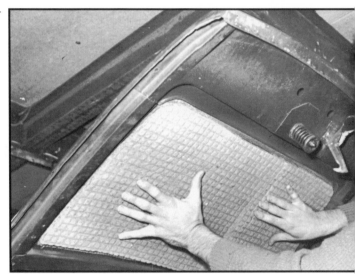

◄ IC8.8
Still in the engine compartment, there are two pieces which stick onto the inner wings. Again they need to be very clean. If you have added any extras, you will have to cut the section appropriately.

IC8.9 ►
The top of the passenger side footwell section is also self-adhesive and is fitted in the same manner as the bonnet.

IC8.10
To prevent the doors from creating vibration by 'drumming' at certain speeds, the Acoustikit comes with four 'Vibrapads' which stick onto the door panels and reduce this unpleasant resonance. They come with a piece of protective backing paper which is peeled off before the pads are stuck down. Again, wipe the panel clean first.
▼

Sharp scissors and an equally sharp craft knife are essential when fitting this kit, as some of the panels have to be trimmed slightly to the exact size. Moto-Build have fitted many of these kits, which are available for all MGB models, and all owners have reported a great decrease in extraneous noise, thus making their steeds much less wearing and much more enjoyable to drive.

◄ IC8.11
The door trim panel has to be taken off, by first removing the window winder handle, trim and armrest. The Vibrapads are extremely sensitive to temperature. If they are not warm enough, they will just crack and break up. On the other hand, if they are at 20 degrees or more, they are supple and easy to fit. Using this Black & Decker Heat Gun is a simple way to ensure the latter. Lightly heating the steel panel also improves 'stickability'!

IC8.12 ►
Fit two in each door, one at the front and one at the rear. There are two 'holes' in the door skin, ideal for fitting the Vibrapads. Once stuck they are there to stay, so you have to get the position right first time!

Electrical accessories

Fitting theft prevention

If you have fitted just a few of the items featured in this book, then you will have a very desirable MG indeed. The problem is that those with less than honest intentions may also admire your handiwork and taste! With the statistics for car theft (and theft **from** cars), rising like a space rocket, it makes sense to protect your pride and joy by fitting an alarm system. According to the latest UK figures, there are 1.5 million break-ins and thefts from cars every year! On average, therefore, a car is vandalised every 20 seconds and every owner has a 1 in 12 chance of being a victim!

There are many makes and models on the market, although those in the Bosch range have a justifiable reputation for being of very high quality. In this section, Moto-Build guide us through just a few of the various types available for your MGB.

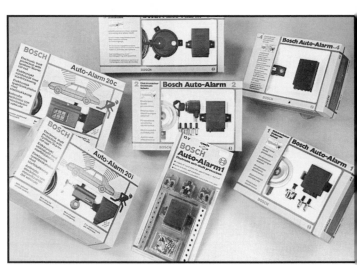

IC9.1►
A selection of various alarm equipment available from Bosch. The wide range includes ultrasonic, remote control, ignition cut-out and keypad systems. The Bosch philosophy is such that each type of alarm is separate. Thus, you can buy a basic set-up and add to it whichever you think is most appropriate for your car. Similarly, you need not buy what you do not need! For example, a Roadster owner would not be well advised to fit an ultrasonic alarm.

◄IC9.2
Here are a few of the integral parts such as senders, control units, etc. Fitting an alarm system, especially if it includes some of the option packs available, is not a job for the fainthearted!

◄IC9.3
With the keypad system, a calculator style pad with six digits has to be fed with the correct four digit code within around 12 seconds of entering the car, otherwise the alarm will be triggered. It can be mounted anywhere convenient, although when fitted in a prominent place, such as the dashboard, it provides a visible warning to any potential thief.

◄IC9.4
The siren is mounted in the engine compartment. It should be positioned where the wiring will reach easily and where it will not be affected by the heat from the engine and exhaust. Also, it should not be in the direct line of spray from the road.

IC9.5 ▶

As an alternative alarm to the keypad, there is the infra-red sensor type. Here, the sensor itself is being mounted at the rear of the car, although Bosch recommend that it should be fitted inside. The hole is being drilled with the Sykes Pickavant 'varicut' variable hole cutter, which makes such a task very simple indeed.

When routing the wiring, great care should be taken to keep all cables away from the exhaust and cooling systems and any moving parts. By using the same cable clips and following the same route as the existing loom, the alarm wiring can be held well out of harm's way.

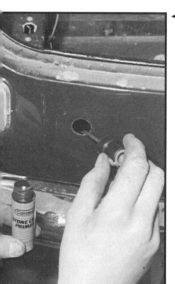

◀IC9.6

As always, the hole **must** be protected against rust. Moto-Build use Corroless Stone Chip Primer for this and brush it well into the hole and surrounding area.

IC9.7 ▶

The infra-red sensor screws into place and ...

◀IC9.8

... is operated by this remote control activator, which doubles as a key ring. It will switch the alarm on or off from a distance of up to ten metres and, as there are 13,000 different codes, there is complete security from outside interference.

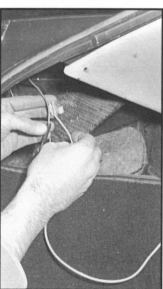

IC9.9 ▶

Wiring the alarm into the MGB indicator system is achieved by the use of 'Scotchlok' connectors, as can be seen here.

Fitting theft prevention

The ultrasonic alarm systems have a sensitivity control which should be set carefully before using the alarm in public. Too sensitive a setting could result in the siren sounding everytime there was a slight wind or someone walked by the car. Your embarrassment could be the least of your worries! Similarly, if your car has a sunroof, do not leave it open as it too could fool the system into being triggered. Even the face-level vents or a slightly open window can allow air movements on a windy day that will trigger the alarm.

IC9.10 ►
The Bosch control units use special plugs. Bosch provide a number of corresponding connectors which are fitted to the relevant wires and which in turn fit into the plugs. A great deal of care has to be taken when wiring these units to ensure the right connections are made.

IC9.11
The Plus 3 microtonic anti-tilt device is a good idea if you have fitted expensive wheels and/or tyres, for a normal ► alarm only triggers if someone tries to gain entry. With such an alarm fitted, jacking up the car and removing the wheels would leave the sytem blissfully unaware that anything was wrong. This sensor unit is being fitted into the boot. It is held by three spring-loaded self-tapping screws. By adjusting these it can be mounted exactly horizontal and the small spirit level type guide in the top shows when this has been achieved. It uses a computer to memorise the exact position of the vehicle in relation to the ground. If the car is moved then the alarm is triggered.

IC9.12
This is the optical ultrasonic detector. It detect movement of air in the ca and thus is advantageou where entry is gained, say by breaking a window. It i not recommended fo drophead cars, as the flexibl nature of the roof could se off the alarm by mistake

◄ IC9.13
Open the door and ... BLAST! It would take a determined thief to stick with this car with the lights flashing and the siren blasting, producing more decibels than a road drill! The standard alarm, in keeping with German regulations, will not flash the car's lights, but a separate module can be fitted which will enable it to do so.

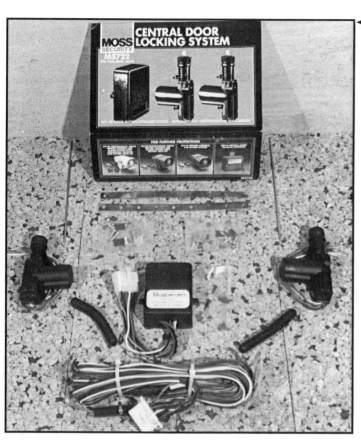

◄ IC10.1
This is what you get. The Moss Security kit laid out, which includes electric drive motors, relay switching unit, cable looms, connectors, linking rods and various ancillary pieces. The MS 722 basic kit includes all that is necessary to fit a two-door car.

Wiring a central locking system is all part of a day's work for the Moto-Build engineers, although you have to have a certain measure of electrical skill to make it a successful DIY project, as this diagram shows. The system is such that it can be operated from either of the front doors.
(Diagram courtesy of Harry Moss International UK Ltd)

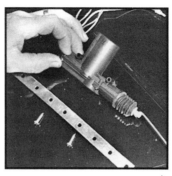

▲ IC10.2
This is the solenoid and mounting strap. The solenoid can, in theory at least, be mounted almost anywhere in the door. However ...

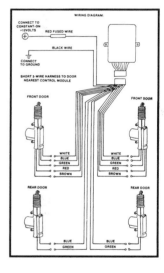

IC10.3 ►
... this is the position that we found best, shown here outside the door skin for clarity. This meant that it could be mounted on the door frame itself. The solenoid operating rod has to be bent so that it takes a straight 'pull' on the original operating rod.

◄ IC10.4
The original operating rod is removed by using a thin bladed screwdriver to prise off this clip which holds the rod to the door latch mechanism.

Fitting central locking

In schematic form, the workings of the Moss system are quite simple. Locking one door locks the other door at the same time. The system can be extended to apply to the rear doors on four-door cars.
(Diagram courtesy of Harry Moss International UK Ltd)

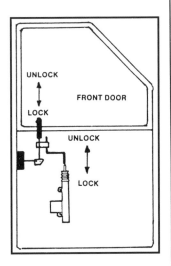

◄IC10.5
The position of the solenoid has to be accurately marked and then the mounting holes drilled. Note the use of the Black & Decker Cordless drill, invaluable for in-car applications.

IC10.6►
The solenoid and operating rod can then be threaded through the door skin. Note that the connecting rod adaptor (near the fitters right hand), has been loosely fitted, so that it will just need tightening when everything else is in position.

IC10.7
The mounting screw being ◄tightened. If you look closely, you will see the top of the solenoid positioned neatly out of the way. When this is secure, the connecting rod adaptor can be tightened, thus making the new solenoid part of the door locking system.

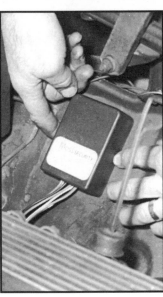

IC10.8►
The 'thinking' part of the central locking system is this black box. It is mounted in the engine compartment, well away from the usual enemies: heat, damp and moving parts. Wiring should also be thoughtfully routed. Before starting to wire up the system, the battery **must** be disconnected.

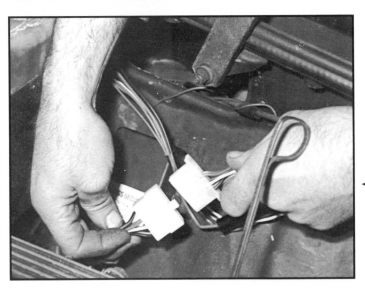

◄IC10.9
The moment of truth. All of the wiring to the black box is via one plug. Once connected, the system, being electrically operated, permits very quick locking and unlocking.

Fitting electric windows

IC11.1►
The kit comes complete with everything required to do the job, except the small window adaptor, seen here at top left. The splines differ from car to car and so Servoglide supply these separately. Servoglide also supply a can of silicone lubricant, which should be used to ensure the smooth, free running of the existing mechanisms before starting work.

So, you're cruising along in your MGB, enjoying the luxurious feel of the new seats and carpets and the sound of your Blaupunkt Berlin and you want the windows down. It is at this point that you'll appreciate the luxury of electric windows! In this section, we follow Moto-Build as they fit a Servoglide electric window conversion kit. Those who cherish the originality of their car will be pleased to know that the Servoglide kit is manufactured by Lucas who supplied much of the MGB's original electrical equipment.

▲
IC11.2
The door trim has to be removed. Note that, although the actual door handle stays in place, the trim around it has come off. The two pieces simply unhook from one another and are not held by any other fixings.

▲
IC11.3
With the window winder handle and the arm rest taken off, the door trim can be removed.

◄IC11.4
The wiring has to pass through from the door to the switches in the car and so a hole has to be drilled. The Black & Decker Cordless drill proves its worth once again. Don't forget that the hole should be rustproofed and that a grommet must be fitted to prevent the wire from chafing.

Fitting electric windows

Connecting the wiring to the motor inside the door skin is not at all difficult, as can be seen from this diagram. All diagrams in the comprehensive Servoglide instruction booklet are schematic, which makes life much simpler for the non-electricians amongst us.

(Diagram courtesy of Lucas Electrical Limited)

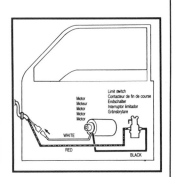

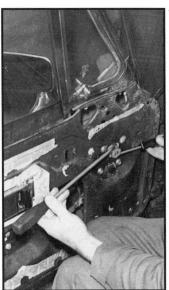

◄IC11.5
Pushed over the later MGB's winder splines is a large, hexagonal nut, which has to be removed. By using screwdrivers as levers the Moto-Build engineer is able to remove it quickly and easily.

IC11.6►
The special adaptor in the engineer's right hand fits onto the splines and facilitates the fitting of the gearbox mechanism which turns the winder spindle.

◄IC11.7
A torque reaction strap has to be fitted. This is mounted on the gearbox to any one of the four holes and to the door, wherever is suitable. The only stipulation is that it must maintain a 90 degree angle to prevent any tendency for the gearbox to rotate about the spindle.

IC11.8►
The drive cable screws into the drive motor as shown here but **not** until the motor has been secured properly in the inner door skin. When routing the cable, it is very important that it should **not** have any tight curves.

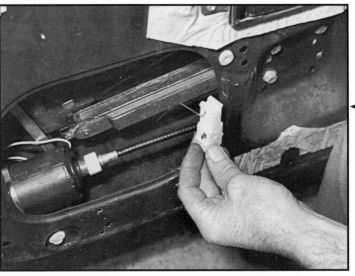

◄IC11.9
With the motor in position and the cable connected, the next step is to fit the limit switch; without it the window could conceivably wind down until it strikes the bottom of the door. It follows that the positioning of the operating arm is vital and could be the difference between electric windows and no windows at all!

◄IC11.10
Before carrying out any wiring, the battery should be disconnected. With the operating mechanisms in position, the trim replaced and the wiring completed, the spindle cover housing can be fitted.

IC11.11►
The second part of the housing is a plastic blanking cover. If, for any reason, it is not possible to use the electric windows, they can still be operated manually by removing this cover and inserting the special tool, as shown. Remember to carry it in the glove locker, just in case!

Moto-Build always check the function of the wiring circuit before actually mounting the switches. Should the motor run in the wrong direction, it is then a simple task to reverse the wires. As can be seen, the wiring of the system from the motors to the switches is only slightly more complex than that of the motors themselves.
(Diagram courtesy of Lucas Electrical Limited)

IC11.12►
The switches, one for each side, can be mounted wherever is convenient. They can be bracket mounted, as here, or positioned under the dash. Alternatively, they can be fitted directly into the dashboard or centre console. A template is included in the instructions should you want to do this.

IC11.13►
The final wiring goes to the fuse box. Sit back, relax and enjoy a touch of luxury!

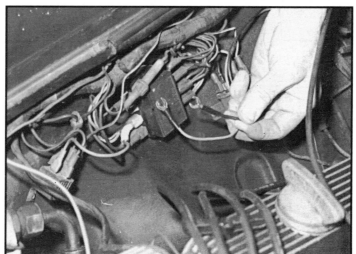

Fitting a cruise control

The Econocruise is an excellent piece of equipment for those of us who have to suffer long, tedious journeys on a regular basis. The electronic 'brain' of the system checks the speed several times per second and adjusts the throttle setting accordingly. Because it is checked and set so often, the speed is almost constant and your MGB thus becomes more economical. A somewhat backhanded advantage (although useful just the same), is that it could well help you hang on to your licence; as most of us know, there is a natural tendency to increase speed when motorway driving, however much we may try to keep to the legal limit. The Econocruise has no such tendencies and will maintain a constant legal speed; provided, of course, that it is **set** for a legal speed ...

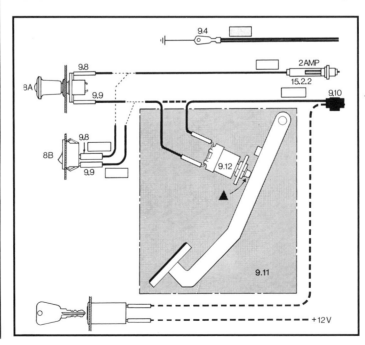

◄ **IC12.1**
The essence of the system is the strap, shown here, which is fixed to the prop shaft. A sensor is placed under the mat and picks up the impulses from the magnets as they spin round. The electronic wizardry of the Econocruise transfers this into a constant speed in mph, by increasing or reducing the throttle setting automatically.

◄ **IC12.2**
Inside the engine compartment, the actuator unit (arrowed), has to be mounted so that the connecting Bowden cable can be fitted in a smooth curve to the carburettors. When the unit is in use, this operates the accelerator pedal which can be quite uncanny to the driver, especially at first!

◄ **IC12.3**
Take your pick: there are three different types of operating switch. From top to bottom they are;
1) a dash-mounted stalk,
2) two dash-mounted switches,
3) a stalk-mounted, self-adhesive switch.
All provide the same function, so it's purely a matter of choice.

◄ **IC12.4**
Just part of the comprehensive schematic instruction booklet. This shows the wiring for the brake cut-out switch. As this is a safety feature, it is vital to check that the brake lamp switch is in good condition and is adjusted so that the lights come on at the start of the pedal movement. Also, the connectors should be totally secure; remember, the brake lamp switch is the primary method of disengaging the system, although there are other 'fail-safe' back-ups.

IC13.1 ▶
This little lot is just a sample of the Link-Sedan instrument range. The individual gauges seen here are: ammeter, econometer, outside temperature, tachometer, water temperature, voltmeter and finally, oil pressure. In the centre are three gauges mounted in a single pod and beneath is an oil pressure pipe, complete with threaded connections.

When fitting extra instruments and/or switches, Moto-Build emphasise that it is important to make sure that their positioning is functional as well as aesthetic; it's no good a new instrument looking good if you bang your knees on a switch every time you get into your car! Also, follow the usual rules with regard to the wiring and routing of your chosen additions. Keep pipes and wires away from excesses of heat, cold and moisture and try to route them without sharp kinks or bends. Always use a grommet when passing a wire through a metal or plastic panel and follow the Link-Sedan instructions with regard to wiring meticulously. Have the work carried out professionally if you're at all unsure.

◄ IC13.2
For mounting extra switches, this Link-Sedan bracket can take up to three of the rocker type, as seen here. The bracket affixes to the underside of the dash, using self-tapping screws.

◄ IC13.3
The switches push into the housing and 'clip' into place. To remove the switch, it is necessary to use a screwdriver to press down the securing tabs.

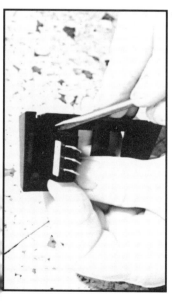

IC13.4 ▶
Standard 52 mm gauges, such as this voltmeter, are a push fit into the brackets, as shown here.

Fitting extra instruments and switches

Before starting to fit extra instruments or switches, it is imperative that you ask your local retailer for details of the full range of Link-Sedan instruments and switches, then sit down with a piece of paper and plan exactly what you intend to do. In this way, you should be able to achieve an attractive and integrated look to the interior of your MGB which compliments the original design. Moto-Build regularly advise owners who are uncertain of how to achieve this. The moral is: if in doubt ... ask!

◄IC13.5
In the case of a single bracket, it can be mounted under the dash on the passenger side. Self-tapping screws are used.

IC13.6►
The gauge is then pushed into the bracket, as shown earlier. The wiring instructions are included with each dial. Clearly, if the information given by a gauge is going to be of great interest to the driver, then fitting it here is not very wise, as he would have to divert too much of his attention from the road.

◄IC13.7
This double mounting bracket can be fitted either under the dash in a horizontal manner, or on its side, as shown here.

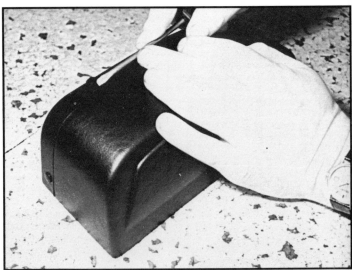

IC13.8►
Whereas the brackets shown earlier are open at the back, leaving the wiring and/or pipework exposed, this pod is totally self-enclosed. By using a screwdriver to remove the plastic rivets ...

IC13.9 ►
... the front can be removed to allow whichever gauges you choose to be fitted. All of the wiring, etc, is neatly out of sight once the pod is reassembled.

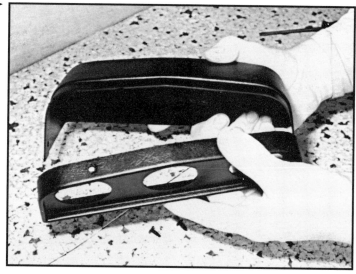

Although it may seem somewhat incongruous in a sports car, those who have regularly driven a car so fitted, will confirm that an econometer is a definite aid to good driving technique. There are, in fact, many times when easing back slightly on the throttle will have no effect on the cruising speed of the car but will be much more economical.

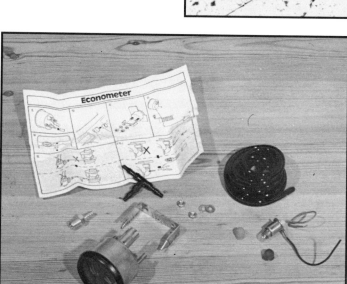

◄ IC13.10
Moto-Build fitted this econometer to a 'B' in their workshops. As always, the first job is to make sure that all the pieces of the kit are present and correct and that you can identify them. Then check the instructions for how and where the gauge should be mounted. The main recommendation with the econometer is that, for it to be of most use, it should be within the driver's line of sight.

◄ IC13.11
Unlike the underdash type of mounting brackets, this single pod necessitates the use of a rubber sealing ring to make a tight fit, as shown here.

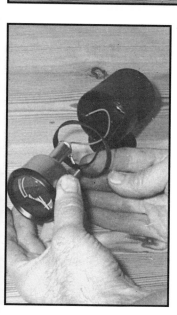

IC13.12 ►
The pod can either be self-tapped into position on the dash for best results, or stuck down, using this self-adhesive pad. A small hole has to be drilled to take the wiring/tubing (unless it can be routed down the side of the dash or through a vent) and, for neatness, it should be covered with the plastic sleeving supplied.

Fitting an intermittent wiper control

There can be few more aggravating situations than driving in damp conditions, where the rain is sufficient to need the windscreen wipers, but not all the time. Constantly flicking them on and off can become very wearing! Moto-Build offer a solution in the form of this Hella intermittent wiper unit. It controls the length of intervals between successive sweeps of the blades and the switch knob can be set, steplessly, to operate them from two to twenty sweeps per minute.

IC14.1▶
This is the basic kit. The instructions are concise and very clear, in typical Hella fashion, and all connectors are supplied.

IC14.2
The electronic 'control' of the system is contained in the switch itself. The wiring to it is achieved by this simple socket. Take note that the size of the switch and the socket dictate a mounting position with plenty of room at the rear.
▼

▲
IC14.3
As shown in the first picture of this sequence, the switch mounting panel comes with the kit. We used it in this instance to mount the switch on the driver's side of the centre console. It is mounted as high as possible to avoid being knocked by a driver's leg when getting in or out of the car.

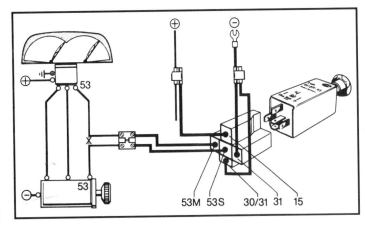

◀IC14.4
The diagram shows that the wiring is relatively simple. All connections are made by using Scotchloks.
(Diagram courtesy of Hella Ltd)

53M 53S   30/31 31 15

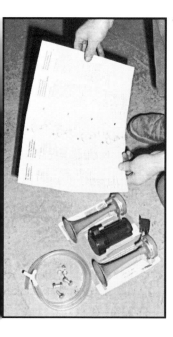

◄IC15.1
As always, read the instructions first. Hella leave nothing to chance and are very thorough. Check also that all parts are present and identify them.

IC15.2►
The compressor unit effectively 'hangs' on this bolt which should be put into place before the unit is offered up. As the mounting nut and bolt are tightened, the bolt is locked into place on the compressor.

If you've ever felt that most of the drivers on Britain's roads are asleep, then why not fit a set of air horns? The Hella set shown here would startle even the most ardent daydreamer back to reality!

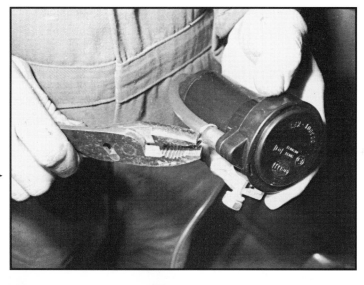

IC15.3►
The air pipe should be fitted now, as it is very difficult to reach when installed in the car. It is held in place by a spring clip which is slackened by using pliers as shown here.

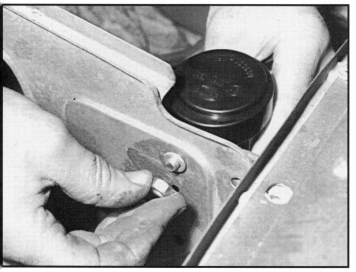

◄IC15.4
Where to mount the compressor is no problem. On the offside of the radiator shroud there is a hole ready and waiting! Mounted here it is ahead of the engine compartment and the associated heat, but to one side of the front grille which protects it from the elements.

Fitting air horns

The wiring of the air horns is not difficult and is explained in detail in the comprehensive instructions.
(Diagram courtesy of Hella Ltd)

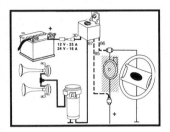

◀ **IC15.5**
The trumpets should be mounted in close proximity to the compressor. A 'Y' piece is supplied to split the single pipe, feeding compressed air to each trumpet.

IC15.6 ▶
The existing horn push should be used to trigger the horns, but the relay provided must be used. Again, it should be mounted close to the compressor. As it is on the offside of the car, it is handy for wiring into the fusebox, which is on the same side of the car near to the bulkhead.

Fitting a maplight

You only have to be lost once on a dark winter's evening to appreciate the wisdom in fitting a maplight! The Hella model shown here is simple to fit and very useful. The unit shown here is permanently mounted in the car and is 195 mm long with a powerful 12V/5W halogen bulb. Other than the metal arm, the rest of the casing is made of glass fibre reinforced plastic. Earlier 'B's have one built in to the dash but this useful feature is absent from later models.
The Hella Map Light is also available with a 500 mm arm for alternative mounting positions.

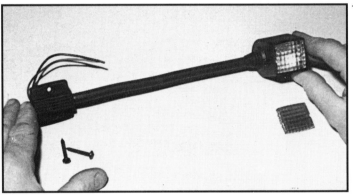

◀ **IC16.1**
The light is mounted on the end of a flexible stalk and comes complete with self-tapping screws and a separate, optional red lens cover to stop excessive glare.

IC16.2 ▶
The mounting position can be anywhere convenient. In most cases, the map reader will be the passenger and so the position should be biased accordingly. As shown here, it will fix under the dash and sit out of the way across the top of the console. The on/off switch is handily mounted in the head of the light.

Fitting inertia reel seat belts

IC17.1 ▶
The kits supplied by Moto-Build come complete with all component parts and mounting brackets, nuts, bolts, washers, etc. Seen here are the necessary parts to convert one side of the car.

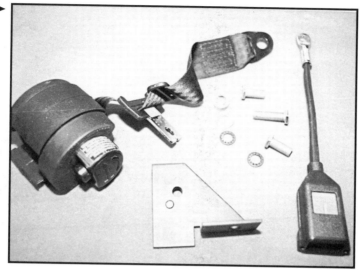

Only later model MGBs are fitted with inertia reel seat belts as standard. For those with static belts, swapping to the later type has many advantages. Not only does it allow free movement in the car (reaching over to the maplight you fitted in Section 16, for example!), but also, it makes life much easier if the car is driven by different people and the static belts have to be manually adjusted to suit. We took a look at how Moto-Build go about fitting inertia belts to a Roadster.

IC17.2 ▶
A close up of the inertia mechanism, showing the plastic cover removed.

IC17.3

As the inertia seat belts mount in three positions, rather than two, a hole has to be drilled by the rear wheel arch in order to mount the mechanism (this is a Roadster don't forget). The hole positions are stamped in the moulding during production. The usual rustproofing procedure should be carried out when the hole has been made. Some models may have mounting nuts held captively, ready and waiting.

▼

IC17.4 ▶
The mechanism can then be mounted on its bracket as shown here. These are safety items and Moto-Build are at great pains to stress the importance of checking and re-checking every nut and bolt, and of ensuring that each mounting point is actually sound. If you have the slightest doubt, seek professional advice.

Fitting inertia reel seat belts

The care of seat belts is often a much neglected task, despite the safety considerations involved. The webbing should always be clean, untangled and in good condition (ie, not frayed). Not only is this an MOT requirement, your life could depend on it! Only wipe seat belts clean, never wash them nor use a propriety cleaner on them.

IC17.5 ▶
The two original mounting points are re-used in order to make up the three point fixing. As can be seen here, it is important to check that the webbing is not twisted in any way. The mechanism can be checked quite simply by tugging at the webbing. When a sharp tug is given, the ratchet system should lock immediately. When pulled gently, it should allow the webbing to reel out smoothly. It is important that nuts, bolts and washers should be used in exactly the right order, to prevent any possibility of the fixings working loose.

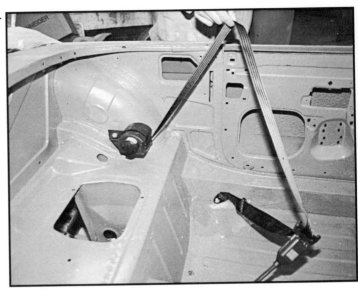

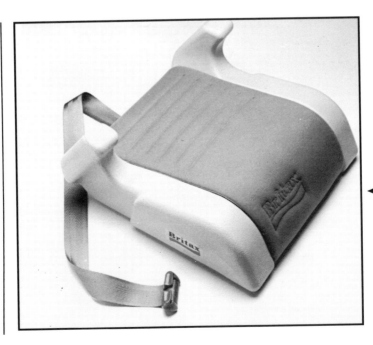

◀ IC17.6
On the GT model, the mechanism is mounted on the top of the wheel arch, as shown here. In this position it does not foul the backrest.

Fitting child seats

When purchasing a child seat, always look for the British Standard 'kite mark'. All Britax seats are approved by this body and, as you would expect from one of the top manufacturers, are produced to a very high standard.

◀ IC18.1
The StarRiser car booster seat is intended for children from approximately four years upwards who would otherwise be sitting too low down for the proper use of conventional seat belts. For use only with the front passenger seat in the case of the MGB.

◄ IC18.2
Full instructions are included with the StarRiser and must be followed carefully. This drawing shows how to position the booster cushion on the seat. (Drawing courtesy of Britax)

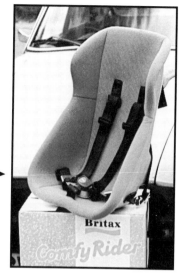

IC18.3 ►
The Britax ComfyRider can be fitted to the rear of an MGB GT **only** (ie, not to the open-topped MGB), and must be fitted with a Straphanger anchor beam in the GT.

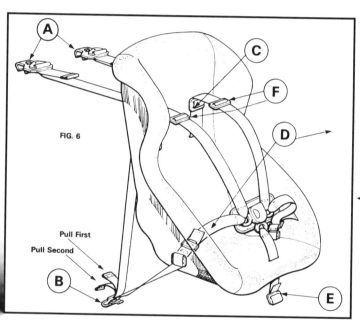

FIG. 6

Pull First

Pull Second

◄ IC18.4
Location points for the attachment straps and details of how to adjust the belts are described in the instructions that accompany the ComfyRider. The hooks 'A' are attached to the Straphanger beam in the rear of the car.

IC18.5 ►
The Straphanger kit includes these components and consists of a bar which is securely located across the rear of the car providing a sound anchorage for the child seat as the car, because of its age, was not fitted with built-in anchorage points from new.

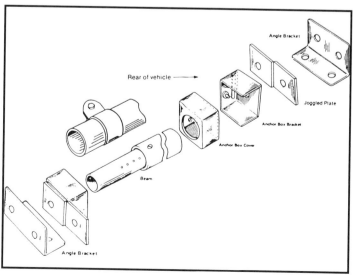

Rear of vehicle

Angle Bracket

Joggled Plate

Anchor Box Bracket

Anchor Box Cover

Beam

Angle Bracket

Britax do not recommend the use of any of their child seats on the rear shelf of an MGB Roadster and only one model of child seat in the rear of the MGB GT. Even then, special fitting requirements have to be followed (see this page). As you will see, there are two more child seats available for use with the front seat and seat belts of the MGB. To be honest, the MGB isn't the most 'family-friendly' car on the road, but if you have to carry a young child, it makes sense to use a child seat. However, it is imperative that you follow the full fitting and use instructions, supplied in clear drawing and note form with each Britax child seat. The drawings shown here are simply to help illustrate what is possible; you **must** consult the full instruction booklet supplied with a Britax or any other make of seat before fitting or use.

Fitting child seats

Before using either of the child seats shown on this page, check with your Britax supplier that it is correct for your particular MGB. Both of these seats have to be used in the MGB in conjunction with the existing front seat belts and it is necessary to ensure that the seat belt anchorage positions are within the areas shown in the seats' instruction booklet.

The same applies to any other make of seat you may choose to use, too. Check with your supplier that it is appropriate to your car before purchasing.

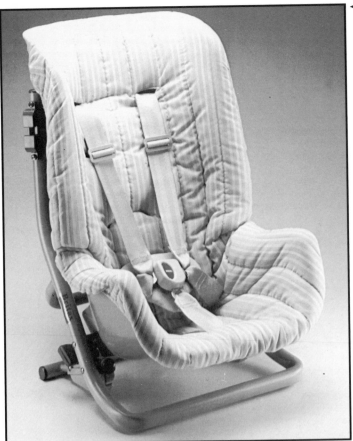

◄IC18.6
The Britax 2-Way can be used in a rearward facing position, for babies up to 10 kg, provided that your MGB is equipped with the appropriate seat belts.

IC18.7
Alternatively, the Britax 2-Way can be used in a forward facing position for children weighing between 9 to 18 kg (20 to 40lb).
▼

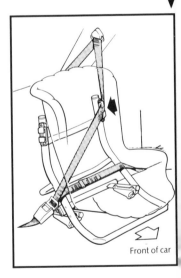

Front of car

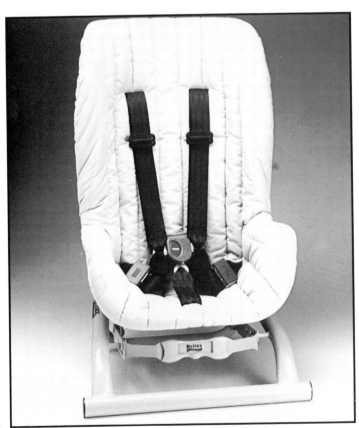

◄IC18.8
The Britax Recliner is also for children weighing from 9 to 18 kg (20 to 40lb) which generally means children aged from approximately six months to four years. As the name would suggest, the seat can be fully reclined, encouraging your child to sleep the journey away.

◄ IC19.1
Moto-Build can supply an Aleybar to suit your car. Three of them are shown here although, if what you want is not available off the shelf for any reason, Aleybars will make up a special for you.

IC19.3
... the bolts are inserted and the retaining nuts tightened. For obvious reasons, if is important that these are torqued up correctly. Use the correct washers as supplied with the Aleybar kit.
▼

IC19.2
◄ All Aleybars come with complete instructions and are precision made to fit individual vehicles. As such, you do not have to worry about whether bolt holes will match up, or if the bodywork will be strong enough at the mounting points, provided that it is not rust weakened. Here, the holes are being drilled through which ...

IC19.4 ►
A more stylish cage is the Aerodynamic model, shown here. It is padded, has a black vinyl finish, and is of double hoop construction which gives more strength and rigidity for the open top MGB. For those with a technical mind, this particular bar is made of 1½ inch OD ERW BS1775 steel!

IC19.5 ►
One, not insignificant point, is that an Aleybar cage allows the hood to be fitted as normal; not a foregone conclusion with some cages! This can be seen quite clearly with this special cage which is fitted to Moto-Build's racing MGB.

It is a terrifying thought but statistics show that in 15 per cent of **real** accidents (ie, not a car park 'ding'), the car actually overturns. Obviously, owners of MGB Roadsters should be particularly concerned here! John Aley has been producing roll cages since 1964 and 'Aleybars' are well respected in motorsport circles. However, the company has a wide range of road-going cages. For a standard road car, no work other than drilling the holes and bolting the cage into place is required. However, if the cage is to be used in a sporting application, then some welding may be needed.

Valeting

Interior valeting

Cleaning the interior of your MGB is made much easier by emptying the car before you start. Take out mats or additional carpets, loose cassettes, pieces of paper, maps, sweets, scrapers, pens, parking tickets, etc ... and you're half way there!

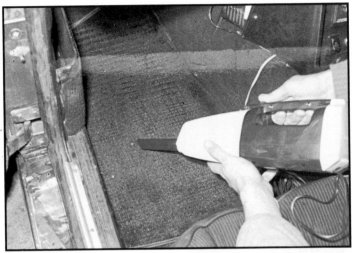

◄IC20.1
Cleaning the carpets and cloth seats is made easier by using a portable vacuum cleaner such as this one from Link Sedan. It works from a cigarette lighter plug or from the battery making it truly portable and its long nozzle means that it can reach into all those awkward little places where the dust usually rests undisturbed.

IC20.2 ►
For stained cloth seats, Comma Interior Clean is the answer. It is poured onto a soft cloth and ...

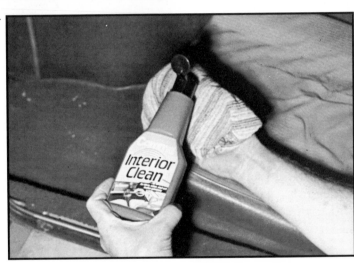

◄IC20.3
... then rubbed well into the area of the stain. It lifts the dirt out of the fabric which can then be wiped away with a damp cloth.

IC20.4 ►
For really stubborn marks, a nailbrush should be used. Interior Clean will not normally harm the fabric, although a small, unseen area should be tested beforehand.

IC20.5 ▶
Comma Cockpit spray is designed specifically for use in the interior of the car. It is silicone based and gives a good, anti-static sheen to the dash, console, etc, whilst removing marks and stains. A tip for getting the dust from those 'tricky to get at' places is to use a paintbrush; dry, of course!

Cleaning the inside of the car is one of those tasks which always seems to be at the bottom of the priority list. Usually, by the time that three weeks accumulation of mud and dirt have been removed from the outside of the car, there isn't much energy left to continue with the inside. However, you should really try to give the interior a good clean out at least once a fortnight. This means that you will be able to keep a general check on the appearance and if any new stains have appeared, you may be able to remove them before they become too ingrained. Those with children will particularly appreciate the wisdom of this last comment! In the long term, an MGB with a clean and obviously well cared for interior will command a much higher market value.

◀ IC20.6
After spray-on application, it should be wiped away using a soft cloth. It makes the car look like new and gives off a pleasant, aromatic scent.

IC20.7 ▶
Not much use to Roadster owners, but Comma Electrocure could be the answer to a GT owner's prayer. It is a liquid agent which is 'painted' onto the rear screen to repair damaged elements in the rear screen heater. Before application, the screen must be totally dirt and grease free. Simple to apply and considerably cheaper than a replacement rear screen!

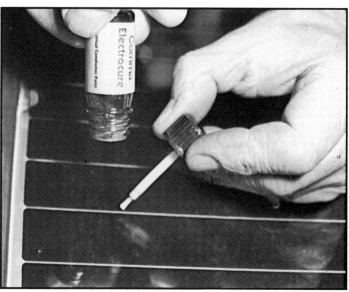

Chapter Three
In-car entertainment

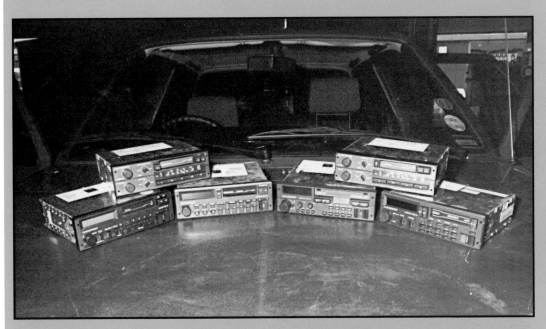

Choosing your in-car entertainment

Some details about the Company

The origins of the Blaupunkt Company date back to 1923 when, trading in Berlin as the Ideal Radio Company, they manufactured detector devices, headphones and radio accessories. The name 'Blaupunkt' became a trademark a year later and the famous 'Blue Spot' came into being, as the headphones were actually marked with a blue spot as they were passed through quality control.

Their first car radio was produced as long ago as 1932 and even that had remote control! Since then, the Company has followed a path of continual development, producing their first FM radio in 1950 and the first push button car radio (called the Omnimat) in Europe, in 1953. In 1969, the 'Frankfurt' model was the first stereo car radio in the world with the electronic car radio being introduced in 1973.

In 1974, they introduced their ARI traffic information and warning system for which they were awarded the ADAC (the German equivalent of the AA) safety prize.

Such a record of technological achievement reflects an unwillingness to accept that a peak has been reached and this clearly shows in the products.

In choosing your ICE you should bear in mind that all MGBs are highly prized vehicles and to fit anything less than high quality audio equipment is doing an injustice to both yourself and your car. This applies even more so if you have spent a great deal of time (and money) in restoring your car.

Over the years, in-car audio has increased massively in popularity. Even a quick glance at any brochure will confirm that the days when this meant slotting any old radio into the dash have long gone. Advising which equipment to fit to your MGB is difficult, almost to the point of being impossible. Everyone has different opinions as to what constitutes a good in-car audio system, from the simple and straightforward to the incredibly sophisticated.

There are a number of limiting factors, not least of which is the amount you can spend, and good quality sound does not come cheap at any level. There is also useage. If the car is only driven four miles a day throughout the year, it makes little sense to load it up with the latest high-tech stereo system.

MGB owners have specific problems in terms of in-car audio fitting compared to their saloon and hatchback cousins. The main one is space, or rather, lack of space. Even in GT form, it could hardly be said that there is copious amounts of it. Also, owners of most cars only ever communicate with the elements via an open window or perhaps a sunroof. However, if you are fortunate enough to have a drophead car, then not only can you have the wind in your hair, but also a few extra difficulties with regard to how to fit your system, how to secure your system and finally how to hear it over the wind noise! A major point is to judge which is best for your personal listening. Although most car fitments are combined radio/cassette units, some people like to listen to the radio and seldom use the cassette player. Thus, a set with particularly advanced radio features but with less sophisticated cassette facilities will appeal. Those who prefer cassette listening will be looking for features such as Dolby noise reduction, metal tape facility, track search, autoreverse, etc. It is worth noting that, by and large, in most combination units, the radio is more advanced than the tape deck and thus a high performance cassette player will usually be accompanied by a high quality radio.

The advent of Compact Disc players has added another facet to the various permutations. Whilst initially an expensive item, the CD player is rapidly becoming more affordable. Although being more limited than tape in some respects (you can't record on a Compact Disc of course) its superb clarity of sound and dynamic range have led to increasing popularity. Whatever the personal choice, it is worth sitting down for a while and deciding exactly what **you** need from a car audio system.

Bear in mind that when improving your in-car audio, uprating one item will almost always mean that another link in the chain has also to be uprated. For example, an uprated radio/cassette deck may require uprated speakers.

In this section we will be looking at some of the options offered by Blaupunkt from their wide range of radio/cassettes. The German company have a well deserved reputation for producing high quality equipment, achieved over more than 60 years in the business. The standard of fit and finish is always high and it is pleasing to note that this applies uniformly to the whole range and not just to the top models.

Because of their attention to detail and, in particular, to the ergonomics of their sets, Blaupunkt equipment will not look out of place in any MGB.

In this Chapter many technical terms and abbreviations are used. In order to save repetitious explanations, we have included a Glossary at the end of this Chapter. It pays to understand the jargon attached to the in-car audio market. Although advertisers love to load their copy with impressive sounding terminology, it is really only impressive if you know what it means! A much more comprehensive glossary of terms appears in the full Blaupunkt catalogue.

(Our thanks are due to Senior Blaupunkt Engineer, George Richardson, for his help in the preparation of this entire Chapter.)

Choosing your in-car entertainment

When buying a radio/cassette unit, one should always remember that at some time in the future, an upgrade of some kind may be desired. The sets featured on this page are all capable 'front end' sets able to utilise additional amplification, speakers, etc.

◄ ICE1.1
Shown here are some of the large range of Blaupunkt radio/cassette models described in this Chapter.

ICE1.2 ►
The Porto is a lower range model which would go nicely with a fairly modest speaker set-up. It has manual tuning with three wavebands (FM Stereo/AM/LW) and 2 x 12W output (music power). The cassette deck is a basic unit offering no form of noise reduction although it does boast a hard permalloy head.

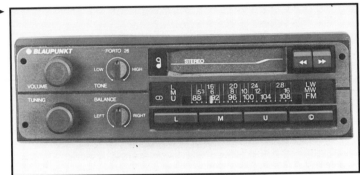

◄ ICE1.3
The Stockholm is visually a very similar set to the Porto, but has several improved features on the cassette deck. The frequency response is increased and autoreverse fitted (very useful in a mobile environment). The output is the same as the Porto.

ICE1.4 ►
Moving to the London is quite a leap, particularly with the tuner, which is the phase-locked-loop type and has a digital readout to display the frequency. Up to five stations can be preset on each of the three wavebands and has manual tune or automatic search facility. As is usual in any manufacturer's range, it is the tuner which benefits first and so it is here, for the cassette deck has no noise reduction or autoreverse. However, the power output goes up to 4 x 6W (music power).

ICE1.6

The Toronto is extremely popular and justifiably so. It takes the specification of the Atlanta a stage further. At the time of writing, it is one of only two sets in the Blaupunkt range with short wave besides the usual three and has a preset facility of five stations on each waveband. As well as Dolby NR, it also has Blaupunkt's own noise reduction system, DNR, which also operates on the radio. One of its major points is the built-in form of theft prevention in that it is code protected. If the power supply is interrupted (if it is ripped from the dash, for instance), the code, known only to the owner, has to be entered before it will work again.

◀ ## ICE1.5

The Atlanta is a well equipped unit in its own right as well as being suitable for adding a whole host of other equipment as part of a system upgrade. Power output is 2 x 21W or 4 x 7W (music power) with a DIN socket pre-amp out. The highly specified tape deck features Metal tape, Dolby NR, Autoreverse, CPS (track search) and Scan. The tuner is similar to that of the London except that there are now six preset stations available on the three wavebands.

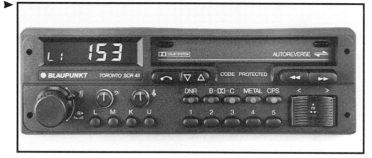

ICE1.7

The Berlin is very much a top of the range set with advanced features abounding which reflect in its price tag. Not surprisingly, it is code protected. It comes complete with a 4 x 20W (music power) amplifier and a high specification tape deck. The latter features autoreverse, scan and CPS (track search) and has an excellent frequency range of 35-18,000 Hz. (The latter represents the sound range the tape deck is capable of dealing with. The wider the range, the better the deck.) The radio, however, is the cherry on the cake. Once switched on, a microprocessor compares any station received with those stored in its memory and, when identified, the name (rather than just the frequency), is displayed. It also has two PLL tuners which operate independently of each other.

One of the Berlin's tuners picks up the station, the other searches for alternatives. The display shows the actual names of the four nearest stations (four more are shown on toushing the 'PCI' key), and the set switches inaudibly to a 'stronger' transmission of the station tuned to, if one becomes available. The database of frequencies/station names are fed into the Berlin via a cassette and thus travelling in another country requires only a simple (two minutes) update to make the set fully operable there. The AVC control is a useful device which measures the amount of noise in the car and increases or decreases the volume of the set as appropriate. It is not possible to cover every aspect of the Berlin, but, as mentioned earlier, this really is **the** set for the radio enthusiast as well as providing a superb, highly specified cassette player. The illustrations show the dual function of the lower range of controls, making the facia simpler and clearer to use. When 'MOD' is pressed, the four lower function controls light up.

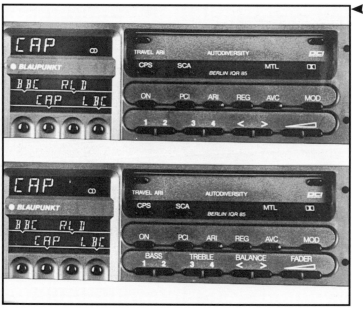

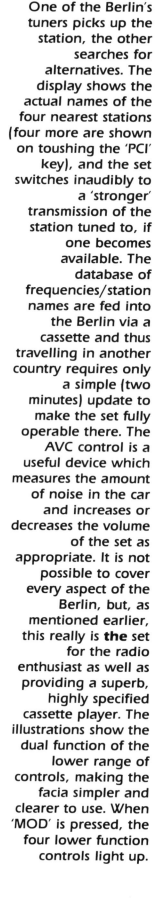

Fitting a radio/cassette player

This part of the book is not **primarily** about DIY, although the fitting of a basic set plus speakers and aerial is certainly a DIY proposition. Anything more complex should be left to a qualified technician, but here is an overview of how Blaupunkt's Chief Engineer, George Richardson, goes about it.

Remember! Always disconnect the battery before starting to fit a radio/cassette player, for although all Blaupunkt and many other sets are internally fused, it is still possible to cause damage to the set and/or to other electrical fitments through just a moment's inattention.

Fitting a radio/cassette player can be easy or difficult, depending on a number of factors, not least of which is the owner's electrical ability and the complexity of the set being fitted. By and large, the average owner should be able to fit an average set with few problems. However, as one progresses towards the top of the Blaupunkt range, the wiring can be somewhat tricky and home fitting cannot really be recommended. For that reason, in this section we are presenting an overview of the sort of work that may typically be required. The car featured here is an MGB GT, although the basic principles apply to all models.

◄ICE2.1
The aperture, ready and waiting. Part of the preparation is the routing and tidying of the wiring. This not only aids wiring up and fault finding, but also contributes to electrical safety. Where there are long pieces of spare cable (for speakers, for example), it is best not to cut them; you may transfer your speakers to another car at a later date and find the leads are then too short! Use electrician's tape to bind them together.

ICE2.2 ►
Not all apertures are DIN size and indeed, this one wasn't. A little trimming with a craft knife (taking great care with the fingers!) soon solved that problem. A little filing may be necessary in some instances.

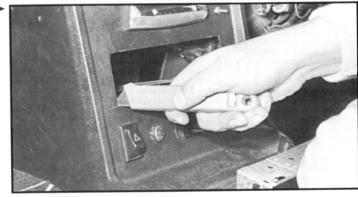

◄ICE2.3
The set to be fitted was a Blaupunkt Cambridge, which required only the standard DIN casing. This fits in the aperture in the console and is held by bending back the metal lugs as shown. For illustration purposes, they are shown here before fitting, although they are actually bent thus after the housing has been inserted.

◄ ICE2.4
With the wiring completed (as per the comprehensive wiring instructions supplied with each set), the unit slots into position and is held there, courtesy of lugs in the housing which align with lugs in the radio/cassette. To remove the set, a couple of special tools push into the four holes on the front of the unit (seen here, two on each side) and disconnect the lugs. This means that, with certain wiring alterations, all Blaupunkt radio/cassette players are interchangeable.

Good quality in-car audio products are not cheap and we would recommend that, having installed the equipment, serious attention is paid to the problem of theft prevention. Security of the set itself is allied to the security of the car, which is dealt with in Chapter Two, Section 9.

ICE2.5 ►
The proof of the pudding! The standard housing has been used here to fit the ultimate in high specification in-car audio, the Berlin. The set is described in detail elsewhere in this Chapter. Even though it is a top line set, it still retains a large measure of subtlety and blends well with the interior of the MGB.

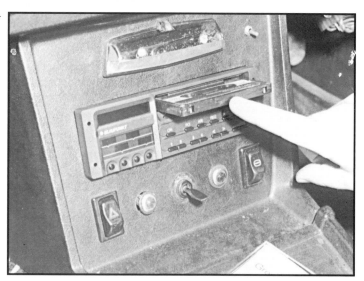

◄ ICE2.6
The lockable cassette requires the fitting of a standard 1.5V (AA) battery which powers the red warning light. When in use, this light flashes constantly as a visible warning to potential thieves. The battery lasts for months of normal use.

Fitting a radio/cassette player

The only certain way to ensure your precious audio equipment is not stolen is to take it with you. The Blaupunkt transportable fitting kit allows instant removal of the radio/cassette for storage in the boot, or better still, safe keeping in the home.

Perhaps the simplest way to keep your radio/cassette actually in **your** car, is to use the Blaupunkt safety cassette. This is a cassette shaped device which slots into the cassette aperture in the normal way. Once in position, it is locked and a metal pin projects from the cassette at right angles, through the radio/cassette unit, through its special fitting frame and into the dashboard/centre console. The special slotted housing required is supplied with the safety cassette.

◄ ICE2.7
With the set out of situ and the lockable cassette in place, the pin can be seen here, projecting through the special DIN casing. Once inserted into a console or dashboard, the pin locks the unit firmly in place.

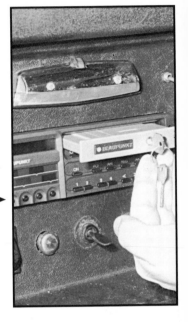

ICE2.8 ►
The safety cassette fits into the player as a normal audio cassette would and once locked into place, renders the unit 'immobile'. In this case it is shown in the Berlin which also has security coding; a doubly safe set!

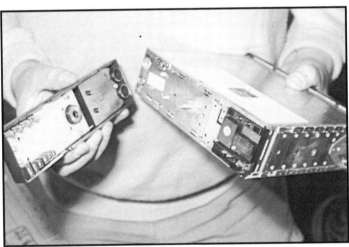

◄ ICE2.9
To convert a 'normal' set to a transportable one, a special backing plate has to be fitted to the rear of the unit. Effectively, this changes the male connections on the rear of the radio/cassette into female ones, which correspond with those in the special DIN housing. There are two versions of this plate, one for mechanically tuned radios and one for those which are electronically tuned. The latter contains a nicad battery which means that pre-set stations on digital units will be retained. The battery has a continuous life of 20 hours and is automatically recharged when the set is replaced in the bracket.

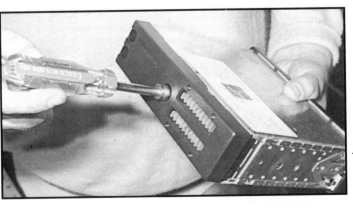

◄ ICE2.10
It is placed in position and held by just one nut. In order to remove the unit ...

ICE2.11 ▶
... a handle has to be fitted. Quite a simple task, it is fitted onto the set from the rear and secured at the front. The carrying handle folds flat when the set is installed and mates with lugs in the frame which prevent the unit from being released unless the handle is raised again. This is a sensible safety measure which prevents the set flying about the car in the event of a crash; typical Blaupunkt thoroughness!

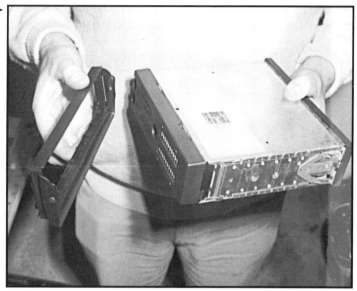

◀ ICE2.12
As with all Blaupunkt accessories, the carrying handle is finished to match the set (in this case, matt black), which avoids that awful 'tagged on afterwards' look, which can occur with some products.

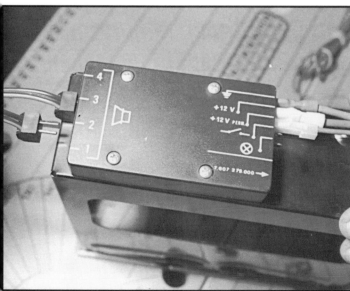

ICE2.13 ▶
A special aerial extension socket has to be used to enable the existing aerial plug to be used.

◀ ICE2.14
The wiring goes from the car to the back of the DIN casing rather than the unit. Seen here, the speaker leads, with standard DIN plugs, are being fitted. Note that the sockets are clearly marked which eliminates the risk of blown fuses, sets and tempers! When the set is inserted, the connections (seen earlier), in the backing plate mate with those in the housing. Simple if you know how!

The Blaupunkt wiring accepts standard DIN plugs. If your car does not have them, you'll have to take a trip to the nearest dealer and obtain some new ones. They clip onto the wire in an ingenious manner which requires no soldering; just a pair of pliers. The wiring of a seven-pin DIN plug, however, does require some soldering work and unless you are an expert (or have infinite patience and actually enjoy burnt finger ends!), it would be wise to entrust this task to a professional. As indicated in the text, fitting one of the more exotic sets ought to be left to your Blaupunkt dealership. A fitting charge pales into insignificance when compared with the cost of replacing a ruined Toronto or Berlin!

Speaker selection and fitting

Take heed all ye who would keep your audio equipment in one piece. Under no circumstances should speaker leads be connected together. To do so could ruin both speakers and amplifiers! For information, the table below should help understanding of some aspects of this and later sections:

Speaker Type	Frequency Response
Bass (Woofer)	35/4,000 Hz
Mid-range	300/12,000 Hz
Tweeter (Treble)	2,000/25,000 Hz

Ever improving on existing technology, Blaupunkt have introduced their Honeycomb range. These speakers radiate all frequencies from an equal, flat surface, regardless of where they are positioned.

The loudspeaker could possibly be regarded as the Cinderella of in-car audio. Time and again we see (and hear!) impressive systems with expensive radio/cassette units, amplifiers and graphic equalizers which are drastically let down by using standard (and thus below par) speakers. This is the audio equivalent of turbocharging your MGB and then running it on cross-ply tyres: not to be advised! Essentially, a speaker is a device for converting the electrical impulses emanating from the radio/cassette into sound waves, capable of being picked up by the human ear. Very simply, the amplifier causes the speaker cone to move in or out and thus create 'waves' of sound.

ICE3.1 ►
All speakers have a '+' and a '-' terminal and it is important that all speakers in any given system be connected in the same way, so as to prevent 'phasing'; one speaker moving in as the other is moving out, with the sound waves produced by each partly counteracting the waves from the other. Blaupunkt speakers have different sized terminals to prevent this from happening.

ICE3.2
There are three basic speaker types plus a new Blaupunkt innovation. The 'Broadband' speaker is the one most usually fitted. As the name suggests, it handles a 'broad' range of frequencies and, as such, is something of a compromise. As can be seen from this cutaway diagram, the single diaphragm reproduces the entire frequency range.
(Diagram courtesy of Robert Bosch Ltd)

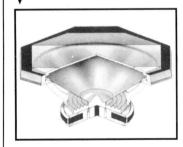

ICE3.3 ►
The next step up is the multiple cone speaker and almost any improvement in an audio system will require at least an upgrade to this type. The speaker enclosure contains more than one speaker. The diagrams here show the more common twin enclosures (co-axial) and the impressive Blaupunkt triple (tri-axial) enclosures, with three speakers, for even better sound production. The alternative to having multi-speaker enclosures is to have separate speakers for each frequency range (tweeters, mid-range, woofers, etc). (Diagram courtesy of Robert Bosch Ltd)

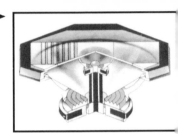
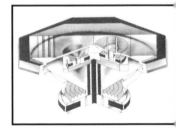

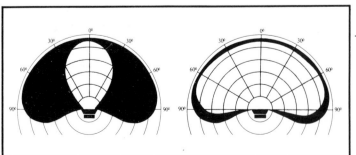

◄ ICE3.4
This diagram clearly shows the advantages of the Honeycomb design (right). The sound is radiated over a much wider area than the conventional speaker, shown here on the left.
(Diagram courtesy of Robert Bosch Ltd)

◄ICE3.5

The choice of door speakers not only depends on available mounting space, but also on power requirements. For sets with modest outputs, this flush-fitting model AL 6547 would be quite adequate. It has a maximum power capability of 8W and a frequency response of 70 to 15,000 Hz. It is a single cone, broadband type.

ICE3.6 ►

The AL 6747 would complement the above, being of the same style, albeit pod mounted. The power handling is a maximum of 15W with a frequency response of 160 to 18,000 Hz. It would fit quite well in this position, as shown in this MGB GT, although locating the wiring unobtrusively would take a little patience!

Speaker installation in an MGB presents us with something of a Hobson's choice; for all practical purposes, they have to go in the doors. Those models with little passenger space, the convertible for example, could manage quite easily with a two, rather than a four, speaker system. If required, a couple of extra speakers could be shoehorned in behind the seats. However, these should really be bass/mid-range speakers as the bass frequencies are not directional (the sound is felt rather than heard), unlike the treble frequencies which are most sensitive to positioning.

ICE3.7 ►

We chose to fit the SL 1230 speaker which is a single cone model. It is a flush fit item designed especially for use in doors. Like all Blaupunkt door speakers, it is protected against the ingress of water by a plastic shield around the electrical connections. Blaupunkt make sure that the all important physical dimensions are clearly listed to ensure that you do not buy a speaker which is not suitable. In this case, the most vital statistic of all, the fitment depth, is 30mm. This, as they say, will do nicely. It has a power handling capacity of 30W maximum and a frequency response of 50 to 22,000 Hz.

ICE3.8 ►

We tried the SL 1230 in the position shown here. We knew that there was a suitable hole behind the trim, but the window winder baulked the speaker cover, as can be seen.

Speaker selection and fitting

Wiring speakers in a car is something of an art. Not only must the connections be correct, but also the routing of the wires must be considered very carefully, so as to avoid using hundreds of yards of speaker cable! When wiring, the basic rule is that the capacity of the speakers must equal the output. In the two diagrams here the output is four ohms.

Fig. ICE.A
With two speakers, they have to be wired in series, as shown.

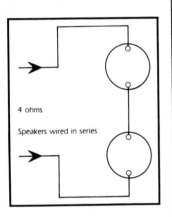

4 ohms

Speakers wired in series

Fig. ICE.B
However, with four speakers, a parallel wiring arrangement is called for.

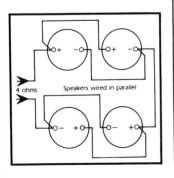

4 ohms   Speakers wired in parallel

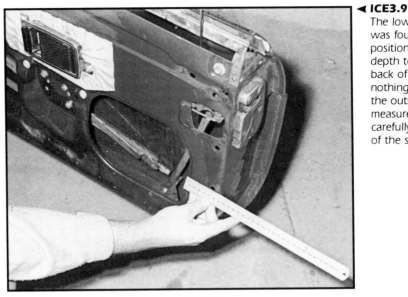

◄ ICE3.9
The lower rear of the door was found to be the best position, having plenty of depth to accommodate the back of the speaker and nothing that would foul on the outside. First task is to measure (and measure carefully!), the exact position of the speaker.

ICE3.10 ►
The measurements can then be transferred to the back of the door trim panel (which is fairly simple to remove, although the window winder, arm rest and handle trim also have to be removed). This is the time to check and double check. Doing the job in a hurry can easily result in holes being cut in the wrong places, and you'll find yourself looking for a replacement trim panel!

◄ ICE3.11
With typical teutonic efficiency, Blaupunkt provide a template on the side of the speaker box, which can be cut out with a sharp craft knife and used to mark the area of trim panel which has to be removed.

ICE3.12 ►
Cutting the trim can also be done with a craft knife, although we cannot place too much emphasise on the need for extreme caution when using these tools. We found that a quicker, simpler and, in many respects, safer method was to drill a small pilot hole and then use the Black and Decker jigsaw to cut the trim, as shown here.

◄ **ICE3.13**
With the speaker aperture cut out, metal clips are slotted onto the edge of the trim so that the self-tapping screws are not just screwed into the relatively weak trim panel. If they protude beyond the speaker cover when fitted, they can be trimmed slightly to fit.

▲ **ICE3.14**
A hole has to be drilled in the door pillar to pass the speaker lead into the car. This was achieved by using the handy Black and Decker cordless drill. Don't forget to deburr (remove the rough, sharp edges), of the hole and to apply a rustproofing treatment straight away. Grommets, to protect the speaker leads, are included in the fitting kit.

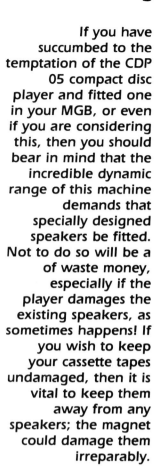

If you have succumbed to the temptation of the CDP 05 compact disc player and fitted one in your MGB, or even if you are considering this, then you should bear in mind that the incredible dynamic range of this machine demands that specially designed speakers be fitted. Not to do so will be a of waste money, especially if the player damages the existing speakers, as sometimes happens! If you wish to keep your cassette tapes undamaged, then it is vital to keep them away from any speakers; the magnet could damage them irreparably.

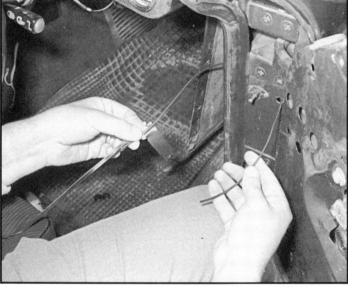

◄ **ICE3.15**
An easy way to thread the thin speaker wire through is to use a 'draw' wire; a piece of stiff wire with the speaker lead attached to it. This saves frayed tempers and frayed fingers!

ICE3.16 ►
The finished article. A neat, unobtrusive fitting, blending well with the MGB interior. Also, unlike a front, lower door position, it is not likely to be kicked every time the occupants leave the car, nor for the high-frequency waves to be absorbed by the occupants' knees.

With certain radio/cassette decks and (at present) all CD players, a separate amplifier is a necessity; they will not work without one. However, there is nothing to stop the enthusiast from boosting the power of his existing system. The principle of in-car amplification is not to reduce your neighbours to tears as you pull onto your driveway or to enable the whole of the High Street to listen to your particular choice in music. It is the same principle as building an engine that produces 130 bhp and then fitting it to your MGB, allowing it the potential to achieve speeds well above the legal maximum. It is being able to listen at reasonable volume levels with an amplifier working well within its capability. It is **quality** and not quantity, that is the keynote.

The graphic equalizer is best described as a more versatile tone control switch. Effectively, your car is its own tone control and because it modifies the sound at random (due to the effects of engine, wind and tyre noise, etc), the chances of getting the sound you would really like are minimal. By using a graphic, you can tune out the problems more accurately.

A crossover unit does as its name implies; it separates the different frequencies (treble, mid-range and bass, etc) and, having done so, it passes them on to the correct speakers. Hence the resulting sound is much purer and cleaner.

There are two important points to note when considering any of the improvements suggested in this section. The first is that none of them will make a poor front end unit work well. In fact, if you have a poor quality radio/cassette, then adding a graphic or amplifier will only serve to make its shortcomings even more obvious. Secondly, all of the products should be matched, preferably by make, but certainly by specification. Uprating the whole system except the speakers, for example, will, at best, give you very little extra performance for your money and at worst, ruin your speakers.

◀ ICE4.1
Here, the BQA 160 amplifier is shown prior to fitting. It can supply 4 x 40W maximum with a frequency range of 20 to 35,000 Hz. As always, the main problem is just where to site the amp. Under the passenger seat is one favourite location, although it can be a little restricted with regard to air circulation and the MGB seat would also need to be raised - which some owners like to do in any case.

◀ ICE4.2
We chose to fit the amp at the back of the facia on the passenger side. In common with many manufacturers, Blaupunkt amplifiers and accessories are designed to connect to each other simply by using 5- or 7-pin DIN plugs. This view shows the DIN socket quite clearly. Note the large cooling fins and also the vents in the amplifier casing.

◀ ICE4.3
If 160W of power is not enough for you, the BSA 247 could be worth a try. It is capable of producing 2 x 120W of stereo sound which can, if required, be bridged to make an incredible mono 240W!

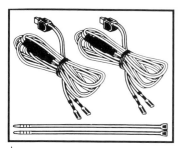

▲ ICE4.4
Blaupunkt produce a full range of ready-made connection cables to allow the accessories in this section to be fitted easily. This is the set for use with tweeters in conjunction with active diplexer SC-XN-A and separate amplifiers.

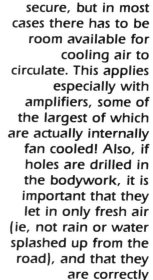

▲ ICE4.5
When it comes to graphic equalizers, Blaupunkt have a varied range to choose from. With limited space and security in mind, we narrowed it down to two. The one we didn't choose is this five-channel remote version. Mounted on a stalk, it allows fitment without the need for a DIN aperture. Being flexibly mounted, it can be adjusted to suit an individual driver's preference. When the car is left for any length of time, it can be bent down along the edge of the seat and out of sight, thus providing no temptation for those with light fingers!

Much thought has to be given to the mounting positions of extra audio equipment. Not only does it have to be secure, but in most cases there has to be room available for cooling air to circulate. This applies especially with amplifiers, some of the largest of which are actually internally fan cooled! Also, if holes are drilled in the bodywork, it is important that they let in only fresh air (ie, not rain or water splashed up from the road), and that they are correctly rustproofed.

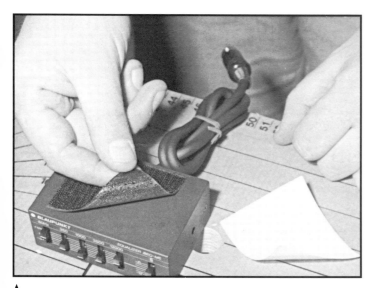

▲ ICE4.6
We decided to fit another five-channel unit, the powerful but compact BEQ-MS. Its small size means that it poses fewer headaches when it comes to mounting it. We used the self-adhesive pad, shown here, which made fitting incredibly easy.

ICE4.7 ▶
Positioned here, alongside the console, on the underside of the passenger side dash, it is convenient for both passenger and driver to use. Also, and very important, it does not foul the passenger's knees!

Graphic equalizers, amplifiers and crossover units

When mounting your audio accessories, there should be no possibility of them getting wet, either directly or indirectly (water dripping off the edge of a bootlid, for example). This applies particularly to soft-top MGB owners, who must always allow for the fact that it is possible to get caught in the rain whilst driving 'al fresco'.

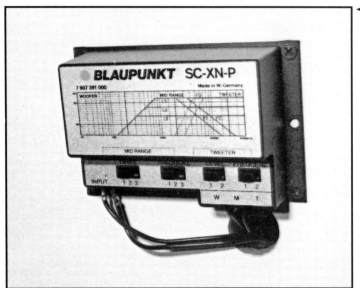

◀ ICE4.8
The Blaupunkt SC-XN-P passive crossover unit. The input and output for mid-range and treble are adjustable, meaning that the effective crossover points can be altered to suit individual taste.

ICE4.9 ▶
Seen here in Blaupunkt's demonstration vehicle, this SC-XN-A crossover unit adds even more to the sound by strengthening the separated signals with separate amplifiers. As can be seen, there is a considerable amount of adjustment available to cater for even the most critical of ears.

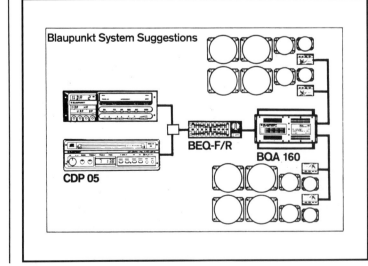

◀ ICE4.10
If dreams were audio coloured they would look like this! Blaupunkt's own idea of the ultimate in-car audio system. Based around the Berlin IQR 85 radio/cassette deck and CDP 05 compact disc player, it adds the following: BEQ FR front/rear nine-channel graphic equalizer, BQA 160W amplifier, four crossover units feeding the delicious sound into no less than 16 speakers. Pure audio magic!

Radio waves are electro-magnetic and move through the air somewhat rapidly: at 300,000,000 metres per second, to be precise! A well designed and built aerial, such as any of those from the Blaupunkt range, is essential to collect these radio waves and provide the good reception required.

The car aerial has one major specific problem, in that the radio is constantly moving around in relation to the transmitted signal. This can lead to poor reception, not only if the signal is too far away, but, ironically, also if it is too close.

If the signal is too far away, there is an opposite problem. (This is particularly noticeable on the FM waveband where the signal tends to travel in straight lines and therefore is easily interrupted by the horizon or tall buildings.) The volume will fall and interference will increase. The **difficulties** associated with all of these phenomena can be largely overcome by having a good tuner and a good aerial.

Contrary to popular belief, good radio reception requires more than just a bent coathanger stuck into the wing! Without the means to collect the radio signal, the expensive tuner that you have just fitted is merely a collection of useless transistors and micro chips.

An aerial 'tip': a light coating of grease on the outside of chrome telescopic models will have a dual effect; it will help to keep rust at bay and also prevent the aerial from sticking.

◄ ICE5.1
Just three of the Bosch range of car antenna on display. By and large, any of the aerials (except the windscreen mounted 'Autofun'), should be mounted in the nearside wing, so that it is away from the main source of interference.

ICE5.2
Bosch offer three different manual telescopic aerials, one of which is seen here. Note that Bosch supply everything required to make fitting easy, including brackets to hold the lower part steady under the wing.
▼

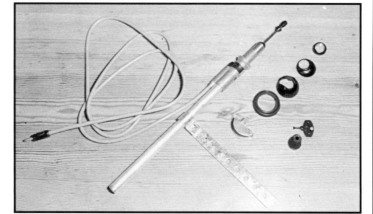

ICE5.3
The Autojet II is in the middle of the Bosch three model aerial range. An electric aerial always costs more than a manual, but it is certainly worth it. There is little as frustrating as joining a motorway and turning the radio on, only to find that the aerial is down! As with most models, the Autojet II extends automatically when the radio is switched on. This feature also makes it vandal (and car washer!) proof. Fitting is very similar to a manual telescopic, although there must be some extra room under the wing to accommodate the motor. Luckily, the MGB is well provided for in this respect. Also, the control box (seen here on the left), must be mounted nearby in a dry place. ►

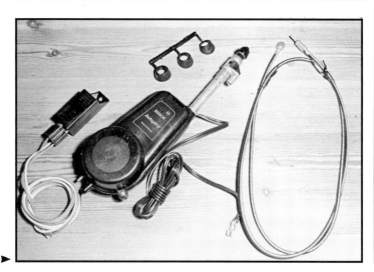

The wiring is quite simple, as can be seen from this diagram.
▼

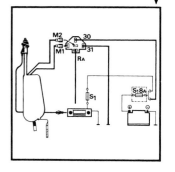

Aerials

If you don't like making holes in your MGB or if you worry about aerial security (who doesn't), or if you just want to keep the clean, smooth lines of your car, then you need the Bosch 'Autofun' windscreen aerial.

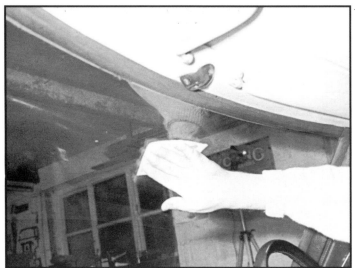

◄ **ICE5.4**
As the aerial element is stuck to the windscreen, the glass should be cleaned with a spirit wipe to remove all traces of dirt and grease.

ICE5.5 ►
A template is supplied with the kit to ensure that the element is aligned correctly with the line of the screen. It also helps to position the amplifier box correctly.

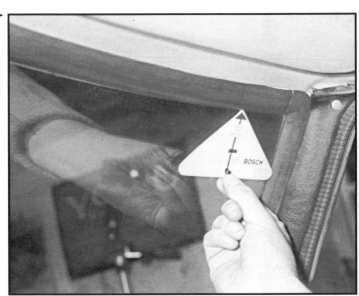

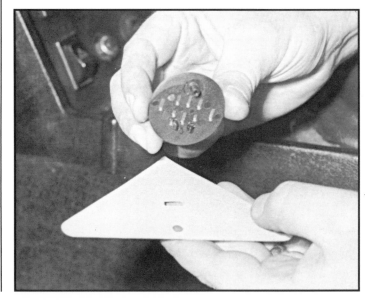

◄ **ICE5.6**
This plastic disc has a peel-off backing which allows it to be stuck to the centre of the screen. Later on, it will be used to mount the heart of the system, the amplifier box.

ICE5.7 ▶
The kit includes several white, self-adhesive spacing strips which are stuck on as shown so that the aerial element can be placed in a straight line.

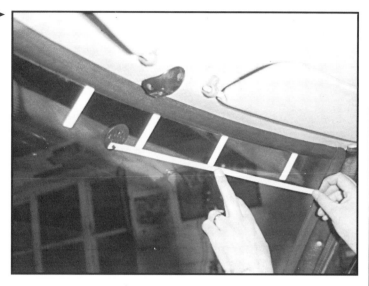

Aerials, like speakers, tend to be the poor relation in the in-car audio family. When fitting a radio, especially an upgraded set, it is always wise to seek professional advice as to which aerial would best suit the characteristics of the unit in question. Try your local Blaupunkt In-Car Entertainment dealership!

◀ **ICE5.8**
When the element is firmly in position, then the backing strip (and later the spacing strips), can be pulled carefully away leaving a barely visible, yet powerful aerial.

ICE5.9 ▶
The small amplifier box can then be 'plugged' into the plastic disc as shown and then secured by a self-tapping screw. Note that the driving mirror has been removed in order that a wire from the amplifier box can be placed under one of the fixing screws in order to make a good solid earth.

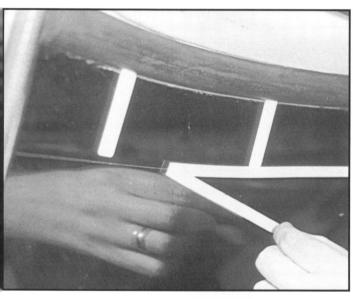

Advanced equipment

As with many of the items covered earlier in this Chapter, the Blaupunkt equipment featured here is not at all well suited to DIY fitment. It would seem silly to spend money on sophisticated ICE equipment only to ruin it by trying to save the cost of main dealer installation.

Compact Disc

In-car Compact Disc players are becoming more and more widely used nowadays. Initial low sales were due largely to the high cost of the machines and of the discs themselves. However, the costs of both have dropped quite dramatically and a CD player can now cost a lot less than some radio/cassette units. Compact Disc has two main assets: first, the sound quality is excellent and second, given a reasonable degree of care, the discs will continue to provide this high quality sound for almost literally as long as you wish. The latter is because the disc is 'played' by a laser beam bouncing off the tracks and therefore the disc is not physically worn during every play in the same way as a conventional record or tape. In terms of quality, the best comparison of tape performance is D.A.T. (Digital Audio Tape). However, like records and existing tapes, D.A.T. tapes, quite simply, start to wear out and thus clarity will suffer. Early CD players were plagued by 'jumping', which was caused by the beam being unsettled by uneven road surfaces. However, this has been eradicated on all except the bumpiest of roads.

Because of its extraordinarily wide dynamic range, a CD player will normally require quite a high-powered amplifier and also matched speakers. Fitting a CD player is also a very good reason for adding a graphic equaliser, again for the same reason.

◄ ICE6.1
If fitted to an MGB with a radio/cassette already in the console, the Blaupunkt CDP 05 compact disc player would have to be fitted under the passenger side dash. Being DIN size, it would fit into the console, if the radio/cassette could be forgone. At present, all CD players need to have a separate amplifier, which could be mounted either at the rear of the console or under the passenger side dash (see earlier this Chapter). Some owners have been known to fit sets behind the lockable glove locker door, after making up a special mounting, for security reasons.

ICE6.2 ►
The CDP 05 uses the unique Blaupunkt system of storing and loading discs. The cartridge system protects the discs from marks and the distortion which can affect standard CD covers at temperatures of over 50 degrees C. The cartridge can withstand temperatures of up to 70 degrees C for 24 hours.

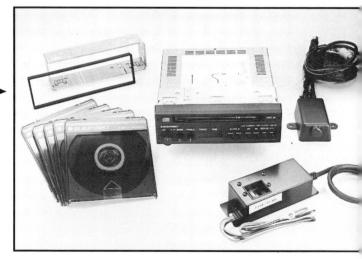

ICE6.3 ▶
Rather upmarket, expensive and difficult to fit, is the in-car phone. The Bosch system seen here does not impinge too much on passenger space, which in the somewhat restricted cabin of the MGB, is a definite plus. It requires, of course, the fitting of a special aerial to the car. This can be mounted on one of the wings, although it is becoming popular to mount one (some are self-adhesive), on the rear window glass.

GLOSSARY OF TERMS

With the help of Blaupunkt, we have listed here some of the most frequently used words and phrases which may prove useful.

AUTOMATIC LOUDNESS — Adapts sound reproduction to the human ear by boosting trebles and bass at low volume.
AUTOMATIC MUTING — Circuit which silences the sound 'between stations' during the tuning search process.
AUTOREVERSE — Automatic reversal of tape direction and track changeover at end of the cassette. The track can be changed manually at any time.
BASS — Sounds in the low frequency range (up to approx 600 Hz).
CPS — The Blaupunkt name for their track search function. When pressed the tape will fast forward or reverse until it comes to the next track when it will stop automatically and play it. Particularly useful in a car environment where most attention should be concentrated on driving.
CHROME DIOXIDE TAPE — Tape with a magnetic coating of chrome dioxide (CrO_2).
CROSSOVER NETWORK — Electronic device for distributing the output of sounds in such a way that different frequencies are handled by different loudspeakers.
DOLBY* NOISE REDUCTION — A system developed by Ray Dolby as a means of reducing tape hiss.
DNR — Dynamic noise reduction. Another system of reducing both tape and FM stereo hiss.
FADER — A control enabling the sound to be distributed between the front and rear speakers in a four-speaker set-up.
FERRIC TAPE — A tape with a magnetic coating of iron oxide particles (Fe_2O_3).
HARD PERMALLOY TAPE HEAD — Tape head that provides extremely high quality sound reproduction and long service life.
HERTZ (Hz) — A unit of measurement for frequency. It measures the number of cycles per second.
MUSIC POWER — The maximum (peak) power available from an amplifier for a short period of time. See also Rated Power.
NR — Abbreviation of 'Noise reduction'; that is, any system for reducing tape hiss (for example, Dolby NR).
NOMINAL POWER RATING — The maximum electric power (in watts) which a loudspeaker can handle continuously.
PLL CIRCUIT (Phase locked loop) — An electronic circuit with a quartz stabilised frequency scanning system, into which station frequencies exactly 'lock' and are held with high stability.
RATED POWER (RMS) — The average continuous maximum output of an amplifier. See Music Power.
SCAN — A helpful feature if you cannot remember what is on a particular tape. When pressed, the SCAN function will seach out the beginning of each track and play ten seconds before progressing to the next track and repeating the operation.
TREBLE — Sounds in the high audio frequency range, approx 4,000 to 20,000 Hz.
TWEETER — A loudspeaker for the reproduction of higher frequencies, approx 4,000 to 20,000 Hz.
TWO-WAY LOUDSPEAKER — Loudspeaker with two different systems in a common housing, eg, woofer/mid-range and a tweeter.
WIDE BAND LOUDSPEAKER — A single system loudspeaker which reproduces the whole audio frequency range.
WOW AND FLUTTER — Unpleasant howling sounds caused by speed variations in the tape transport system.

*DOLBY IS THE TRADE MARK OF DOLBY LABORATORIES.

It pays to try to understand some of the jargon attached to the in-car audio market, especially when comparing features which can vary (in name) quite a lot.

Chapter Four
Mechanical uprating

Don't just launch into mechanically modifying your MGB in a random fashion, bolting on bits as your whim takes you; instead, take a rational view of what you want from your 'B' and plan accordingly. Some owners want to keep their cars as near original as possible, but improve them for easier use in today's driving conditions, while others want to go the whole hog and turn their cars into roaring, fire breathing monsters. Either way, you'll find plenty of advice on these pages and there's some general advice on what it takes to race an MGB in Chapter 6. But do have a plan in mind of where you want to go, and you won't find yourself wasting money on parts and services that may be superfluous. Do make sure, before carrying out any tuning work, that your car is structurally sound, that brakes and suspension are in tip-top condition - it may pay to take professional advice - and remember to notify your insurers of all changes you have carried out, otherwise your insurance could be invalid.

Many advances have been made in terms of motoring performance since the venerable MGB was first introduced and a first step should be to take advantage of those that relate to safety. In the view of this writer, this should take priority over such things as 'concours' originality; after all, what's the point of a car that wins prizes but which is not as safe as it could be? What price life and limb? Thus, the first areas to receive attention should be brakes, where inexpensive (and often indistinguishable from original) modifications can be carried out, and tyres, because the car's contact with the road is where it is at its most vulnerable. In first-class condition, the MGB's suspension system is adequate for normal driving, but there is most certainly room for improvement. The alterations detailed in this chapter show just what can be done. Next come engine modifications. In its basic form, the MGB engine is not exactly over powerful but some very noticeable and worthwhile improvements can be made just by paying attention to air filters, exhaust manifold and exhaust system.

IMP1 ►

This heavily modified MGC makes clear to the world that there is more beneath the skin. Some owners prefer to drive a wolf in sheep's clothing. (Photo courtesy of Pearl McGlen)

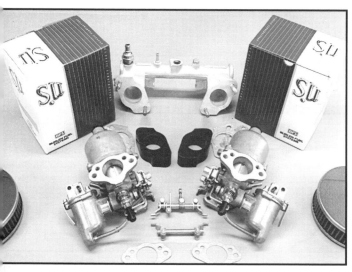

◄ IMP2

First step to increasing power must be to ensure that what you already have gives of its best. Overhauled carbs are a must.

◄ IMP3

The original, cast iron exhaust manifold robs your engine of bhp just by being there; a modern, tubular job releases the potential.

IMP4 ►

At the other end of the scale comes a complete engine replacement with a far more powerful and flexible 2-litre conversion of the original block.

Introduction

If you become really serious about making your MGB 'go', you may wish to install a bigger B-series engine, or even convert the car to V8 spec. Make no mistake, however, that such conversions are very costly and, in the latter case, major structural work has to be carried out. You might, after all, simply decide to add an electric fan, a set of alloy wheels and stop at that. The choice, after all, is all yours ...

◄ IMP5
Apply the same principles of a carb swap (this is a Holley), and better tubular manifolds to a V8 engine and the performance gains are nothing short of startling. But then you'd have to improve suspension; and the diff and gearbox; and ...

IMP6 ►
Efficient front shock absorbers are crucial factors in the MGB's ability to get round corners quickly and safely. If they're worn, replace with new standard units, new uprated (all round) shock absorbers or replacement telescopic units. And remember that suspension and brakes come first!

Fitting an engine pre-heater

The Kenlowe pre-heater is an interesting device which could save you a lot of trouble through the icy winter months and wear on the engine throughout the whole year.

The Kenlowe pre-heater basically comprises a pump and a heater element, which is mounted inside the car. Approximately ten minutes before the car is required, the pump should be connected to the mains and switched on. When you are ready to leave, the cable can be removed and your car will have a nice, warm engine. This means that the heater will function straight away and also, there will be no need to use the choke. As such, the usual early morning 'washing of the bores' will not take place and this could make a massive difference to engine life if used regularly. Whilst not altogether necessary, a garage with a power supply would make regular use of the pre-heater, much easier. Also, by wiring it up the previous evening, an accurate timer could be used to switch it on automatically.

MU2.1
The component parts of the system. The pump/heater element is seen here in the centre. All the necessary plugs, pipework and fixings are included in the kit.
▼

MU2.2 ►
The pump assembly being offered up inside the engine compartment. It must be situated below the level of the car's top hose in order to avoid air locks. Moto-Build sometimes use the shelf below the windscreen washer bottle, re-siting the latter, although this would not apply to cars with servos. The heater controls have to be set to 'HOT' for the system to function correctly.

Fitting an electric cooling fan

MU3.1 ▶
The kit as it comes, which includes the fan itself and mounting brackets, the thermostat control, manual override switch, temperature sensor and all electrical cable, nuts, bolts, etc.

The Kenlowe thermostatic cooling fan is an excellent way of bringing your MGB bang up to date, for many modern cars are fitted with a similar system as standard. Moto-Build find that with the fan fitted, the choke is used less, fuel consumption is improved, power is increased and noise reduced. Obviously, the original belt-driven fan should be removed before installing the Kenlowe kit.

MU3.2
The motor/fan should be assembled loosely with the brackets and offered up to ascertain the exact mounting position. Make sure that the fan doesn't foul the radiator and that the blades have about 1/4 inch clearance. Make sure also that the bonnet will shut before drilling the required 5/16 inch holes for mounting brackets! The Kenlowe wiring diagrams are clear and concise.

MU3.3 ▶
This is the temperature sensor which switches the fan on automatically as the engine gets too hot (in heavy, slow moving traffic, for example). It is actually fitted **into** the top hose and the slotted sleeving in the mechanic's left hand is used to ensure that there are no leaks when the jubilee clip is re-tightened.

MU3.4
This warning/manual override switch should be mounted within easy reach of the driver. The yellow ◀ warning light comes on with the fan and the switch can be used to switch on the fan manually (when towing, for instance).

MU3.5 ▶
The thermostat control can be mounted wherever is convenient on the bracket supplied. Moto-Build find that one of the best places is actually on the radiator shroud. It is set by running the engine until the gauge reads 'hot' and then turning the knob until the fan cuts in; that's it, it's set! In practice, the Kenlowe fan will operate for around two minutes before cutting out again.

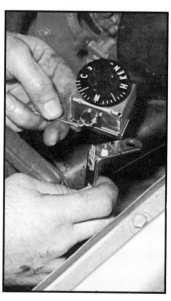

Fitting an oil cooler

Even though most MGBs had an oil cooler fitted as standard, there are many that have had it removed altogether by penny-pinching owners who have found the high cost of an original equipment replacement too high when the oil cooler that came with the car has failed. Although this may save money in the short term, it is not a good idea with an MGB, for the car benefits greatly from the presence of an oil cooler. Moto-Build are shown here fitting one of the 'Clova' range of oil coolers from Pacet, which are all tested at the factory to at least 250 psi (17 bar), so reliabilty should be no problem! The 19mm end tank throughway ensures a reserve of capacity, which then passes down the 35 mm gallery. Turbulators brazed along the whole length give contact at all points for maximum heat dissipation.

MU4.1 ▶
The Pacet cooler fits onto standard captive nuts. The standard Sykes-Pickavant socket being used here shows off its useful ability to operate at an angle on the nut; a readily available 'UJ' facility.

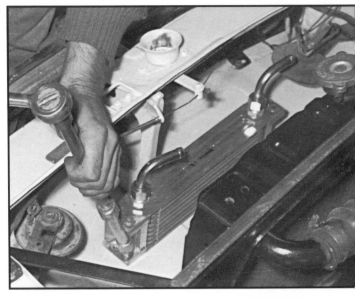

MU4.2
The hose has to be carefully measured and cut to length before fitting to the oil cooler via the 90 degree joints. It should be fitted over the end and then the jubilee clip tightened. The nuts holding the joint to the cooler should only be tightened when the exact angle and position of the pipes is correct. ▶

MU4.3
Top quality hose, to SAE standard 100 R6, is used in all Pacet oil cooler kits. The new hoses pass through existing holes and grommets in the radiator shroud. It is important that the hoses have no sharp bends in their routing. They can either go to the original oil cooler mounting positions on the engine and oil filter housing or, ...
▼

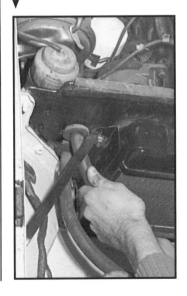

MU4.4 ▶
... for the tiny number of cars which are not so equipped, Pacet produce a 'sandwich' plate which fits between the oil filter housing. This plate is equipped with a rubber sealing ring. This benefits from a smear of grease on both sides which helps to make it totally oil tight. When the job is finished, the Moto-Build engineers check all connections once more, just to make sure, and then run the car for a while to ensure that none of the oil tries to escape!

Fitting a free-flow air filter

MU5.1 ▶
On the left is a complete filter assembly, whilst on the right it has been broken down into its components. It includes a base plate, chrome cover, washable filter and spring clip.

MU5.2
In addition to the above, blanking plugs are provided for fitment to vehicles which do not need to use the breather holes. The MGB is one of them and so the Moto-Build mechanic inserted a plug as shown.

▼

◀ MU5.3
The base plate bolts into position as shown here, using the existing horseshoe shaped 'captive nuts' and the new bolts supplied with the Ram-Flo kit. Assembling the filters is the work of a few minutes, although we found that the overflow pipes needed re-routing slightly to avoid fouling the new filters.

The main aim of fitting a non-standard air filter is to improve the air flow into the carburettor and let the engine breathe more easily. Small power increases can be obtained, although the main benefit is better engine response. The Peco supplied Ram-Flo filter shown here has a removable, washable element. It is cost effective to use a filter which can be re-used rather than thrown away, but it must only be washed with soapy water and **not** petrol!

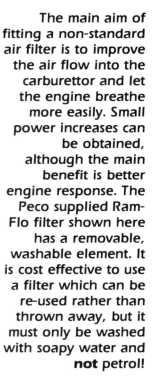

◀ MU5.4
The chrome covers are held in place by simple, but effective, spring clips. Peco's Ram-Flo filters certainly improve the appearance in the engine bay and add a little something to the performance as well.

Fitting a modified exhaust system

Out of sight, out of mind, seems to be the order of the day with exhaust systems. However, it is important to remember that having a good, solid, efficient exhaust system is a legal requirement. Also, as well as creating extra noise (and losing valuable bhp!), a leaking system or silencer box could well be dangerous, allowing poisonous exhaust fumes into the car. Moto-Build are able to supply many Peco systems and/or boxes for the MGB, which range from the two non-standard systems featured here, to a straightforward replacement.

MU6.1
This is the Peco TBB/5 complete system, with twin 2¼ inch tailpipes. It is a direct replacement for the original system as can be seen with the system laid out alongside this Roadster.

MU6.3
The atttractive twin chrome pipes give a more meaningful look to the rear end of the car and the throaty rasp is a bonus. It fits to the original bracket by means of a small adaptor plate. This is available separately and can be fitted with the original system if it is just your back box which has rotted.

◄ **MU6.2**
The new pipes fit onto the standard exhaust manifold as shown in this shot, obviously out of situ for clarity.

◄ **MU6.4**
The Peco MG/6 system is for those who require some more power. It includes a greatly improved mild steel exhaust manifold and there are no prizes for spotting that the centre box is missing. This tends to sap the power of the standard system and so for the sake of a little extra noise, it can be worth getting rid of.

MU6.5 ►
The big bore tubular steel manifold/downpipe fitted to an engine out of the car for illustrative purposes.

MU6.6
You don't have to be an engineer to see that the Peco free-flow system allows the gas to flow much more easily than the standard exhaust manifold.
▼

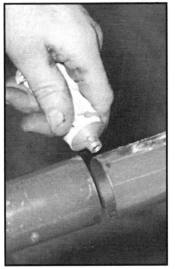

▲
MU6.7
When fitting the various pipes together, Moto-Build always use a smear of exhaust sealing paste to ensure a totally leakproof joint.

When removing the standard exhaust from the manifold, there is a good chance that one or more of the studs will shear or just refuse to budge. Add to that the general awkwardness of their position and you will see why Moto-Build recommend removing the manifold from the car altogether. Although this may sound long-winded, once the carburettors have been removed, access is far better than it is between the manifold and exhaust system. Once off the car, any really stubborn nuts can be properly treated with releasing fluid and as a last resort, heat can be applied to ease the studs out. In the long run, this can be a much quicker method since it would certainly **not** be safe to apply heat to the manifold in position on the car.

◄ **MU6.8**
Held alongside the original centre box, it is quite apparent that the gases have a much smoother ride on their journey to the outside world via the Peco straight-through system. The shape and run of the intermediate pipe is such that it still complies with the underbody contours of the MGB and utilises the original mounting brackets.

Fitting a modified exhaust system

It is quite possible to change your own exhaust system or parts of it, although a full garage ramp to get the car high into the air makes the job considerably easier.

Moto-Build recommend that all mounting rubbers be renewed as a matter of course.

There are various safety rules which must be followed. Bear in mind that by their nature, exhausts can be hot, so let it cool before touching any part of it. Also, a two or three year old exhaust will have lots of flaky rust on it, all ready to drop into your unprotected eyes; so wear some form of eye protection! You'll need lots of releasing agent to be able to turn some of the nuts and probably a saw for the clamps which don't want to move of their own accord. When replacing your exhaust, always use quality replacement parts, such as Peco, as buying cheaper 'pattern' parts can be false economy; they are often made of thinner metal and to wider tolerances meaning that they would be harder to fit and then not last as long! **Never** work beneath a car supported solely by a jack. Use axle stands and securely chock the wheels on the ground. Work on level, hard ground.

▲
MU6.9
No mistaking which is which here; the new system is absolutely massive by comparison!

MU6.10 ▶
Seen from underneath the car, this is the standard silencer, showing the mounting bracket and rubber.

SU carburettors: swaps and overhaul

SU carburettors were fitted as standard to MGBs, which means that for the originality-conscious MGB modifier, moving up a size of SU carburettor will maintain some of this originality, especially since larger SU carburettors were recommended contemporaneously by Leyland 'Special Tuning'. Also, unlike many modern carbs, SUs are able to be maintained and repaired quite easily.

Burlen Fuel Systems are well versed in the whys and wherefores of the SU (not least because they now market through their network of dealers the full range of SU products). Burlen Fuel Systems provide full after-market support functions including technical back-up to the SU factory and along with Moto-Build, they have provided the technical know-how for this section. They were keen to point out that, whilst overhauling a carburettor in the manner shown here is within the range of most DIY enthusiasts, it is vital to maintain a high level of cleanliness and that no small measure of patience and dexterity is required. Carburettors are precision instruments and do not take kindly to heavy-handed treatment.

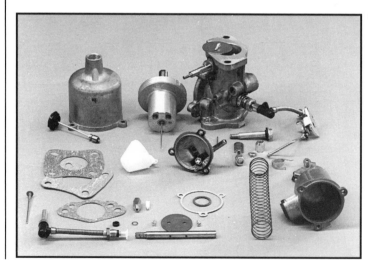

◀ **MU7.1**
A Burlen Fuel System kit seen here alongside a dismantled HS4 carb.

MU7.2
When putting the HS4 back together again, don't forget to open the split screw end in order to lock the disc in place
▼

◄ **MU7.3**
Having replaced the throttle lever, interconnection lever tab washer and nut, and tightened them, don't forget to bend the tab washer down to lock the nut.

MU7.4 ►
Before putting the new jet in place, ensure that all of the old rubber gland is removed from the outlet at the bottom of the float chamber.

If your car is still running on its standard carbs, then they are going to be pretty worn by now! Rebuilding would doubtless put some sparkle back into your motoring and probably give some extra mpg as well. In terms of performance, carrying out Aldon Engineering and Moto-Build's engine modifications without paying attention to the carbs is absolutely pointless and a waste of time and money.

MU7.5 ►
When fitting the new jet, ensure that the gland nut, metal washer and rubber gland are in the correct order and tighten in place.

◄ **MU7.6**
If the carbs on your car have a wire jet linkage, push on the new retaining clip with a small socket spanner. Other flat linkages use a small self-tapping screw.

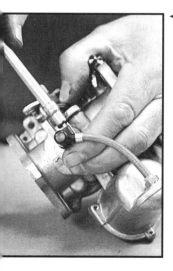

MU7.7 ►
Ideally, the new needle valve should be fitted with the special Burlen Fuel Systems key, as shown here. However, a 'thin wall' socket spanner will do.

SU carburettors: swaps and overhaul

Fitting larger SU carburettors on their own, say Moto-Build, will give only a mild increase in performance and one which, for the most part, will be barely noticeable. A substantial increase in 'urge' will materialise, however, when you fit larger SUs to allow the engine to reap full benefit from other engine mods. But what of the cost? Well, in the old days (the good old days?), a pair of SU carbs would have cost you around £300 if purchased from BL. Burlen Fuel Systems sell them today for around a third of that; now **that's** progress! They can also supply whatever manifold is required to effect your particular choice of carburettor, together with larger capacity fuel pumps for very high performance and racing engines.

◄MU7.8
When refitting the float, be sure to push in the pin so that it is central.

MU7.9►
When screwing down the float chamber lid, replace the alloy tag which includes the carburettor specification number. This is vital to enable the carburettor dealer to obtain the correct parts the next time the carb is serviced.

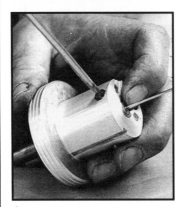

▲ MU7.10
Hold the needle with the base of the shoulder flush with the base of the piston, whilst tightening up the fixing screw.

▲ MU7.11
Take care to line up the keyway in the piston with the tag on the body and at the same time, ensure that the needle enters the jet

◄MU7.12
Don't forget the piston spring when reassembling the suction chamber. Then check that the piston lifts and drops smoothly. Early carbs with fixed needles may need the jet centering.

◀MU7.13
Finally, replace the damper in the dashpot.

MU7.14 ▶
At the top are a pair of HS4 carbs complete with linkage. These are a direct replacement for the later HIF type, seen below.

The number on an SU carb indicates the bore size and the number of '1/8 inch' increments by which it exceeds one inch. Therefore a HS4 carb, which was fitted to very early MGBs, would be a 1½ inch bore (1 inch plus 4 x 1/8 inch), whereas the HS6 carb is 1¾ inch bore. Simple isn't it? Burlen Fuel Systems can supply an HS4 conversion kit for those owners who are cursed with Solex equipped cars. (Solex were used in an effort to meet American emission regulations.) They will also supply a similar kit for owners wishing to move from the later HIF4 carbs back to the HS4. You pays your money ...

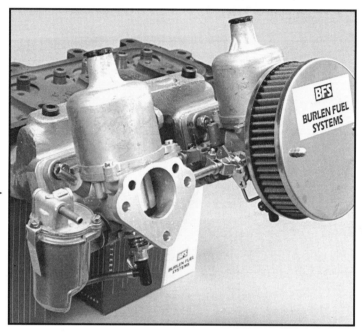

MU7.15 ▶
Rather tasty; this pair of HS6 SU carbs are exactly the same as the originals from Leyland Special Tuning and are available today from Burlen Fuel Systems. They are on a special manifold on an MGB head at Moto-Build, who have considerable experience in these things.

Larger capacity fuel pumps

MU8.1 ▶
The best carbs in the world are not much use if the petrol doesn't reach them. Once again, Burlen are the suppliers of either the standard pump, seen here on the left, or the larger capacity double unit alongside it. The latter is particularly recommended for those owners of highly tuned or uprated cars, especially those involved in competition.

If your pump is of any age, then it is a wise move to replace this item before it fails you. Burlen Fuel Systems now market a range of pump repair kits to enable you to rebuild your own pump.

Fitting a twin-choke carburettor

In this section we show the folk at Moto-Build fitting twin-choke carburettors from Dellorto. These carburettors demand a lot more of the fitter than the fitting of SUs, and unless you are particularly well versed in the art of fuel system maintenance, you would be best advised to leave the tuning to an expert, preferably someone with a rolling road facility, such as Aldon Engineering. Altering the settings on an SU, for example, is relatively simple, whereas the same task on the Dellorto equivalent requires the changing of jets and is, therefore, much more complex and impossible to achieve satisfactorily at home. You could fit the carbs yourself, but you cannot hope to set them up correctly.

MU9.1 ▶
A Dellorto twin-choke unit for the MGB, complete with manifold and twin cables, etc.

MU9.2
Here the assembly is being offered up in the engine bay. Note the distinct lack of space when compared with the SU carburettor set-up. ▼

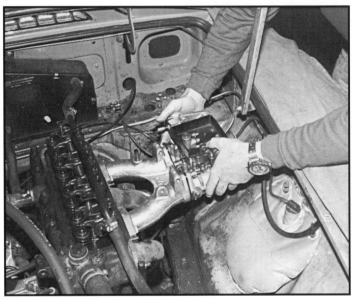

▲
MU9.3
This curious looking object is, in fact, the special accelerator pedal adaptor which is needed for operating the twin throttle cables.

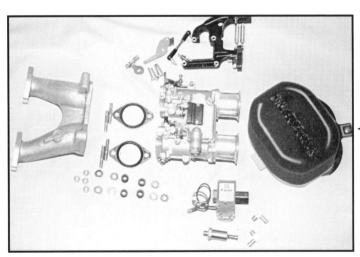

◀ MU9.4
This is Moto-Build's twin-choke conversion kit, laid out in all its glory. The Dellorto system is similar to that produced by Weber, and both give more immediate 'thump' under acceleration than SUs, but both are considerably less economical.

▲ MU9.5
This is very important; these carburettor inlet manifold lugs are deeper than those of the exhaust. As the nuts and washers hold both manifolds in place, it follows that when they are tightened they will only secure the inlet manifold and not the exhaust. In this instance, the height of the exhaust manifold lugs have been made level with those of the inlet manifold by welding on shims. **Do not** file the lugs of the inlet manifold as this would dangerously weaken it.

◄ MU9.6
No, the bellmouth on this carb is not faulty! It has been adapted to fit the contours of the MGB inner wing. If this piece hadn't been removed, the carburettor would have touched the inner wing as the engine moved under acceleration.

MU9.7
As can be seen here, the Dellorto carb needs considerably more depth than the SU originals.
▼

Moto-Build mechanics insist that it is essential to remember the safety rules when working with any part of the fuel system. Petrol and petrol vapour are highly flammable and can be ignited from the smallest spark. **Do not smoke or allow anyone else to whilst you are working in the engine compartment.** Similarly, if you are doing extensive work on your carbs, it would pay to disconnect the battery, as there is always the risk of a short circuit occurring.

Fitting a stainless steel fuel tank

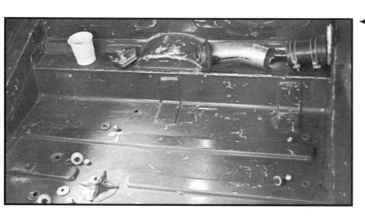

◄ MU10.1
Removing the old tank is not difficult, although some of the nuts, accessible from the inside of the boot, may need a little encouragement in the form of releasing fluid. You will end up with the various nuts, bolts, washers and pipes, seen here. You may not, necessarily, end up with the coffee cup, which is an MS-N optional extra!

In this Section, we take a look at how Murray Scott-Nelson go about installing a stainless steel fuel tank. They took great care throughout the fitting because of the potential danger involved when working with petrol. The battery was disconnected, absolutely **no** smoking was allowed and the tank was drained of its petrol. It is not wise to use the last of the petrol from the old tank as you run the risk of picking up bits from the bottom which could end up in the carburettors!

MU10.2 ►
Swapping the fuel tank is probably the only time that you will see the bottom of the boot floor. Grasp this opportunity to give it a good blast over with underseal or something similar such as Corroless rust-proofing fluid.

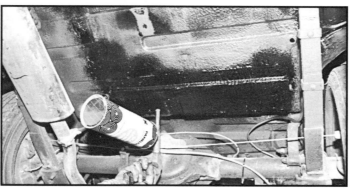

Fitting a stainless steel fuel tank

Place a hose pipe into the old tank and wash it through with running water for some time before disposing of it. A discarded fuel tank full of fumes is, in effect, a bomb waiting to go off.

The standard mild steel fuel tank in the MGB is under attack by rust from all sides, eating through from the inside and even more on the outside, where it is encouraged by road dirt and spray. The accumulation of dirt and grime between the floor of the boot and the tank top rarely dries out fully. Thus, the tank will eventually begin to leak, sometimes around the fuel gauge sender, but more usually around the top edges. Tell-tale signs to look for are: the smell of petrol fumes, loss of fuel when the tank is full, and damp patches in dry weather on the outer surfaces of the tank. A good quality stainless tank (available from both Murray Scott-Nelson and Moto-Build) is an excellent investment and much cheaper in the long run.

◄MU10.3
Even if you are using the old fuel tank sender, you will still need a new seal for the locking ring. Also, a new pipe from tank to fuel pump is a good idea, as the original will doubtless be well rusted.

MU10.4►
With the new rubber seal in place, the fuel gauge sender can be positioned ...

◄MU10.5
... and the locking ring tapped securely into place. Do not use too much force at this stage otherwise the tank or sender, or both, could be damaged. Don't forget to replace the foam rubber gasket which forms a collar around the filler neck, as this stops fumes entering the car.

MU10.6►
Before refitting the tank, the rubber strips which sit on top of the tank have to be replaced. Use either the originals or, if they have deteriorated, pieces of old inner tube will do just as well.

◄MU10.7
Nearly finished. Two people (or a little ingenuity!), are required to play 'replacing the fuel tank'. Here are the rules. You draw lots and the loser lies on his back holding the tank steady, whilst the winner sits on the boot floor and fits the fastenings! Murray Scott-Nelson recommend that the car should be left in the air whilst the tank is filled with petrol, so that any leaks can be detected more easily.

MU11.1 ▶
This is the early, 25D type, distributor as fitted to MGBs up to the late 60s/early 70s. If you have one of these and wish to rebuild it, then go ahead, although few professionals would bother. Since so many parts will be worn, it would be better to replace it with a new Aldon Automotive distributor, as supplied by Moto-Build, with a greatly improved 'advance' curve and better performance.

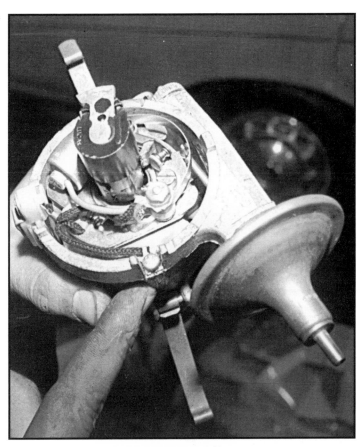

Many owners only know distributors as being the domed-shaped things which house the points! However, they are far more complex than that, as this diagram of the Lucas 45D4 shows. Getting deeply involved is only recommended for those who are proficient at DIY mechanics. Aldon Engineering, who are acknowledged B-series tuning experts and suppliers to Moto-Build, show what is involved in rebuilding or replacement.

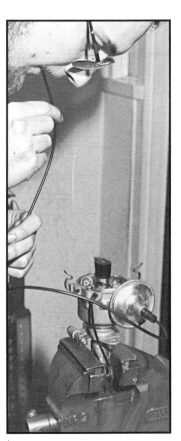

▲
MU11.2
Here, Aldon's Don is sucking on the vacuum pipe which shows whether or not the vacuum diaphragm is punctured.

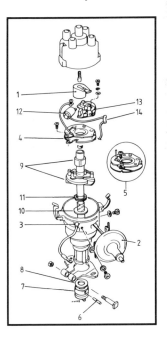

MU11.3 ▶
This highly complex (and expensive!), machine allows Don Loughlin to plot very accurately, the advance curve on an Aldon competition modified distributor.

Distributors

Whether you are fitting a big-bore engine, modifying your existing unit or just trying to get the best from your standard motor, Moto-Build are adamant that getting the spark in the right place at the right time, and therefore obtaining an efficient distributor, is absolutely crucial. Thus, rebuilding the unit you have or buying a new one is definitely a good move.

Full details of how to dismantle and rebuild an MGB distributor are given in both the relevant Haynes manual and also in Lindsay Porter's 'MGB: Guide to Purchase and Restoration'.

MU11.4 ►
To work efficiently, all of the distributor wiring must be in tip-top shape. In this MGB V8 unit, a wire has been discovered with almost non-existent sheathing. Clearly this could lead to a short circuit.

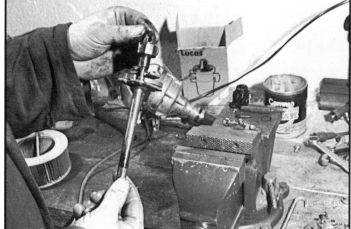

◄MU11.5
Actually dismantling and rebuilding your distributor is not a task for the fainthearted. In real terms, it is probably much better to replace the unit altogether. Certainly, specialists such as Aldon do not find it cost effective to rebuild them, which is why they and Moto-Build sell so many of Aldon's new (improved!) replacement distributors.

MU11.6 ►
This shows the 101 BY1 distributor which Aldon supply for all the chrome bumper MGBs. For all others, they use the 101 BY2 unit.

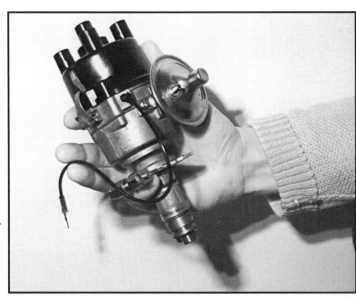

Fitting contactless electronic ignition

MU12.1►
This is the contactless kit needed for a standard 1800cc MGB. Piranha produce an almost infinite range of ignition systems, including heavy duty units for race, rally and tuned engines, and a unit with rev limit facility. The latter is available for either road or competition engines; all are supplied by Moto-Build.

Fitting a Piranha Contactless electronic ignition system is a fairly simple means of improving the efficiency of your MGB. The system uses an optical trigger to energise the coil. A slotted disc fitted over the distributor cam revolves between an infra-red light emitting diode and a photo transistor. This, in turn, triggers the electronic circuitry to switch off the coil and produce a spark. At high speeds, it allows up to three times longer for the coil to charge than is available with a standard points system. This means that there is always a powerful spark, even at high speeds. Obviously, as there are no contacting moving parts, wear and tear are eliminated and thus the timing stays accurate almost indefinitely. By burning the fuel more effectively than any contact breaker points system, the benefits are; reduced fuel consumption, increased power, improved starting, better reliability, less exhaust pollution and smoother running.

◄MU12.2
The old contact breaker points have to be removed in order to fit the contactless ignition. A simple task, the Moto-Build mechanic pointed out, having first removed the distributor cap (but leaving the leads in place), and rotor. With the points taken out, the base plate can be removed by undoing these two cross-head screws.

▲ MU12.3
The Moto-Build mechanic then places the optical trigger into position, using the same cross-head screws. On top of the trigger is the scanning disc, seen here already fitted to the distributor shaft.

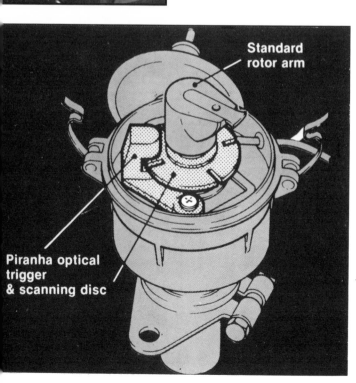

Standard rotor arm

Piranha optical trigger & scanning disc

◄MU12.4
This diagram shows the simplicity of the contactless ignition system. Note that the standard rotor arm is retained.
(Diagram courtesy of Piranha Ignition Systems Ltd)

Fitting contactless electronic ignition

There are Piranha systems available from Moto-Build and many other outlets for all MGB models, but you must get the right one for your particular car. For 1800cc models from 1962 to 1980, with the Lucas LU 25D distributor, the kit reference number is TO1A. For later models with the Lucas LU 45D distributor, the reference number is TO9A. Those lucky owners with double the numbers of cylinders beneath the bonnet need reference number TO5A.

MU12.5 ►
Beneath the new base plate, the vacuum advance return spring must be connected.

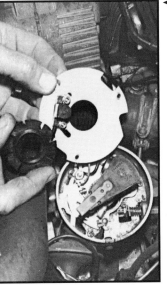

◄ MU12.6
The kit for the V8 engined MGB is outwardly very similar, but is specific to that model. Its advantages are particularly welcome with this big engine.

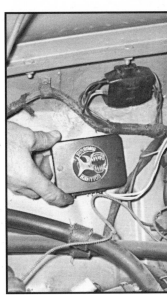

MU12.7 ►
The all important 'black box' containing the electronic magic which makes the ignition work, has to be mounted in the engine compartment. It must be mounted away from extreme sources of heat, dirt and moisture. Once installed, the system will require no maintenance.

◄ MU12.8
This graph shows how much more efficient the new system is, especially in the higher rev range. (Diagram courtesy of Piranha Systems Ignition Ltd)

Modifying a cylinder head

MU13.1 ▶
The head at the top is a unit which has two bosses, in the positions shown here. These were cast in place for the US car's air injector ports. Its value in the UK is that the bosses provide the head with more rigidity and strength. The lower head is an earlier unit, without the air injector port bosses.

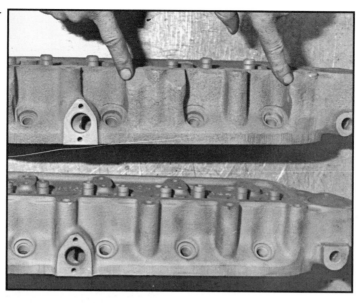

Aldon Engineering take a great deal of time and care over the preparation of their cylinder heads. Under Don Loughlin's management, they use the latest in hi-tech machinery together with skill and experience gained over many years of working with MGBs. The former can be bought but not the latter. These modified heads can be obtained from Aldon direct or through Moto-Build.

◀ MU13.2
If your cylinder head is cracked, the odds are that it is here, on the exhaust seats on cylinders two and three. Can you spot the difference between the heads? Note the slight change in the heart-shaped combustion chambers. The upper head is an early (up to 1970) unit.

MU13.3 ▶
Very early heads have this large protusion in the combustion chamber which causes less efficient gas flow.

Modifying a cylinder head

Working on the cylinder head is a task which requires accuracy, skill and patience in equal amounts. Best results also demand that magic ingredient, **experience,** which is why Moto-Build and others 'in the know', set so much store by the Aldon Automotive workmanship shown here.

MU13.4 ▶
As can be seen here, the combustion chamber of this head has been considerably modified! This is not an Aldon Engineering head and Don's opinion was that perhaps the modification was a little extreme. Removing such a large amount of metal from the far side of the chamber may well be counter productive, as the most important factor is to get the gas flowing correctly from the valves to the spark plugs.

◀ MU13.5
Here, Don is using a purpose-made template to mark out the exact shape of a revised combustion chamber for one of Aldon's uprated heads.

MU13.6 ▶
When the shape has been marked, Don can then grind the bottom and sides of the combustion chamber with this special tool which is, in effect, a metalworking 'router'. The tool is specially shaped to form the curved sides of the chamber.

MU13.7 ▶
When the shape has been formed, polishing is done using this power tool with a flat wheel. Smooth is the name of the game in order to obtain a really good gas flow.

At all times Don was most careful with his handling of the head and its associated ancillaries. Most of all, cleaniness was stressed. After every operation, the head was thoroughly cleaned and the oilways, etc, blown through using an airline.

◀ MU13.8
Here, Don is using a rotary tungsten carbide burr to grind metal out of the ports. Again, this is part of the chase for improved gas flow.

◀ MU13.9
The top of the port is also enlarged, allowing gases to flow smoothly right into the combustion chamber.

MU13.10 ▶
This simple looking device is, in fact, an extremely sensitive and expensive Swiss valve seat cutting tool. Here, the magnetic base of the tool has been affixed to the metal table and the spigot holding the tungsten carbide cutting bit is being positioned correctly on the seat.

Modifying a cylinder head

The Aldon valves shown in this section are larger than standard, as shown here, allowing greater flow, more readily accomplished.

Inlet
Standard	1.56
Aldon Eng.	1.70

Exhaust
Standard	1.34
Aldon Eng.	1.45

Sizes relate to the diameter of the valve in inches.

Moto-Build's experience is that an Aldon head fitted to a standard 1800 engine will give a very noticeable increase in performance.

MU13.11► The seat cutting tool in operation. Note the swarf around the cutting bit. It is important that all of this kind of debris is cleaned out from all internal passages before refitting the head.

◄MU13.12 The next task is to check combustion chambers for volumetric capacity. This is done by using a burette to drop paraffin into the chambers. The amount taken by each chamber should be exactly the same. If not, it may be necessary to remove some more metal from the chambers. For a road engine, a difference of around half a cc spread over the four cylinders is more than accurate enough. However, when preparing a racing engine, Aldon would look to be even more accurate! Here, Don is using a face mill to ensure that the head is absolutely level.

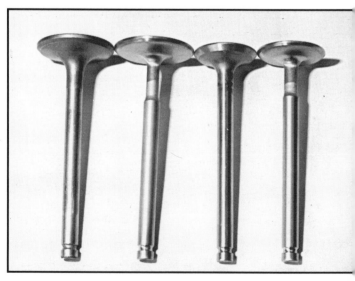

MU13.13 ► Four valves; two inlet and two exhausts. From the left is; Aldon's 'waisted stem' exhaust valve which improves gas flow, alongside a standard exhaust valve for comparison, then a similar 'waisted stem' inlet valve, alongside its standard counterpart, on the far right.

MU13.14▶
A pair of reinforced rocker posts help to avoid flexing of the rocker shaft. This can occur because the shaft overhangs the end of the pedestal and tends to 'bend' upwards. These would normally only be used on a racing engine, using a high valve lift cam, stronger springs and sustained high revs.

MU13.15
The HRG alloy crossflow head, originally made for the MGA series, never really caught on, although in principle it offered many benefits over the standard head. On a standard head, the inlet and exhaust ports are on the same side, which means that the inlet ports ▶ have to be siamesed. Also, the centre two exhaust ports have to be joined together. The HRG design gets away from multiple ports and ...

MU13.16
... as can be seen here, the inlet ports are now separate and on the side of the spark plugs. Although the HRG company ceased production some time ago, the heads are being manufactured once more by a company who have bought the pattern rights. The 'new' head achieves what the old originally failed to do, it actually **improves** performance!
▼

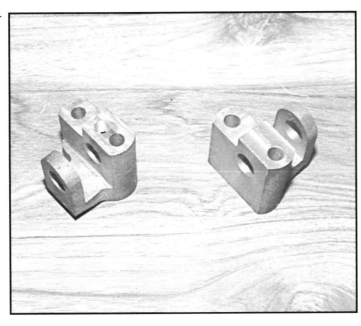

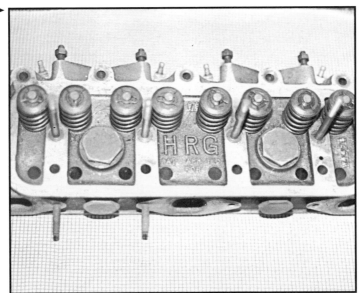

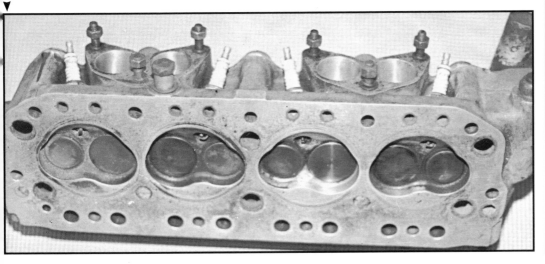

Don was at pains to emphasise the need for continued care when fitting the reworked head. It is only too common for Aldon to supply a beautiful 'new' cylinder head to an owner, only to have it returned some time later because it has been damaged during installation. Moto-Build add that it is essential that the nuts should be tightened in the order recommended in the manual and, once they begin to go 'home', by only half a turn at a time.

Fitting a reworked cylinder head

Even if you have had your cylinder head rebuilt by a professional, you may wish to fit it yourself. This is clearly not beyond the means of most DIY owners, although the new (or reworked) head must be treated with respect to avoid damaging the newly machined surfaces. Likewise, everything must be kept spotlessly clean. Here's how Moto-Build go about fitting an Aldon head.

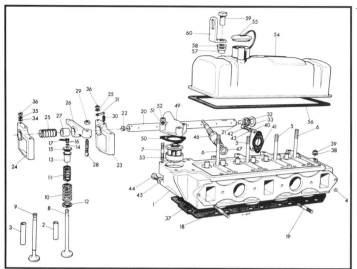

◄ **MU14.1**
For those who feel moderately competent, full details of how to dismantle and rebuild the MGB head are contained in either your Haynes Owners Workshop Manual or Lindsay Porter's 'MGB: Guide to Purchase and DIY Restoration'.

MU14.2 ►
The key to successful assembly is meticulous care and cleanliness. Before even thinking about refitting your cylinder head, it must be totally clean and swarf-free. You must always work with clean hands and tools and in clean surroundings, regarding even the slightest speck of dirt as Enemy No. 1. Moto-Build's mechanics always have the oil can ready and here the cam followers are being liberally doused. All moving components must receive this treatment as assembly takes place.

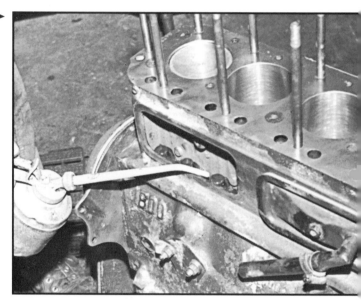

◄ **MU14.3**
A new gasket, naturally. The head is lowered very carefully onto the block. Take note that hands are not underneath the cylinder head. Doing so is a sure way to get very sore and squashed fingers!

Building a big bore engine

MU15.1 ▶
How would you fancy **this** engine under your MGB's bonnet? This is the Aldon Engineering two litre conversion designed to give your tired old 'B' a little extra sparkle. It looks surprisingly standard, although the Aldon badge on the rocker cover gives the game away. Specialists such as Moto-Build can supply to order.

The Aldon 'big bore' conversion featured here brings the engine's capacity up to 1948cc although, naturally, it is referred to as a 'two litre' engine. It is an ideal answer for those owners who have a very worn engine and were thinking of a rebuild. The extra power, torque and flexibility of the bigger unit makes it well worth the relatively small extra cost over a standard rebuilt unit, when rebuild time comes around.

◀ MU15.2
Here Aldon's Don Loughlin bores the block out to suit the new piston size and give an overall capacity of 1948cc.

MU15.3 ▶
With the cylinder block now the correct size, the bores have to be honed to a smooth finish. Here the machine is being set up and ...

◀ MU15.4
... this is a close-up of the hones in action. Although the bore looks smooth after the boring bar has been used, when checked through a microscope, something resembling a large screw thread would be seen! This helps the new piston rings to 'bed in'. Note the use of honing oil to keep things cool.

Building a big bore engine

A very important point to bear in mind is insurance. You must inform your company about any modifications you make, especially when they are as radical as a two litre engine! Some companies may refuse to insure a highly modified car, so it is wise to check beforehand. Also, an Engineer's report will probably be required.

MU15.5▶
The top of the block is skimmed to make sure that it is absolutely true and to bring the pistons to the correct height in the bore.

◀MU15.6
Here, Don is lightening the back of the (standard) flywheel. The object of this exercise is to improve acceleration in the lower gears by helping the engine to rev more easily. In technical terms, it reduces the 'moment of inertia'!

MU15.7▶
The crank has to be perfectly in balance and this is achieved by using some more of Aldon's hi-tech machinery. Don has a crankshaft already mounted in the beam balance.

MU15.8▶
Where a crank is out of balance, metal has to be ground away from the heaviest parts.

At every stage of the engine preparation, cleanliness was the keyword. Great care was taken to ensure that there was no danger of dirt or swarf ending up in the finished unit.

MU15.9
Having balanced the crankshaft, the flywheel and 'heavy duty' Peco clutch are then added and the balancing process repeated. The three holes in the clutch cover are standard. However, if the cover needs lightening...
▼

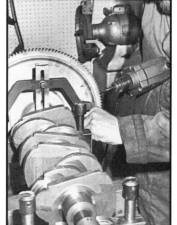

◀MU15.10
... the answer is to drill one or two more in the appropriate places. It is Aldon's practice to punch alignment marks on crankshaft, clutch cover and flywheel, so that if future dismantling is necessary, they can be re-aligned without the need for further rebalancing.

MU15.11
Three different connecting rods have been used in MGB engines. On the left is an early type with an angled, split big-end. These are very heavy and thus Aldon do not use them in their big bore conversions. They were fitted to engines up to the end of 1968. After this the manufacturers fitted the rod seen here in the centre. It is much lighter but still has a small end bush in the little end and uses a gudgeon pin which is retained in the piston by circlips. This was used for less than a year before the rod shown on the right was adopted. This is the same except that the gudgeon pins are press-fitted into the little end. Either of the two on the right are acceptable for tuned MGB engines, although Aldon favour the latter.

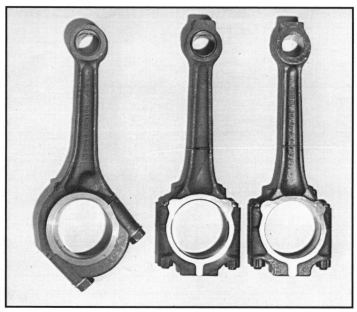

Building a big bore engine

This diagram shows the press fit gudgeon pin type of piston and con rod in detail.

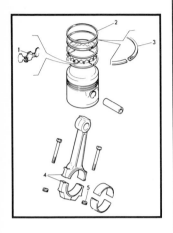

◄MU15.12
The con rods have to be balanced and here Don is performing the task on a simple balance jig. They are weighed 'end to end', ie, the big-ends and the little ends all weigh the same. Not every engine tuner is quite as thorough as Aldon in this respect.

MU15.13►
Where weights are not equal, the grinder is used once more to remove a little metal. The amounts involved are very small but infinitely important. This kind of thoroughness explains why specialist suppliers like Moto-Build rate specialist tuners like Aldon so highly!

MU15.14►
On the left is a standard piston and on the right is the soon-to-be-fitted big bore piston.

◄MU15.15
As mentioned earlier, Don prefers to use the latest type of MGB con rods. However, as the pistons were not designed for rods with a press fit gudgeon pin, the gudgeon pin bosses have to be honed out to suit

MU15.16
When finished, the gudgeon pin can be fitted into place as shown here. Some tuners use heat to fit them, but in Aldon's experience it is better not to.

Aldon use only highest quality replacement parts which are fitted with equally high quality tools and equipment. In conjunction with the skill of the Aldon engineers, a superb result is guaranteed, which is why Moto-Build are so happy with the results ...

▲
MU15.17
The Duplex double row timing chain, seen here on the left, was fitted to pre-1968 MGB's as standard. After this, the single row chain was fitted to all 18V type MGB engines. Wherever possible, Aldon prefer to use the Duplex chain on their tuned units.

MU15.18
The uprated cam for the bigger engine is shown at the top with the standard cam below. Spot the difference!
▼

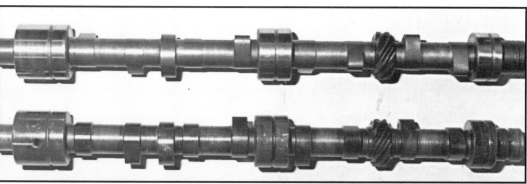

◄**MU15.19**
A lovely, clean engine, awaiting a head. The shiny finish on the bores, etc, is not for show. The smooth surfaces will provide smoother running, more power and a longer lasting engine.

Building a big bore engine

With a new and bigger motor, your braking system has to come in for some attention. New pads/shoes will be fitted as a matter of course and whilst you're there, check the condition of the discs. If they too are worn, replacement is a must; the extra 'go' of the two litre engine will leave no room for error. Moto-Build can build improved front disc brake assemblies while at less cost, Mintex brake pads, described on page 164, give a noticeable improvement.

MU15.20 ►
More capacity and power means more stresses and strain on the clutch. At the top is a Peco heavy duty clutch assembly, far better suited to handling the uprated two litre Aldon motor than the standard one, seen below.

◄ MU15.21
When fitting a new clutch, a mandrel **must** be used to line up the 'HD' Peco clutch driven plate. The MGB engine is especially hard to locate onto the gearbox if the clutch is not correctly aligned.

MU15.22 ►
With the mandrel holding the driven plate in position, the pressure plate is held in place on the flywheel.

◄ MU15.23
Here the Peco clutch retaining bolts are being tightened up. They should be tightened in diagonal order and to a torque figure of around 25/30 lb/ft (34/41 Nm).

MU15.24 ▶
The end result; almost a work of art for some lucky owner. The two litre unit gives the sort of performance the MGB can really use without going to the extreme of fitting the 3.5 litre, Rover V8 unit, with the enormous degree of complex work involved.

Don't forget that the new engine will place extra strain on the ancillaries. Items like the oil cooler and radiator should be checked and replaced if required. All the parts you require may be obtained from your MG specialist, such as Moto-Build, who are the featured company in this Chapter.

◀ **MU15.25**
Another example of Aldon's thoroughness is this core plug strap. There was never much likelihood of the plug coming adrift, but now there isn't any! These straps are considered to be a non-essential optional extra.

MU15.26 ▶
Having obtained your super, new, powerful motor, it makes lots of sense to use one of Aldon's competition type distributors. Getting the spark to the right place at the right time is vital on any engine and especially so on a tuned unit like this. The best type of distributor was that fitted to very early MGBs from approximately 1964 to 1968. Obviously, such a distributor will now be considerably worn, but Aldon's own model has a very similar advance curve.

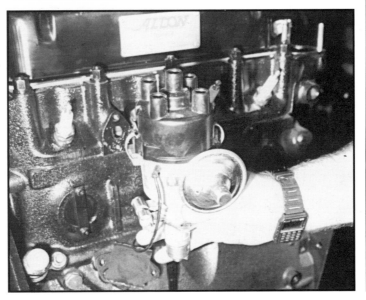

Engine fitting

In this section we are covering the fitting of an engine once it has been uprated, although not in any great detail. For more thorough coverage of this subject refer to Lindsay Porter's 'MGB: Guide to Purchase and DIY Restoration'.

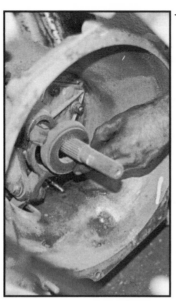

◄ MU16.1
Before fitting the new Aldon engine, Moto-Build strongly recommend that you fit a new clutch release bearing, as replacement is an 'engine out' task and the cost of a new release bearing is relatively low in any case.

MU16.2 ►
There is no need to totally remove the exhaust manifold. By judicious use of a strong twine, it can be tied back against the inner wing. This particular manifold is a tuned Peco unit, useful with the old standard engine, but even more so with the two litre motor on its way!

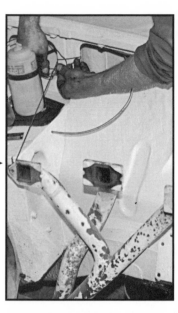

MU16.3 ►
Here the Moto-Build mechanics are lowering the uprated Aldon engine gently into position. This is best achieved by using a purpose made engine lift. As can be seen, the bonnet does not have to be removed to lower the engine into place although it may be best to do so to avoid any risk of damage. Note the angle at which the unit is being offered up to the gearbox, which has to be jacked up slightly, so that the engine slides neatly onto the gearbox splines.

◄ MU16.4
Once the gearbox and engine have been bolted together, the engine mountings are fitted to the engine front plate first, and then the bolts pass through the plate into the mounting on the chassis. New mounting rubbers are always used.

MU16.5 ►
Almost home! The engine ancillaries, distributor, carburettors, etc, can now be fitted.

As MGB specialists, Moto-Build are able to supply and fit uprated engines to those owners who want more than just a power 'tweak'. The engines they supply are manufactured by Aldon Engineering, to the same high standard as we have seen on the previous pages.

◄ MU16.6
The final test. Having installed the engine, it makes a great deal of sense to have the car set up on a rolling road, such as the one at Aldon Engineering. This is even more desirable with a tuned motor such as the two litre unit seen earlier, as most of the manufacturer settings do not apply.

Fitting an aluminium rocker box cover

MU17.1 ►
One of the simplest items in this book to fit, the Kimble cover shown here is a straight replacement for the original, requiring very little mechanical knowledge. It certainly looks a lot better but also, aluminium being the excellent sound absorbing metal that it is, the engine's tappet noise is reduced.

Whenever they fit, or supply, a Kimble aluminium rocker box, Moto-Build always include a new gasket. Refitting the original gasket with the new rocker box cover is guaranteed to encourage leaks.

V8 engine conversion - overview

As you may imagine, fitting a V8 engine into the somewhat crowded confines of the MGB engine compartment can be a very complicated task, although made feasible by the conversion components produced by the V8 Conversion Company. This applies especially to earlier models. That being the case, we have prepared this section as an overview, rather than as a detailed blow-by-blow account. More work is required than could be described in detail here.

MU18.1▶
This is the standard V8, in fine original order, once owned by Lindsay Porter. The standard V8 was a discrete car, with only the small badges on the rear tailgate and nearside front wing giving notice of intent.

MU18.2
The standard V8 engine in situ. Note the enormous air filters with chambers on their ends, containing temperature ▶ sensitive bimetal strips. These enable the engine to draw heated air from the exhaust manifolds when the engine is cold and cooler air from the engine bay when the engine is warm.

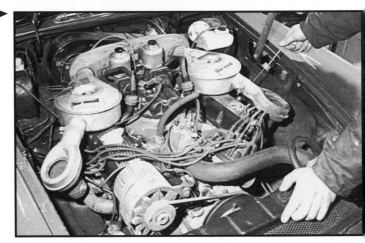

MU18.3
A nice, pristine engine in the process of being fitted into a late model 'B' by the V8 Conversion Company. The radiator mountings, which are well forward compared to earlier models, denote ▶ that this is a later '75-on car and thus one of the (relatively!) simpler cars to convert.

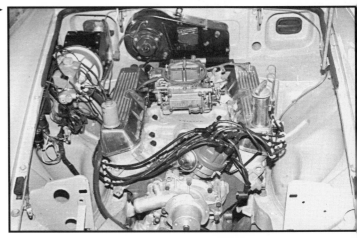

MU18.4
This picture shows the modifications necessary to the nearside bulkhead of a chrome bumper MGB. Those cars, pre-1975, are the most difficult to convert. After 1975, the same 'V8' body shell was used for all models.
▼

MU18.5▶
The gearbox tunnel must be modified to accept the five speed gearbox. This goes to show just how much bodywork, as well as mechanical work, is required, especially on these earlier cars.

MU18.6►
This is the Offenhauser dual port inlet manifold offered by the V8 Conversion Company.

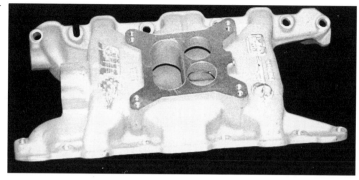

MU18.7
Better gas flow is achieved ► by using tubular exhaust manifolds rather than cast. The shape is very important because of the lack of space for routing. The V8 C.C. supply all of the necessary fittings and gaskets to suit. (Cast manifolds are far harder to obtain, as well as being very resrictive to the engine's efficiency.)

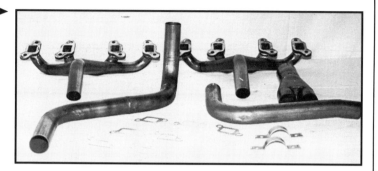

MU18.9►
Cooling the big, eight-cylinder motor is obviously of paramount importance, using these components. Note the twin fans.

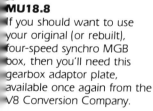

▲
MU18.8
If you should want to use your original (or rebuilt), four-speed synchro MGB box, then you'll need this gearbox adaptor plate, available once again from the V8 Conversion Company.

MU18.10
If you do fit the five-speed SD1 gearbox, you will need another propshaft, crossmember mounts and speedo cable. The V8 Conversion Company can supply their own specially produced propshafts to suit the MGB.
▼

MU18.11
More power **always** requires uprated brakes. The V8 Conversion Company always fit these thicker discs, together with uprated calipers to suit. High performance pads are used.
▼

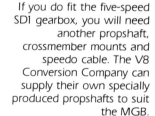

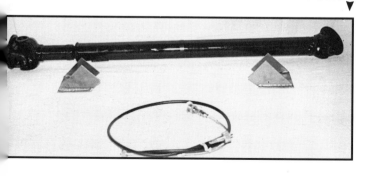

Moto-Build are insistent that the standard gearbox, as fitted to the factory prepared V8s, is not really up to handling the extra power. First gear often stripped its cogs and the overdrive had to be blanked off from third gear. The Rover five-speed box is far better and when undertaking a conversion, this is always recommended. On this page we show some of the parts fitted by the V8 Conversion Company and some of the optional extras available. You'll also need a V8 or MGC differential to prevent the poor engine from using far too many revs for any given road speed.

V8 engine conversion - overview

Don't forget the insurance angle when doubling the number of MGB cylinders. Many companies will not handle any cars which are non-standard in any way and most will demand an engineer's report that it is safe. The V8 Conversion Company have no qualms about the safety of their cars, although they cannot help you with the final point ... paying the increased premium!

MU18.12►
The offside bulkhead has to be modified, along with the steering on this chrome bumper model.

MU18.13►
Looking further down the same car, showing more of the modified steering system and the revised engine mountings.

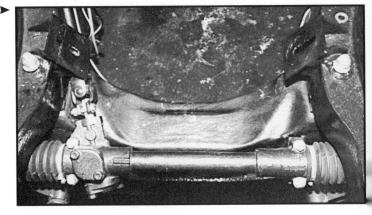

MU18.14
If you don't want twin carbs (and associated pipework etc), then you can have this single Holley carb instead.
▼

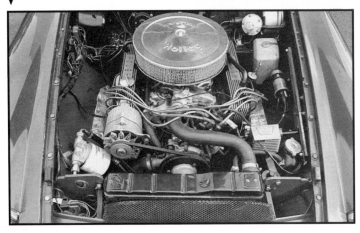

MU18.15
Made to make your mouth water! An absolutely beautiful, Holley carb-equipped MGB V8 Roadster. Never actually made by British Leyland, the V8 Conversion Company have rectified that serious omission by producing the parts for the car you see here. Note that, like the factory cars, the engine fit under the bonnet without the need for a bulge; this is something that not all conversions can boast.

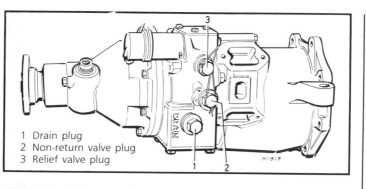

MU19.1►
The D-type overdrive unit, fitted to earlier 3-synchromesh gearboxes, can be added later but only if you change the gearboxes' 3rd motion shaft as well.

1 Drain plug
2 Non-return valve plug
3 Relief valve plug

An overdrive can be fitted to any MGB. It functions not only on top gear, but also on third, which effectively gives the car six gears! Benefits of overdrive are considerable, as can be seen by the modern trend of building cars with five gears as standard. They include better fuel consumption, longer engine life and quieter high speed cruising. Moto-Build gives some insight into how to make the swap.

MU19.2►
This is the later 4-synchromesh gearbox which came with the LH-type overdrive unit as an optional extra.

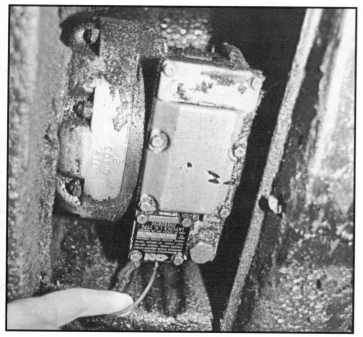

◄MU19.3
A D-type overdrive unit in place beneath the dirt and debris of ages. Probably the best time to consider changing to overdrive is when your existing box is in need of an overhaul. Then you can buy a second-hand gearbox with overdrive and have that overhauled instead.

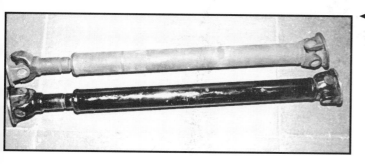

MU19.4
When overdrive is fitted, a different propshaft is called for. The top one here is the overdrive unit, whereas the lower one is not. They look interchangeable but the locating splines are not in the same longitudinal position and mixing them could be potentially very damaging.

Fitting an overdrive

Two types of overdrive units were fitted as standard to MGBs. The earlier 'D'-type was fitted to cars with three-synchromesh gearboxes, whilst the later 'LH'-type was fitted to cars equipped with four-synchro gears. They are not interchangeable.

MU19.5 ▶
Over the years the shape if the gearbox tunnel has changed. This makes life difficult for those owners of early, three-synchro, MGBs, who want to fit later, four-synchro, overdrive gearboxes, since later gearboxes will not fit within the confines of the earlier cars' transmission tunnels.

◀ MU19.6
Wiring for the overdrive is simple. In their wisdom, the manufacturers installed overdrive wiring into **every** car, regardless of whether overdrive was fitted. If you are adding an overdrive some of the wiring is here, alongside the steering column.

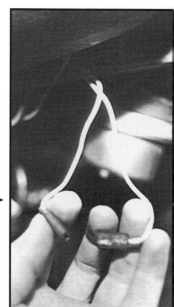

MU19.7 ▶
The wiring for the switch is found underneath the dashboard, on the right-hand side. The two wires are usually taped up out of the way. The Moto-Build mechanic pulls them down so that they can be ...

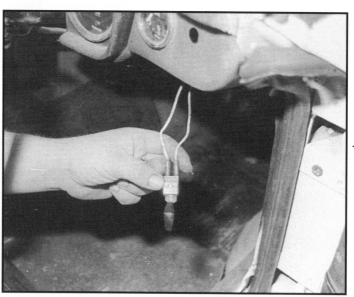

◀ MU19.8
... connected to the switch. This can then be positioned as shown in this photo. Later MGBs had a Triumph type overdrive switch on the gearknob, a much more practical method of actuating the overdrive. It is perfectly feasible to retro-fit this, rather than use the dashboard mounted switch.

Brakes and suspension

Braking system modifications

MU20.1 ▶
Just some of the vast Automec range of braking components available. On the left is a copper brake pipe replacement kit, which is well worth fitting to virtually any MGB, as the originals will doubtless have seen better days. The new ones are easy to bend to shape and will **never** rust!

MU20.2 ▶
Here, one of the rear brake pipes is being removed ready for replacement. As you will see if you take a glance under your own car, they really do take a hammering down there. Consider that your life is at stake and make sure that the **whole** of your braking system is in first class order.

MU20.3
Moto-Build recommend swapping the brake fluid to the latest Automec silicone type. Normal fluid has a tendency to absorb water and thus decreases the efficiency of the braking system and could even, in extreme circumstances, cause you to 'lose' your brakes completely. However, the silicone fluid is non-hygroscopic, which alleviates this problem. Although Silicone fluid will mix, it only provides full benefit when uncontaminated with normal fluid. The tag supplied with the one litre pack is hung around the master cylinder, as a reminder that only Silicone fluid should be used to top up. ▶

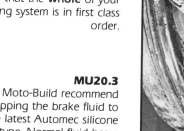

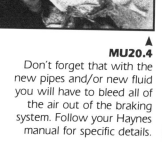

▲ MU20.4
Don't forget that with the new pipes and/or new fluid you will have to bleed all of the air out of the braking system. Follow your Haynes manual for specific details.

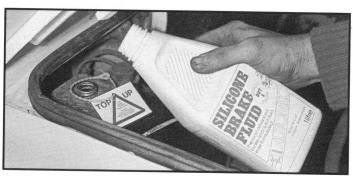

Out of sight, out of mind. Moto-Build have a large repertoire of stories, and some non-too pleasant, of owners who just 'never thought' to check their braking system components. It is all too easy to ignore the brakes: the pipes, fluid and various cylinders are tucked away where no-one ever sees them and brake pads wear away so slowly that one adapts to less effective brakes without any conscious effort. It is only when an emergency stop is required that you realise that they aren't, perhaps, what they should be. Don't let your car be one of Moto-Build's 'crash repair' cases. The Automec copper brake pipes featured here come ready labelled, showing you just where each length of pipe has to be fitted, and all the correct ends and connections are pre-fitted by the manufacturer.

Braking system modifications

Always take great care if you deal with your brakes on a DIY basis and have your work checked over by a trained mechanic before using the car on the road. Make sure that the car is supported by axle stands, with the wheels chocked and that no oil or grease finds its way on to brake pads or linings. If in doubt, contact the specialists. An additional benefit of Automec Silicone fluid, by the way, is that master and wheel cylinders will not rust internally and so last much longer.

MU20.5 ▶
When an owner wants to upgrade his MGB's braking performance, Moto-Build fit Mintex Don D171 brake pads. In addition, less pedal pressure is required, which is handy for those cars without servos.

MU20.6 ▶
The Mintex D171 pads are fitted in the normal way, as per the Haynes manual.

MU20.7
For vastly increased stopping power, Moto-Build can fit the MGB V8 discs, which are much thicker than their four-cylinder counterparts. New calipers are also required.
▼

MU20.8 ▶
Whilst fitting your new brake pipes, it may be as well to check a few other sections of pipework. Automec manufacture copper replacements for clutch and petrol pipes, which also have a habit of rusting away, just like their braking relatives. Once again, they're easily bent and fitted into place.

MU21.1►
Moto-Build can supply this Lockheed servo kit which comes complete with everything required, including a most explicit set of instructions and clear diagrams.

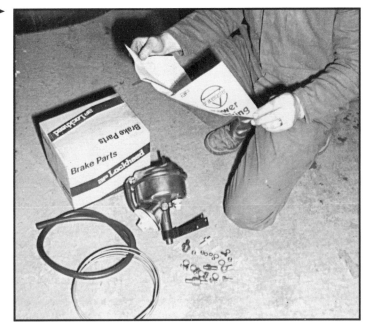

MU21.2
This is the usual mounting place; in front of the bulkhead on the nearside. The actual choice of location will depend on whatever else you may have already added to your car.

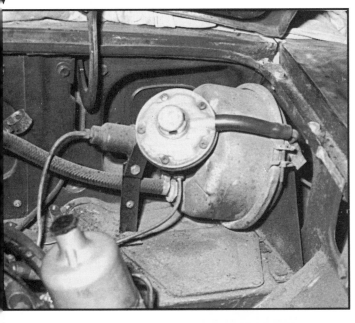

Fitting a servo to the braking system of the MGB can be very beneficial, reducing the pedal pressure and giving much more 'feel' to the brakes. This applies especially to those who find non-servo assisted brakes on the 'B' somewhat hard work. As well as the vacuum connections described here, there are several hydraulic connections which must be made. As always, when the brake hydraulic system has been opened, it **must** be bled correctly before using the car. Check your Haynes manual for full details. This would be an ideal time to change your brake fluid, preferably for the Automec Silicone type as described on pages 163 and 164. This section applies only to cars with a single brake circuit and NOT tandem master cylinder cars. You should note, however, that a servo will not actually increase the **efficiency** of your brakes.

▲
MU21.3
This non-return valve is supplied with the kit and has to be inserted somewhere in the vacuum pipe. The valve is marked very clearly as to which way round it should be fitted. Clearly, this is absolutely vital to the correct functioning of the servo unit. The net result of fitting the servo will be brakes that are very much more pleasant to use around town and that allow stopping from higher speeds without feeling the need to place both feet on the brake pedal!

MU21.4►
The vaccum pipe connects to the inlet manifold as shown here. If your car is not so fitted, it would be possible to drill and tap the manifold and fit the requisite connection. However, it would probably be easier to pick up a secondhand manifold from an MG specialist with the connection already in place.

Stiffer lever arm dampers

If you find that you're hanging onto the steering wheel like grim death when cornering your MGB, then it's time to check out your suspension! Suspension items are among the more commonly ignored parts of any car, but ironically, they are some of the most important. Worn, or damaged, shock absorber units will, at least, give a poor ride and at worst they can kill! They are also an MOT failure point. Replacing them with stiffer or uprated Spax lever arm units can be very beneficial, giving better cornering abilities and, in some cases, increased longevity.

MU22.2 ▶
These are modified uprated Spax lever arm shock absorbers. They are stiffer by around 20 per cent, which is achieved by using different internal valves. Moto-Build would not recommend uprating them any more than 20 per cent for normal road use, as this would place a great strain on the mechanism, with a higher risk of failure. Although, theoretically, removing and replacing a lever arm is a 'bolt-off, bolt-on' task, it is likely that years of being exposed to the elements will make them somewhat reluctant to leave their happy homes. Patience, the correct sockets and gallons of releasing agent are the answer. Full details are given in your Haynes manual.

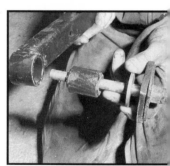

MU22.2 ▶
These are MGB V8 suspension bushes being fitted. They are a worthwhile addition to any MGB. Being much stiffer than standard, they improve cornering by preventing the very long wishbone suspension arms from flexing too much and they also last considerably longer.

Fitting an anti-roll bar

An anti-roll bar is self descriptive. It is basically a piece of round bar which connects across the underside at the front (and in some cases, the rear as well), of the car between the suspensions. It follows that the stiffer the bar, the less tendency there will be for the car to roll when cornering. Apart from the first few, rubber bumper MGB's were fitted with a rear anti-roll bar, which reduced the amount of roll quite dramatically.

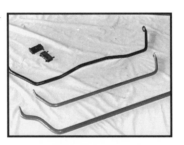

MU23.1 ▶
Moto-Build supply a whole range of replacement anti-roll bars, including the unit shown here. The standard bars are either 5/8 inch or even a mere 9/16 inch on some cars. An uprated unit will be a much more meaty 3/4 inch. The one at the foreground of this picture is an uprated bar for the MGB. At the top is a pair of solid anti-roll bar mountings which are ideal for racing. They are not really suitable for road use as they make the suspension very stiff and also, being fitted with grease nipples, they need servicing every thousand miles. (For those of a curious nature, the bar at centre is for an MG Midget and at top is an MGC item. Happy now?)

MU23.2
The anti-roll bar bolts onto arms which link with the suspension wishbone. Undo these bolts here, which are more than likely to need a spot of releasing agent, and then ...

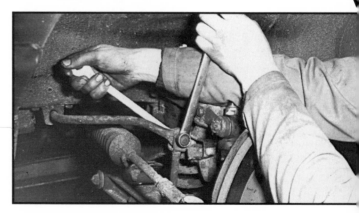

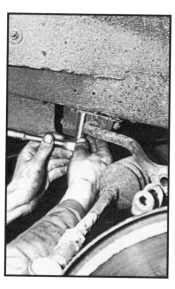

◄ MU23.3
... undo the rubber bush mounting brackets, which hold the centre section of the bar.

MU23.4 ►
Here, the bracket is being removed. The dismantling and replacement procedure is mirrored for the offside of the car.

MU23.5 ►
Having removed the old bar, the new, stiffer, unit can be wriggled into position. Note also that Spax telescopic shock absorbers are fitted to this car.

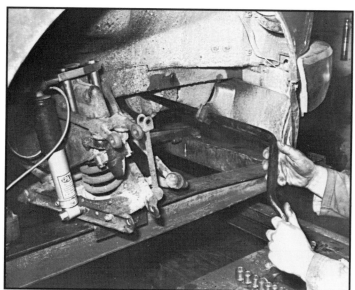

Fitting a thicker anti-roll bar is regarded by Moto-Build as probably the single most effective suspension modification you can make. MGBs can roll somewhat at the front and thus a thicker stiffer bar is a great aid to 'flatter' cornering. It will also add to any understeering tendencies the car has. Depending on how you drive this will counteract the oversteer caused by a heavy right foot.

◄ MU23.6
Bolting the new bar onto position is a reversal of the removal instructions. Note that new mounting rubbers should **always** be used.

Fitting a telescopic shock absorber kit

By the standards of the end-of-the-century, the handling of the MGB leaves something to be desired, although it's not all that bad when you consider that it is based on a pre-war design by one Alec Issigonis! The main problems are; the type of shock absorbers fitted as standard (ie, lever arm), and the use of a 'live' rear axle. In this section, Moto-Build show how to fit a set of the excellent Spax telescopic shock absorbers which prove that the 'B' can be made to behave itself!

MU24.1▶
The high quality Spax components laid out prior to fitting. The 'hardware' is zinc plated for corrosion resistance and the flexible hoses (needed to re-route the brake lines away from the new shock absorbers), are of the braided 'aircraft' type.

◀MU24.2
Here, the valve is being removed from the bottom of the shock absorber unit. In this case, the Moto-Build engineers had removed the kingpin as part of another task. This is not actually necessary, although it makes access somewhat easier. The shock absorber body has to be physically sound with no side play in the top spindle. It actually forms the top link of the front suspension and thus is retained.

◀MU24.3
The valve is separated from the plug and discarded and ...

MU24.4▶
... after the plug has been replaced, the shock absorber should be re-filled with fluid so that the spindle is properly lubricated, although there will no longer be any 'damping effect', of course.

MU24.5 ▶
The lever arm units are held on by four bolts. The outer two are removed and the thread of the crossmember, into which they fit, should be cleaned up. The top mounting arm, supplied with the Spax kit, is secured by these two long bolts and grip washers. The Moto-Build engineers were very careful when screwing these into place, bearing in mind the probable build-up of rust and other debris in the thread. They screwed them in three turns forward and two turns back, to ensure that the screw was not cross-threaded. Better still, you could use a thread tap first.

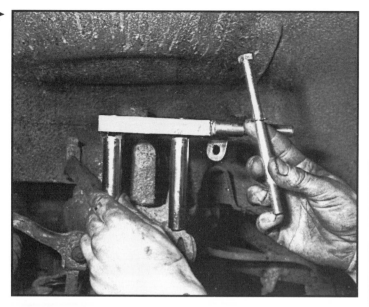

Whenever your MGB has less than four wheels firmly on the ground, you **must** take safety precautions. The 'B' is not a light vehicle at the best of times and it will seem even less so should it land on your person! **Always** use axle stands and chock the wheels. **Never** work under, or even near, a car supported only by a jack. Only raise the car when on hard, level ground.

◀ MU24.6
The nuts, bolts and washers securing the spring pan are removed and the new bottom shock absorber mounting bracket is fitted using the same holes, but with the longer bolts supplied with the kit.

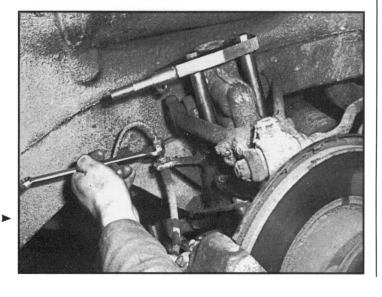

MU24.7 ▶
The old flexible brake hose has to be removed; first from the bracket and then from the caliper.

Fitting a telescopic shock absorber kit

The Spax shock absorbers fitted in this section are adjustable, meaning that the owner can have a ride as hard or as soft as he wishes. It follows that the handling characteristics also can be adopted to suit a particular driver or driving style. The Spax units can be so adjusted to give, at one end of the scale, understeer (a tendency for the car to want to go straight on in corners) or, at the other, oversteer (an over-reaction of the steered wheels compared to the steering wheel input). Naturally, a point somewhere in between, in order to gain neutral handling, can also be selected. Moto-Build's Darryl also claims that the type of front anti-roll bar you use will affect the front damper settings required. A thick anti-roll bar could necessitate the lowest Spax damper setting.

MU24.8 ▶
The new copper brake pipe (again supplied with the Spax kit), is fitted to the existing brake line at the bulkhead and then run along to the new top mounting bracket. The braided hose, also supplied, can then be put **loosely** into position.

◀ MU24.9
Once the positioning of the hoses has been checked, the washer can be placed on the bracket ready ...

MU24.10 ▶
... to accept the new shock absorber, which ...

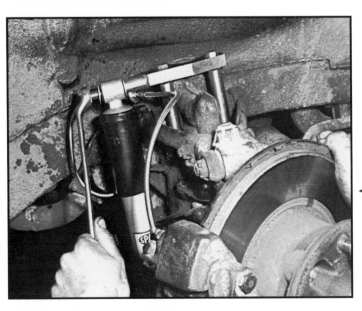

◀ MU24.11
... can then be tightened up in the usual manner. Check the brake hoses one more time before tightening them also. Don't forget that, having opened the hydraulic braking system, it must now be bled.

MU24.12 ►
As can be seen here, the Spax kit for the rear of the car is considerably simpler!

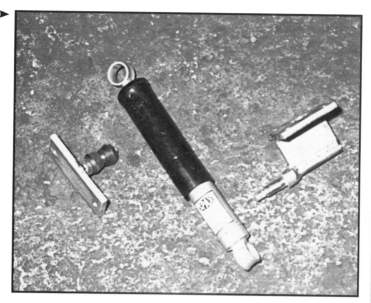

Fitting a set of Spax telescopics on the MGB has a number of effects. It drastically reduces the car's body roll and keeps the tyres on the tarmac, especially on bumpy roads. Moto-Build point out that they also improve the location of the long wishbones on the front suspension, which helps to prevent wind-up during heavy braking. This is particularly noticeable on the MGB V8, where the high power output and better brakes usually mean that more use is made of both!

◄ MU24.13
The nuts and bolts holding the rear shock absorber in place are removed. If you are doing this yourself, don't forget that the car must be properly supported as described on page 169.

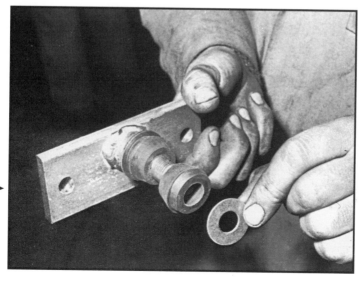

MU24.14 ►
A photo, prior to fitting, of the new top shock absorber mounting bracket. As can be seen, Spax supply the brackets with all relevant nuts and washers.

Fitting a telescopic shock absorber kit

It should be remembered that better cornering and handling in general, is not only a question of uprating the shock absorbers. The tyres should be in good condition, as should the wheels, especially if they are wires. If you suspect spokes of working loose or the wheels of running out of true, have a specialist check them. In many cases, the higher cornering speeds available prompt owners to uprate the tyres along with the shockers. The tracking should be checked as a matter of course, as should the wheel balance. Finally, as speeds from A to B will undoubtedly increase, you would be well advised to take a long hard look at your brakes. Good quality standard discs/drums and pads/linings are a minimum. Depending on your driving style, says Moto-Build's Darryl, you may find it necessary to uprate the brakes also.

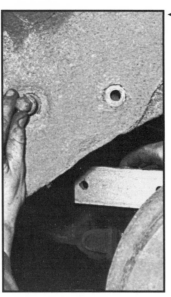

◄ MU24.15
The new bracket from the Spax kit is fitted in place of the original shock absorbers. Then the spring clamp plate can be removed from the U-bolts, although you will undoubtedly have to use more than a little releasing agent.

MU24.16 ►
The bottom plate can then be fitted. Note that Moto-Build have already fitted the shock absorber, which saves having to remove the exhaust. It's easy when you know how!

MU14.17 ►
With everything in place, all of the nuts are checked. They should be checked again after a few hundred miles and thereafter at regular service intervals.

◄ MU24.18
And that's it; the job finished. The bottom brackets look to be very low, although, as Moto-Build point out, they are very close to the wheel and so are unlikely ever to catch on anything and Spax confirm that this has never given any problem. The kit as a whole, however, makes the most dramatic improvement to the handling of your MGB.

MU25.1 ▶

The change in ride height was achieved by fitting a different crossmember at the front. The later type is seen here at right, alongside the earlier type. It follows that, to be absolutely correct, the way to lower the ride is to swap the crossmember. However, this is a truly mammoth task and also involves changing all of the front suspension.

According to Moto-Build, the cars which benefit most from a suspension lowering exercise are the post-1975, rubber bumper models. These are an inch higher than previously, as American regulations required an increased ride height at that time.

MU25.2

A considerably easier way of getting the car a little lower, is to use Moto-Build's shorter coil springs. The shock absorber travel has to be checked beforehand to ascertain whether telescopic shock absorbers should also be fitted.

▼

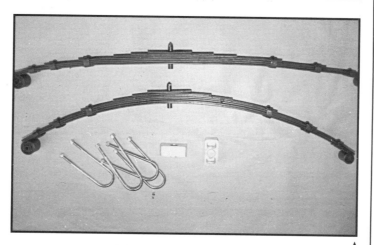

▲

MU25.3

At the back of the car, leaf springs are used. The lower one here is the uprated and lowered unit. If lever arm shock absorbers are being used, you must check that the travel is sufficient. With all of Moto-Build's replacement leaf springs, new 'U' bolts are supplied which ...

◀ **MU25.4**

... is just as well, as the originals are likely to be somewhat the worse for wear. The Moto-Build mechanic makes light work of removing this 'U' bolt with his pneumatic socket.

On the road

The first thing noticed when driving an MGB equipped with the Aldon two litre engine is the deeper engine note. 'That's good', you think, 'the engine actually **sounds** more powerful!' Then, when you pull away, the bigger engine's second impact is made. You will find there's so much more torque than the old engine ever had, that you can change up a gear earlier, and you don't even need to change **down** so often. This makes driving in and out of town on 'give-and-take' roads, a far greater pleasure than experienced before in an MGB. With what seems like a touch on the throttle, instead of having to stir the gearbox and wait, the car grunts past slower traffic and sails up hills in a refreshing fashion. Then, when you need to accelerate, such as when overtaking, you find there are more revs on tap than before. This could be function of the lighter flywheel (it certainly helps the car to rev more quickly), or the larger valves and flowed head, but Moto-Build's Darryl reckons that it has

The combination of Moto-Build expertise in racing and running rapid MGs, Aldon Engineering's famed abilities in extracting extra, reliable power from an MGB engine and the 'chassis' tuning equipment offered by people such as Spax, all contribute towards helping the MGB owner equip his or her MGB with extra 'bite' **and** with extra on-the road safety. After all, an engine that is giving all it's got when the driver is confronted with an overtaking situation where more is needed is a liability, to say the least. And while the MGB's power plant was fine for the early '60s, endowing the car with true sporting performance for its day, the car certainly benefits from the Aldon/Moto-Build treatment today! Having made it go faster, the extra cornering abilities and braking performance shown in this Chapter become essential attributes.

◄OR1
Just the addition of a front spoiler to the front of Lindsay Porter's V8 was enough to set off its appearance. More significant were the Spax shockers and stiffer front anti-roll bar which transformed the road holding without, in his view, making the suspension **too** stiff.

OR2 ►
Those who own a very early MGB are most unlikely to want to modify the car's appearance but the sort of bolt-on (and thus, by implication, bolt-off again, if you should wish), mechanical mods shown in this Chapter can make the car so much more pleasurable as well as safer to drive.

◄OR3
The popularity of front spoilers is indicated in this huge MGB line-up taken at an MGOC event.

◄ OR4
This GT has been fitted with V8 wheels (or those from a Jubilee; they're essentially the same), and sprayed in two-tone paintwork.

OR5 ►
One specialist, advertising in the MGOC magazine, offers this GT conversion which makes the car a 2+2 convertible. Too drastic perhaps?

◄ OR6
Even more dramatic is the Cobra look-alike kit car option for those with a totally rotten bodyshell who don't fancy restoration. The completely new bodyshell, produced by Heritage (an arm of Rover Group), and built on the original press tools and jigs looks likely to make this option redundant.

more to do with Aldon's engine balancing allowing the engine to rev higher which vibration previously ruled out of bounds. The balancing ought to make tickover smoother but the counter-effect of a 'hotter' cam more than offsets the beneficial effects of the engine balancing. On this test car, a Weber carb was fitted and that certainly didn't help tickover smoothness. Nor did it help economy! You'd expect the larger engine to use more petrol and the way the right foot keeps enjoying itself doesn't help matters, but the Weber plays a big part in knocking consumption down to below 25 mpg. Mind you, it also plays a part in providing that enjoyable extra spurt of acceleration when the throttle is pressed. The test car was fitted with Spax telescopics, Moto-Build's stiffer anti-roll bar and Pirelli tyres. Compared with a standard 'B', handling was totally transformed. The car cornered flatter, the tyre grip allowed exhilarating driving, but the relationship between front and rear suspension left just a touch to be desired, not having been finally set up. Moto-Build claim that

On the road

with a thicker front anti-roll bar, you can turn the rear Spax shockers up, turn the front right down and get rid of the mild understeer that characterised this car. Of course, you don't get 'owt' for 'nowt' and the flip side of this coin is that the suspension is so much firmer than it was before. However, the extra comfort of the shaped seats, allowing faster cornering with a greater feeling of security, rather made up for it. Brakes were similarly improved. Mintex M171 pads gave an impressive amount of extra brake 'bite' when the pedal is first depressed and the effect is even greater when V8 brakes are fitted. The extra value of the larger V8 brakes is that brake fade, which is not an inherent problem with the 'B' in any case, is virtually eliminated. A modified MGB on the road is a greatly superior car to the standard item. The test car tried here **looked** good (the MGB still catches the passer-by's eye, in any case; the tastefully modified car much more so), **felt** good, because of the trim improvements made and by golly, it went so well that it **did** you good, too ...

◀ **OR7**
This American car has been subtly and tastefully modified with chrome wire wheels and a chrome plated edging strip extending all around the car, including the edges of the front spoiler. Most attractive!

OR8 ▶
Modification for racing is beyond the scope of this book, unless you want to go in for a level of Clubman racing where only simple modifications are allowed. See Chapter 6.

◀ **OR9**
The history of modified MGBs is a strong one. This is a Costello MGB V8, one of the cars fitted with the V8 engine before MG got round to doing the job themselves. This car also wears Sebring headlamp cowls, deep front spoiler and chrome sill covers. (Photo courtesy of Pearl McGlen)

Fitting alternative wheels

◄ MU27.1
This Moto-Build supplied wheel looks for all the world like the Mini-Lite wheels which were popular in the late '60s and early '70s. However, this one is made by GB wheels and very nice it looks too.

MU27.2 ►
GB Wheels make these specifically for the MGB and so no complicated adaptors are necessary, they just bolt-on as normal.

MU27.3 ►
This rather attractive multi-spoke alloy wheel is produced by Cosmic with the MGB very much in mind. Now is the time to turn the page for locking wheel nuts!

MU27.4
Keeping your wheels clean and free from road dirt and mud is hard enough without having brake dust to ► contend with as well. These 'Wheel Clean' discs, from Carflow, solve the problem. The metal centre pushes onto the hub, over the wheel mounting studs, and then the rubber surround is cut to suit the particular size of wheel. The brake dust is then deflected away from the expensive alloys you have just fitted. The disc has passed many official Government tests to make sure that it does not interfere with braking efficiency. When fitted, it is simply clamped between wheel and hub.

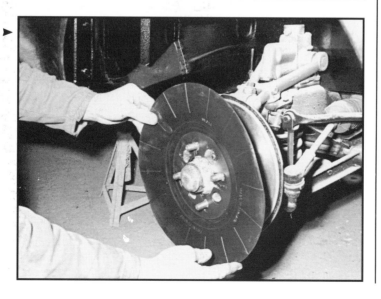

Little will improve the appearance of your MGB more dramatically than a set of alloy wheels. They are, of course, more expensive than steel ones, but do look considerably better. Many companies do not produce wheels for the 'B' nowadays, so you may have to shop around. In this section, we look at two who do. The cleaning of most modern alloy wheels is limited to washing with warm soapy water, along with the rest of the car. As they are covered with a thin coating of clear lacquer, it is vital that no strong solvents are used for cleaning as these would probably dissolve the lacquer! Don't forget to adjust the insurance value of your car to cover the cost of the new wheels.

Fitting locking wheel nuts

Having fitted alloy wheels and possibly a new set of tyres as well, you will doubtless want to keep them on your car. Even those who have steel wheels may well have expensive tyres which would be just as tempting to the would be thief especially, as London-based Moto-Build know, in the bigger cities! These Carflow locking wheel nuts make it almost impossible for anyone to remove the wheels without the special socket 'key'.

MU28.1▶
This is what you get. The kit comprises one nut for each wheel, a 'key' for fitting and removal, a stainless steel cover and a plastic device for removing it. Carflow nuts are available for all MGB models.

◀MU28.2
Close up, it can be seen that the holes in the top of the nut correspond with the pins in the end of the key. There is a massive number of possible variations of hole and pin positions. All keys have a special code number with which you can order a replacement should you lose yours. Carflow provide a sticker with this on which can be stuck anywhere convenient in the car or in your handbook.

MU28.3▶
Once in position, the key allows the nut to be tightened just like any standard nut. You must remember to keep the 'key' in the car at all times; a puncture without it will immobilize the car!

Little can give a more sporty and distinctly 'period' feel to the MGB than the addition of wire wheels. Definitely a trip down memory lane to the days of British Racing Green and all that! However, if your car is used on British roads on a regular basis, you will have to allow time out each week for cleaning purposes! Here, a Moto-Build mechanic demonstrates some of the work entailed.

MU29.1
This shows the front hub being changed from a disc wheel type to a wire wheel type. After taking out the split pin and removing the nut, the hub can be pulled off the stub axle. Note that the usual safety precautions should be taken when the car is jacked up.

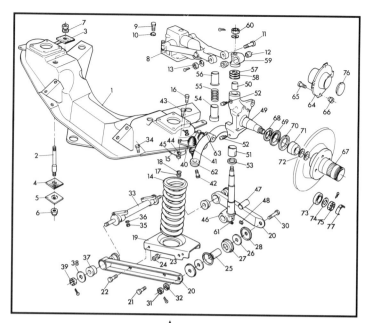

MU29.2
This diagram should make things clearer. The disc wheel hub (64) is removed and the wire wheel hub (67) is put on in its place. Note the extra length of the latter.

MU29.3
At the rear the best approach is to use a Moss Motors conversion kit which retains the original track width.

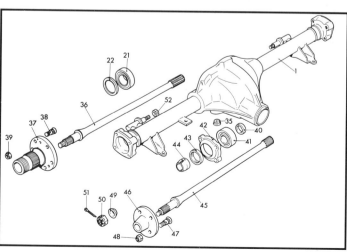

◄MU29.4
Axles for wire wheel cars are almost 2″ narrower than those for disc or rostyle wheels. You could swap the hub (item 46) for the wire wheel hub (item 37), but the rear wheels will probably foul the wheel arches. Using the Moss conversion system is far simpler and cheaper!

Fitting wire wheels

Moto-Build point out that wire wheels are not as robust as steel 'disc' wheels and will need rebuilding every few years. Just like the wheels on your bicycle, the spokes become loose after a time and require re-tensioning and the wheels balanced and trued. It is essential that inner tubes are used with wire wheels, since the air inside tubeless tyres will escape through the spoke holes.

◄MU29.5
A wire wheel hub with all the brake components reassembled around it. See your Haynes manual for details.

MU29.6►
If you want to cheat, you can buy these wire wheel adaptors, which simply bolt into place. The only problem which may occur, is that the tyres may rub against the rear wheel arch, because of the slightly widened track, especially if the springs are a little worn or the 'U' bolts are loose.

MU29.7►
An even quicker way of cheating is to use these Moto-Build supplied wires, which look like the real thing but which are, in fact, bolted on just like a disc wheel. Look closely and you'll see!

◄MU29.8
This **is** the real thing, gleaming in the sunshine. Worth all the effort of keeping them clean? That's up to you! In fact chrome wire wheels were never fitted as standard and are a real labour of love. Moto-Build can supply rebuilt, stove enamalled 'original' wires, too.

Fitting wheel trim rings

MU30.1▶
So you have steel 'Rostyle' wheels and little cash but would like to make your wheels look more interesting. How about ...

It is important that the fitting of wheel trims and wheel trim rings is properly carried out. It is easy to fit them in such a way that they look as if they are seated correctly but, in fact, are not. This could lead to them flying off whilst the car is moving. If you're lucky, you will just lose the trim; if not, the consequences could be much worse, for it would be quite possible for someone to be injured should they be struck by an errant trim.

◀MU30.2
... a set of chrome wheel trim rings? This particular set is from the excellent range supplied by the MG Owners Club direct to Members. They are also fitted and/or supplied by Moto-Build to many customers who wish to add a little extra sparkle. The rings are of high quality and certainly give a sparkle to the wheels on the 'B'.

◀MU30.3
The rings simply clip into place and require some heavy pressure with the flat of your hand to push them on flush. Make sure that the cut-out in the ring matches the valve stem.

Understanding ...

Tyres

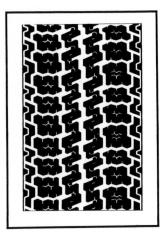

A Pirelli tyre contact patch, shown in the diagram, illustrates how the road would 'see' the tyre.

When you realise that your car's 'footprint' - the area in touch with the road - is in fact no bigger than a man's hand, you begin to see how crucial the selection and care of tyres can be. All your car's power and performance will come to nothing unless the tyres keep the car safely on the road.

Converting to ultra low profile tyres is one of the most effective and economical ways of enhancing many cars' looks and handling. However, don't choose on looks alone. At the extreme, you could end up with tyres that foul the bodywork or that cause a deterioration in wet weather grip, particularly at speed. You must also ensure that the tyre is not too wide for the width of wheel rim you are using and that the circumference is not so different from standard that the speedometer reading is greatly affected.

Specification

The tyre sidewall markings relate to both size designation and service description. Taking, for example, the groups of letters and numbers contained in the tyre description: 185/65R14 82H and reading from left to right:

'185' refers to the nominal section width of the tyre, whilst the '65' represents the aspect ratio. Aspect ratio is the ratio of nominal section width to section height. In this case it means, roughly speaking, that the distance from the bead of the tyre to the tread, is 65 per cent of the tyre's width. The lower the tyre's aspect ratio, the less sidewall flexing will occur, improving cornering grip and steering response. On the other hand, the tyre is less able to absorb bumps and could allow more road noise to be transmitted, while the ride could be a little firmer - although this is something that some owners prefer.

'R' indicates the tyre construction. Here, 'R' stands for Radial.

'14' refers to the wheel diameter in inches.

'82' is the load index, which is a numerical code associated with the maximum load the tyre can carry at the speed indicated by the speed symbol.

Finally, 'H' is the speed symbol. This is an alphabetical code indicating the speed at which the tyre can carry a load corresponding to the load index.

Tyre Choice

Car tyres purchased as replacements should have at least the same speed rating as those fitted as original equipment. The load index is also very important. While most ultra low profile tyres have at least the same load capacity as the base tyre, this should be checked before purchasing your replacement tyres.

When considering converting to ultra low profile tyres it is recommended that the overall diameter of the wheel/tyre package should not vary more than plus 3 per cent to minus 5 per cent from the original equipment tyre fitment. Remember, the percentage difference in the overall diameter will result in the same percentage difference in the overall gearing and speedometer reading. Larger tyres give lower speedometer readings; smaller tyres give higher speedometer readings. Most tyres fit a range of rim widths which will help you to choose the most suitable package for your needs, and for this, you need to speak to your supplier.

By increasing the 'tyre performance' on your car, with ultra low profile tyres, the wear rate may be affected due to your relying on the improved handling of the car. The more technologically advanced the tyre and car the more responsive the handling will become. However, you should remember that the latest generation of tyres - designed decades after the MGB's front suspension - may alter your car's handling characteristics in ways you may not have anticipated!

It is worth re-emphasizing that you should only deal with expert tyre dealers who will give you the best service and advice, such as Standard Motorists Centres or Central Tyre Company. Remember that quality of service is especially important when having expensive tyres fitted to 'exotic' wheels.

Early MGBs were fitted with 155R14 tyres on 4J wheels. The largest permissible tyre size for fitting to these wheels is 165/7014. Where cars were fitted originally with 155R14 tyres on 4½J wheels, the largest permissible tyre size is 185/7014.

MU31.1▶
The Metro 6R4 was MG's latest racing car, its dramatically effective 4WD traction assisted by Pirelli tyres.

65-Series tyres and below should **not** be fitted with tubes and thus should never be used with wire wheels, since you must **always** use inner tubes with wire wheels. In addition, Pirelli recommend that only wheels with safety-type rims should be used.

◀MU31.2
Nowadays, on the track, Pirelli tyres are a firm favourite among MGB racers.

◀MU31.3
The P4 is an everyday, 'family' tyre giving good grip, comfort and longevity.

MU31.4▶
P6 is a high performance tyre with outstanding levels of performance.

◀MU31.5
P600 is part of Pirelli's 'second generation' of ultra low profile tyres, developed for the modern car market.

Pirelli are strongly associated with the AH4 (asymmetric hump) safety rim. Whereas a punctured tyre normally collapses into the rim (left), the AH4 holds the tyre in place, offering limited run flat properties while still using normal tyres.

MU31.6▶
P Zero uses an asymmetric tread pattern, giving a normal block pattern across the inner 50 per cent of the tread width, an intermediate area for 28 per cent of width, and racing-type performance from the outer 22 per cent. These are not suitable for the MGBs but demonstrate the extent of Pirelli's techological prowess.

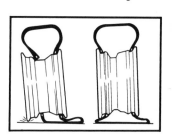

Tyres

Pirelli produce a Car Tyre Fitment and Conversions booklet for the tyre dealer to advise you in your tyre choice. Some confusion may arise from time to time regarding ultra low profile conversions and in these instances, you should contact the Pirelli Performance Bureau where advice on the most suitable tyre fitment, for your vehicle and pocket, will be offered (see end of book for telephone contact).

This chart, produced by the Pirelli Performance Bureau, shows size for size conversions of a base tyre size of 165R14. These tyres were fitted to a 5J wheel. For MGBs fitted as standard with narrower wheels and tyres, owners **must** note the maximum permitted tyre sizes shown in the margin note on page 182.

These are not recommendations but possible sizes based on overall diameter between the plus three and minus five per cent variation shown below. It is recommended that the overall diameter of the wheel/tyre package should not vary more than plus three to minus five per cent from the original equipment tyre fitment.

MGB original tyre size 165/R14, 622mm diameter.

Alternative tyre sizes and diameters shown below

OPTIONAL SIZES	-5%	-3%	+2%	+3%	RIM SIZES IN INCHES
175R14 P4			633		5
175R14 P5			633		5
175/70R14 P4		604			5
175/70R14 P5		604			5
175/70R14 P6					5
185/70R14 P4		620			5
185/70R14 P5			623		5
205/70R14 P6			624		5
195/70R14 P3*				635	5.5
195/70R14 P5*				635	5.5
195/70R14 P6*				635	5.5
185/65R14 P6	598				5
185/65R14 P600	599				5
195/65R14 P6*		606			5.5
195/65R14 P8*		611			5.5
195/65R14 P600*		612			5.5
205/65R14 P8+			628		5.5
195/60R14 P6*	593				5.5
195/60R14 P600*	592				5.5
205/60R14 P6+		605			5.5

* Fouling will probably occur on bodywork arches, suspension, and steering especially in a fully loaded condition.
+ Bodywork modification will be required.
Only 70 series are tried and approved!

Lubrication - oils, greases and fluids

Duckhams have been famous for producing the very best in engine oil, gear oil, grease and other associated products for a very long time.

Understanding lubrication

Back in the days of yore when knights were bold and rivers froze over in winter, the motorist didn't trouble his head about the type of lubricant in engine or gearbox. As long as there was plenty of the stuff around, the engine and gearbox chugged and ground along quite contentedly. Nowadays, the enthusiastic owner knows better! With increased performance, longer journeys and higher speeds, the demands on lubricants can be quite considerable and can be well beyond the capabilities of many of the 'economy' oils on the market. The wise owner gets to know what is required in a lubricant and makes darned sure that he or she uses only the best available. After all, to reduce the working life of an engine or gearbox because of penny-pinching or because of selecting the wrong lubricant for the job is not what any MGB owner wants. Cheap 'n' nasty oils are best left to the cars to which they are best suited!

Engine oils

This section leans on the expertise of Duckhams, a company right at the forefront in oil technology. They have invested an enormous amount of resources in producing a range of engine oils that satisfies the requirements of all engines, including the most advanced, with some to spare. Before explaining how they have done so, it is necessary to take a look at some of the criteria that are applied to modern oils.

Many years ago, all engine oil was 'single grade'. It was given an 'SAE' rating which described how 'viscous' or 'thick' it was. An SAE 20 oil, being 'thin' was used in the winter months when the oil became heavier, making it more difficult to start the engine, while in the summer months a 'thicker' oil, perhaps SAE 40 or 50 was used so that the oil did not become too 'watery' to do its job. Then along came multigrade oils, introduced first by Duckhams themselves, way back at the beginning of the 1950s, and covering the spectrum from SAE 20 to 50 all the year round. These oils are still universally available, of course, along with variations such as 15w/50, 10w/40 and even 5w/50 in some cases.

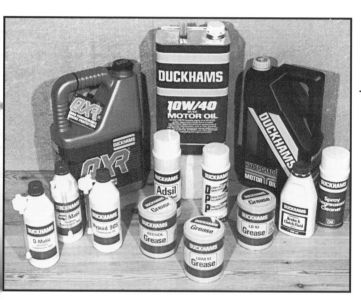

◄UO1
Mention Duckhams, and most people immediately think of oil. However, there's also Spray Degreasant Cleaner, DPP penetrating and lubricating fluid, and Adsil Silicone Fluid which is wonderful for lubricating sliding rubbing parts. All come in aerosol packs. Check in your handbook to find which grade of Duckhams engine oil or transmission fluid will be required for your MGB.

Where the lower 'drag' factor of a lower viscosity oil is required but without the additional features of QXR, Duckhams also produce '10w/40 Motor Oil'. Excellent for easier winter starting and marginally improved fuel economy when used with a newer engine, 10w/40 is not intended to replace Hypergrade 15w/50 in an older or high-mileage engine. Oil consumption could deteriorate noticeably if 10w/40 is used because it can find its way more easily past worn bores, piston rings and valve guides.

It's relatively easy to make an oil which gives a viscosity of 20w/50 while it is new. The manufacturer just adds something called a 'polymer' which acts as a 'thickener' as the oil gets hotter. There is, however, a wide choice of polymers available and the old rule of 'you get what you pay for' applies. Cheap polymers lose their effectiveness quite rapidly as they are subjected to heat and 'shearing' effects inside the engine. The net result of using cheap polymers is that a 20w/50 oil loses the SAE 50 part of its viscosity which removes much of its effectiveness when the engine is working hard. The only way of avoiding the potential damage that this can cause is to only use a top-name brand. Companies like Duckhams only use the best polymers in their multigrade oils because, they claim, they expect even more from their engine oils ...

Top brand 15w/50 oils, such as 'Hypergrade', are designed to satisfy the technical requirements of every engine used today. However, there is another oil, known as QXR, designed with the owners of modern high-performance cars in mind. These are probably fuel-injected engines in the majority of cases, quite possibly with multi-valve heads, while some are turbocharged, although of course, any engines powering the cars shown in this book can enjoy the benefits of QXR. The idea behind QXR was to develop an oil to meet the extra demands placed on a lubricant by these high-performance engines. Such an oil would cost more to buy than conventional oils, but would offer the very best protection from wear, the greatest possible freedom from deposits, excellent oil consumption control and the ability to perform really well over the widest extremes of temperatures and motoring conditions.

QXR is a 10w/40 oil, offering all the protection that could possibly be required along with a reduction in the 'drag' effect suffered inside an engine when 'thicker' oils are used. Ordinarily, a 10w/40 oil would have two huge disadvantages over conventional

Lubrication - oils, greases and fluids

Oil companies are fond of saying that proprietary oil additives are at best useless and at worst harmful. After all, if there was a better additive, they would use it themselves! If you want the best possible level of additive in your oil, buy the more expensive oil: it's that simple! Take a look at the oil's designation number to determine additive level. For instance, the Duckhams swing ticket indicates that its 'API' classification is API SF and CD in the case of both QXR and 'Hypergrade'. The last letter indicates the degree of specification; the last-but-one indicates 'S' for petrol engines; 'C' for diesel engines.

oils: it would tend to lose viscosity at higher temperatures, and it would tend to vapourise at high temperatures because 10w/40 oils are normally so much more volatile.

The most expensive solution, and one which prices the oil beyond many enthusiasts pockets, is to use a synthetic lubricant in place of the usual mineral base oils. However, the route chosen by Duckhams is interesting! They have developed a special process through which the normal mineral oil is put at the refining stage to give it all the properties required but at far lower cost than that of synthetics.

Best of all, the tests which Duckhams carried out during development showed that in terms of performance, QXR proved to be comparable to highly expensive synthetic oils in some respects - and in other respects, even better! Pat Lelliott, Duckham's Technical Service Manager, is so proud of QXR that he says, 'Achieve all those standards and you have an oil of the high-performance class, such as QXR. Look around and see how many products attain such levels. There aren't many!'

◄ UO2
As this section indicates, Duckhams QXR is the very finest choice for high-performance engines. Here, it's being used in an MGB.

UO3 ►
As well as being available in the large 'oil change' packs, QXR is also available in smaller top-up packs.

Gearboxes (manual)

The oil specification demanded by a gearbox varies according to its design and such factors as power transmitted, ease of gear selection and sealing, for instance. In the case of the MGB, the same type of oil that is used in the engine should be used in the gearbox, provided that the viscosity is not lower than 15w/50. In other words, 'Hypergrade' oil is perfect for the job. On the other hand, if the car is used in very cold temperatures, leading to a 'sticky' gearchange, Duckhams 10w/40 Motor Oil could be used.

Rear axles

An oil such as Duckhams Hypoid 90S is, quite simply, all that is required to withstand the extraordinary 'shear' forces involved. Look at the specification of the oil. API GL4 is fine for every normal use, but if an oil with a higher level of additives is required, API GL5 may be considered, a higher last number indicating a higher level of additive treatment.

UO4 ►
There is a wide range of Duckhams grease types available and once again, you should check that you are purchasing the right type by checking in the vehicle handbook.

Spark Plugs

Carl Benz, father of the motor car, called automobile ignition the problem to end all problems. "If the spark fails", he said, "then everything else is useless however sophisticated the design". Bosch pride themselves on having supplied that spark as early as 1902, though things have progressed just a little since then ...

Often under-rated and overlooked, the spark plug plays a decisive part in the efficient operation of any engine, and for a high-performance engine, the demands placed upon it are amazingly tough. At a working pressure of up to 50 bar and in gas temperatures of up to 3000 degrees Celcius, the spark plug is expected to deliver 30,000 volts and above, no less than 100 times **every second** when the car is at speed. Not only that but the poor thing is expected to work happily, hot or cold, for months and thousands of miles on end: Indeed, some modern cars' service intervals now demand a spark plug that will work well over a 20,000 mile period, and Bosch engineers have come up with a range of plugs that fulfil even that criterion.

MU33.1

Three types of Bosch spark plug on display here are (left to right): the triple electrode plug specially developed to give highly extended service intervals for some modern cars; platinum tipped plugs which are dearer to buy but are a good deal more efficient provided that they are accurately gapped before use and the standard Bosch Super plug, produced to original equipment specification.

MU33.2 ▶

Advantages of Platinum plugs are: ignition conditions remain practically constant all through recommended service life of plug; plugs warm up more quickly and so 'self-clean' earlier; heat transfer properties are improved; the centre electrode is virtually wear resistant; the property of platinum.
A Very long insulator nose ensures extension of the thermal operating range.
B 0.3mm dia. platinum centre electrode
C Platignum centre electrode sintered gas tight in insulator nose.

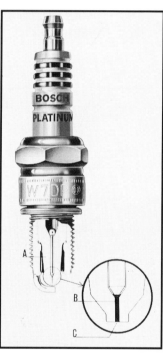

SPARK PLUG TYPES

Some spark plugs have a flat seating surface and make use of a sealing gasket; others have a conical surface and are self-sealing. Clearly, the correct type of plug seating designed for the engine has to be used; they are not interchangeable. Some types of spark plug are interchangeable, however. Where radio interference from spark plugs is a problem (which is unusual, to say the least, in the case of 'our' cars - although with radio interference, anything can happen!), it is possible to buy Bosch plugs with interference suppression (those plugs with an in-built resistor have an 'R' in the type number) and even fully shielded plugs.

Other special plugs include those with multiple electrodes to satisfy some manufacturers' extremely long service intervals, and those with precious metal electrodes. These plugs, with either silver ('S' identification) or platinum ('P' identification) electrodes are inherently more efficient than ordinary plugs, and the extra efficiency is especially useful in high performance engines, right up to racing spec.

Spark plugs

PLUGS IN PRACTICE

Spark plugs tend to break down, in the main, for one of two or three reasons. One is that the plugs internal insulation fails leading to internal shorting out, although this is usually because another problem has occurred. A plug working outside its optimum working temperature range will be prone to failing in this way, so it's important that the correct heat range is used in your particular car. If the engine is standard, just use the correct plug, the designation of which will have been determined by Bosch and the vehicle manufacturer. If the engine is tuned, however, the specialist concerned should be able to advise.

Leaving the plug in place for too long can also cause breakdown of the plug, of course. Again, the insulation can fail, or the centre electrode can become contaminated leading to reduced efficiency, or the electrode can become eroded.

TYPE NUMBERS AND FITTING

You can identify a Bosch plug by the type number on the box and on the body of the plug itself. Take a typical number, such as W 7 DP. (Plugs with resistors would have an additional 'R' after the 'W', by the way.) 'W' indicates the type of thread and seat, this being the most common flat seat, M 14 x 1.25 thread. '7' indicates the heat range - a critical measure, because to use a plug outside the correct heat range could damage the engine. 'D' shows that the plug thread length is, in this case, 19mm (or 17.5 mm if the plug is tapered), while the last letter indicates the electrode material, where 'C' would indicate the standard plug with copper electrode. You will find an application list detailing the correct plugs for your car wherever the plugs are sold.

MU33.3 ►
Ensure that the plug threads in the head are clear. Use a Sykes-Pickavant thread chaser if necessary (see 'Engine conversion'). Screw plug in by hand until it is seated. New plugs with flat seats are turned a further 90 degrees with a spark plug wrench. Already used flat-seat plugs, and conical seat plugs, are turned by a further 15 degrees with the wrench. (Courtesty of Robert Bosch Ltd)

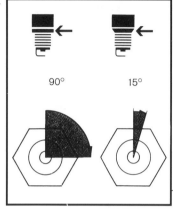

MU33.4
Using the Bosch spark plug gap-gauge
A. Measuring the electrode gap. The measuring wire should pass through with only the slightest resistance
B. Checking platinum plugs for wear: Bend the side electrode back; push measuring wire into hole in insulator nose; when wire goes in as far as plastic stop wear limit has been reached
C. Opening the electrode gap with the 'bottle opener' type bending devide on the Bosch measuring tool
D. Close the gap by tapping lightly and carefully on a smooth, hard surface ▼

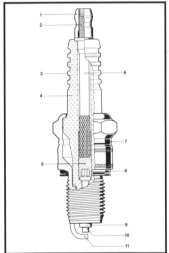
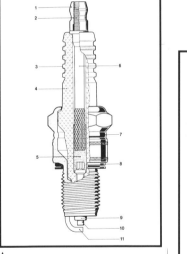

▲
MU33.5
CONSTRUCTION OF SPARK PLUG
1 Terminal nut
2 Thread
3 Current leak barrier
4 Insulator
5 Conductive seal
6 Terminal stud
7 Fitting: swaged & heat shrunk
8 Gasket (flat seat)
9 Insulator tip
10 Centre electrode
11 Ground electrode

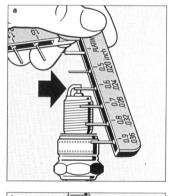

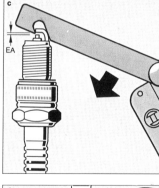
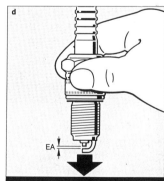

Improving engine bay appearance

MU34.1 ►
It is truly amazing just how much oil and grease can end up in an engine bay, even where there is no specific oil leak. Using Comma Hyperclean degreasant is one of the simplest ways to deal with this. It is in aerosol form and can be sprayed at the affected areas with great accuracy. For best results it should be left for five minutes to break down the oil. Then it can be washed off, either by using water with a stiff brush or better still, by using ...

Cleaning and protecting the engine bay is an oft neglected but very important task. When the working area is dirty and oily, it can sometimes discourage the DIY owner from keeping up with those regular maintenance tasks. The true importance of this is usually discovered at 2.30 am, on a wild and rainy winter's morning, ten miles from anywhere in a car with failed spark plugs! On a more serious note, excessive dirt and oil could easily conceal potentially dangerous items, such as loose nuts, worn cables or hoses. Moto-Build demonstrate some products from the excellent Comma range.

MU34.2 ►
... the KEW Hobby pressure washer. This is not only invaluable for cleaning the car bodywork and chassis, it can also be extremely useful when it comes to cleaning the engine bay. It is connected to both mains water and electricity supplies, so obviously some care should be taken to keep them apart! It should not be used when the engine is hot (for obvious reasons), or just before you want to go out: when you have finished cleaning your engine bay, there will be a lot of water about, and the 'electrics' will need some time to dry out. In particular, the distributor cap may have to be removed and wiped dry, inside and out.

MU34.3
Unorthodox ideas Part 1: Rubber and plastic 'blackwork' inside the engine bay can be rejuvenated with Comma Trim Black, intended for black rubber (and plastic) bumpers. It can also bring up rubber mats a treat!

MU34.4 ►
Unorthodox ideas Part 2: Comma's Cockpit Spray, intended for use in the car's interior, gives an attractive sheen to everything in the engine bay, from wiring and hoses to rocker box cover and ancillaries.

Chapter Five
Techniques and tools

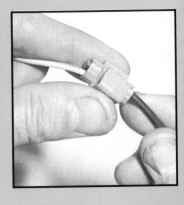

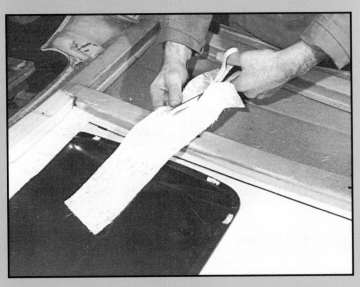

Workshop skills and equipment

Hand tools

There seem to be two approaches when it comes to buying hand tools. One is to buy the cheapest Far East produced tools that can be found, preferably on special offer at the local filling station and, better still, given away free with 5 litres of engine oil; while the other approach is to buy tools with a sense of quality about them, tools that will last a lifetime. Some of the finest tools that can be had are made in the UK by Sykes-Pickavant, who are also the producers of the Speedline economy range. We examine some of them here.

It's possible to produce a higher standard of work with high quality tools than with poor ones. Not only do they fit better, causing no damage to the components that you are working on, such as nuts and bolts, but they're also designed to work efficiently. In addition there's the psychological benefit of working with high quality tools in your hands.

HT1 ▶

One of the exceptions to the 'Made in Britain' rule is the wide range of tool boxes and chests, which are made for Sykes-Pickavant in Canada. They're made of tough heavy gauge steel, are lockable, and contain separate 'filing cabinet' type drawers for tool storage. Some of the units are stackable.

HT2

Castors and fixing nuts and bolts come as part of the kit. Two of the castors swivel and are lockable, providing a stable base if you wish to use the cabinet top as a workbench.
▼

HT3

You have to pull out the top drawer and bolt the push-pull handle to the side of the cabinet.
▼

HT4 ▶

A nice touch this: SP also provide trim finishes for the drawer fronts which give an attractive appearance and do away with sharp edges. The Space Maker Chest seen in HT1 contains six smaller drawers and a lift out tote tray. It's designed to fit neatly on top of the cabinet bench.

Hand tools

With Sykes-Pickavant's surface drive sockets (see top figure), force is applied on the 'flats', not the corners, reducing socket and fastener wear and avoiding 'rounding-off'. The arrows in the lower figure show those parts of the nut or bolt where the socket applies its turning force.

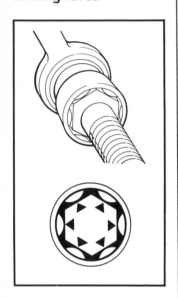

HT5 ▶
The tote tray from the Space Maker Chest with a selection of Speedline SP tools. Speedline are still of a very high quality, needless to say, but are designed to satisfy the enthusiastic DIYer's pocket.

◀ HT6
There are no better looking or better handling ratchet sets than SP's Speedline tools. The 3/8 inch drive socket set is so well built that it's easily tough enough for most jobs yet it's lighter, easier to handle and less expensive than its 1/2 inch drive counterparts. Buy sockets in sets or individually bubble packed as shown.

HT7 ▶
In the old days everyone bought open-ended or ring spanners. Now we buy combination sets like the Speedline spanners pictured in the background. The extension set, pictured right, has a wonderful semi-universal joint end on each one; a boon in awkward spots.

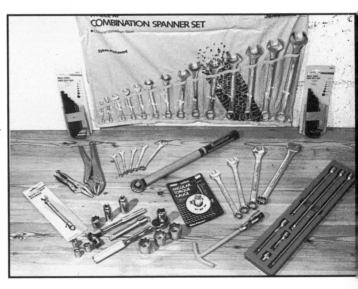

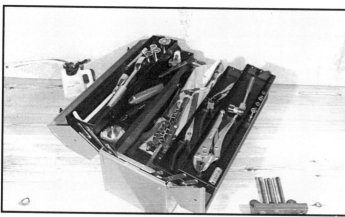

HT8

The SP Mechanic's Box has four cantilevered trays and an extra deep lower compartment. It's superbly built and there's no comparison between this and the average short-life accessory shop tool box.

HT9 ▶

You can use an SP Compression Tester to check the health of an engine before deciding whether it's a suitable case for modification or whether some reconditioning will be needed first.

Engine diagnosis and tuning is relevant to engine modifications in two ways. First, it enables you to tell whether any reconditioning work will be required on the engine before uprating its performance, and second, it allows you to keep the engine in prime condition thereafter.

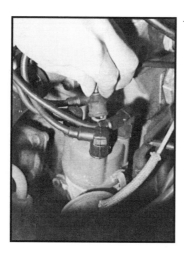

◀ **HT10**

The engine will have to be cranked so it's important to remove the HT lead from the distributor cap to avoid the risk of an electric shock.

HT11

The Speedline spark plug spanner has a universal joint which enables you to give extra leverage and aids access in awkward spots. See 'Understanding Spark Plugs' for correct tightening procedure.

▼

HT12 ▶

Faulty valves or piston rings will give variable compression readings and this indicates that some reconditioning may be necessary. A blown cylinder head gasket or - horror of horrors! - a holed piston, will also give distinctive compression readings. Deep seated plugs require the accessory extension set shown here.

Hand tools

Here's a typical application of the 6-24V circuit tester, testing continuity in the ignition circuit. The ignition switch is in the 'start' position. You can also check for breaks in a suspect wire by clipping the crocodile clip to a good earth and pushing the sharp end of the probe through the insulation at various points.

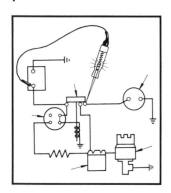

HT13 ▶
Apart from the compression tester and circuit tester already mentioned and the spark plug thread chaser (bottom right), there's a huge range of other SP engine tools. Bottom left is the carburettor tool overhaul set while along the top (from right) are: oil filter remover, feeler gauges, piston ring compressor, and the odd-looking but extremely useful cylinder head stands.

HT14 ▶
For 'chassis' work, there's the Speedline disc brake pad puller, a nut splitter (a better alternative to a sheared bolt), and ball joint remover.

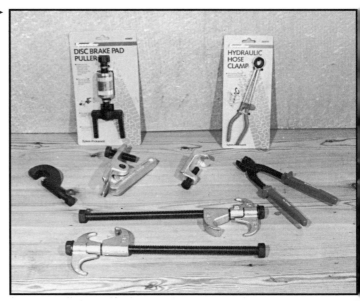

◀ HT15
Torx fasteners are found in a variety of applications on modern vehicles such as door hinges, locks and striker plates, window regulators, wiper motors, seat fixings, bumpers, etc. SP Speedline Torx drive bit sets solve the problem.

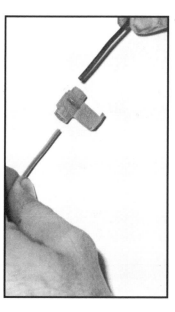

◄ HT16
Even professional electricians now often use wiring clips like the one shown for joining two pieces of wire together called 'Scotchloks'. These connectors will also join the end of one wire into the 'run' of another.

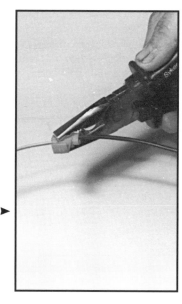

HT17 ►
Speedline insulated grip pliers are shown here squeezing the clip and making contact between the two lengths of wire. It's as simple as that!

A Speedline long reach riveter will be invaluable when fitting body kits. When selecting rivets remember that the rivet should be 4mm (5/32 in) longer than the thickness of the material to be riveted.

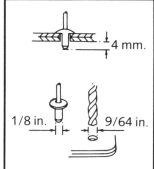

HT18 ►
The finished job is possibly only just about tolerable from the aesthetic point of view, but the electrical contact is perfectly acceptable.

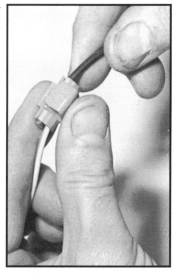

The correct selection of drill size is important: it should be 0.1mm (1/64 in) larger than the rivet.
(Figures courtesy of Sykes-Pickavant)

HT19
Sedan market an extremely useful box of wiring clips and fasteners shown in the background. The SP crimping tool is used to pinch a spade terminal to the end of a bared piece of wire. No soldering necessary.

HT20
Last in this sequence but perhaps first in priority, especially in respect of some of the items to come, is the Speedline safety kit. Goggles, gloves, efficient breathing mask and earplugs.

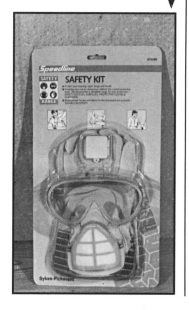

Arc, MIG and spot welding

Here is one of the latest developments in arc 'welding' technology, although in fact, plasma cutting is but a distant relative of the arc welder as such. Costs of the smaller plasma cutters, such as the Clarke Plasma King 25, have fallen to the level where the keen restoration enthusiast who intends carrying out more than one job could afford to buy one.

It's only a few short years ago that the only way of cutting and welding steel was with messy and relatively dangerous oxyacetylene welding. Now there's electric arc and MIG and spot welding and even electric cutting: quick, clean and efficient and, best of all, affordable to the keen DIYer. For a combination of quality and economy the smaller Clarke units shown here take some beating!

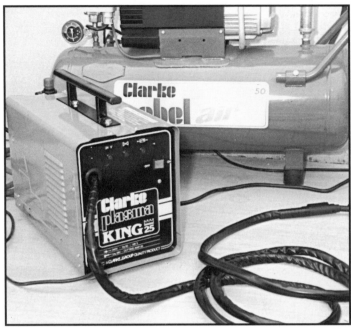

◄ **W1**
Plasma cutters demand coupling to a compressor to supply cooling air to the torch and cutting area. This cuts down significantly on distortion. Conveniently, the jet of plasma which carries out the cutting operation, is also formed from air; no gasses here!

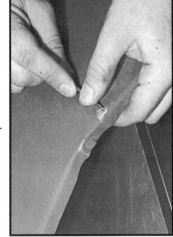

W3
Once you start (note gloves and head shield), cutting is amazingly quick and clean. Edges are clean with no grinding required and none of the mess that oxyacetylene cutting produces.

W2 ►
Because electrical contact is needed, it is best to start cutting on a piece of paint-free metal with the smaller models. However, the King 25 model shown here will even start cutting on a painted surface.

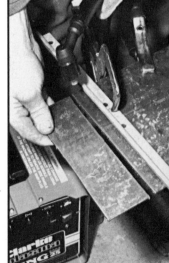

W4 ►
Here, we used a straight-edge to guide the edge of the cutter, clamping the edge to the work piece before commencing work. This gives a edge that is not only clean but one which is true and straight.

◄ W5
Most of us are more interested in the practicalities of MIG and arc welding, however. This MGB owner studies the handbook that accompanies his Clarke arc welder. Full operating instructions are included with every Clarke set and must be carefully studied and understood before commencing work.

If you try MIG welding in windy conditions, the shielding gas, which is supposed to surround the weld, will be blown away leaving a weak and truly horrible-looking weld. Weld indoors or put a wind shield around the weld area. Alternatively, you could invest in one of the new Clarke 'no-gas' MIG welders which contains the materials for producing its own shield in its specially cored welding wire.

W6 ►
Most DIY MIG users are happy to use the small disposable gas canisters as shown here and which are available from many DIY and auto-accessory outlets. If you give the machine a lot of use, save money by obtaining a large cylinder from one of the major gas companies.

Clarke's newest MIG is the 100E Turbo 'no-gas' machine. Flux cored wire produces its own gas shroud allowing the MIG to weld car body panels and mild steel up to 5mm thick. This makes it especially useful for outdoor work. There is also a 140 amp model available.

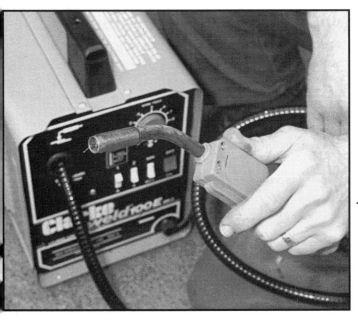

◄ W7
In the background, the Clarke Weld 100E MIG machine. With a MIG welder, welding wire appears out of the end of the torch when the trigger is squeezed and that's where welding takes place.

Arc, MIG and spot welding

You'll probably find it easiest to hold the torch at the angle shown and move it steadily in the direction indicated.

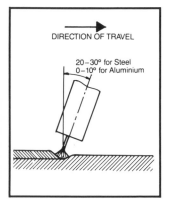

DIRECTION OF TRAVEL

20–30° for Steel
0–10° for Aluminium

W8

The MIG welder in use. After a little experimentation the correct settings will be very quickly established. Tack-weld your two work pieces together at regularly spaced intervals, then go back to the start and run a continuous seam weld end to end. It has to be the simplest form of welding!

W9

You can even plug-spot weld two pieces of steel together. Drill a 1/8 inch hole through the top sheet, then weld down to the sheet beneath, 'plugging' the hole. The Sykes-Pickavant side cutters, shown alongside, are an ideal means of trimming wire to the right length before starting to weld.

W10

The wire feed mechanism inside the machine. Wire is pushed along the feed pipe by the two rollers being pointed out here. Shielding gas travels along its own pipe contained with the torch assembly.

W11 ►

Disposable cartridges of shielding gas, varying types, thicknesses and quantities of welding wire, gauges and fittings are all available from Clarke equipment stockists.

198

◄ W12
Setting a MIG welder up for use is simple! Follow the guide to settings given in the handbook, then make adjustments, one at a time, to suit the job in hand and your own preference.

W13
As stated earlier, you must start by tack welding the two pieces of metal together. Here, we used a Sykes-Pickavant clamp to grip the work pieces securely while the tack welding was carried out.
▼

One of the smaller Clarke spot welders also has a timer which consistently regulates the duration of the spot weld. It automatically compensates for slight rusting, paint residues and zinc coating for best results. A spot welder can seem rather an extravagant piece of equipment until you realise just how neat and tidy a true spot weld appears and also when you accept that, on most parts of an MGB's bodywork, spot welds are 'original' whereas other types of weld are not. Having said that, of course, it is not always possible to use spot welding because of access problems.

◄ W14
Then, the 'spaces' between the tack welds can be filled in. Don't just start at one end and continue through to the other; weld in one place, then another until the run is complete, spreading the heat around and reducing further the risk of distortion.

W15 ►
Though MIG causes little distortion, spot welders cause even less. This is the simplest Clarke spot welder with a selection of welding arms designed, cleverly, to clear obstructions and allow you to weld up more of an MGB's bodywork than you would without them.

Arc, MIG and spot welding

'Strike an arc' by either stroking the end of the rod on the work piece or strike a blow with the end of the rod allowing it to bounce up to the correct distance away. It must be said that the procedure takes more practice than for MIG welding. Another problem is that you can't arc weld really thin sheet steel but the welders themselves start at less than half the price of a MIG.

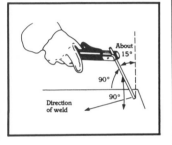

◄W16
Current settings are easily controlled by using the sliding scale. In the background is a 140E, while being adjusted is a fan 160 Turbo.

W17
As with MIG, you have to tack weld first. The slag which forms on the top of an arc weld has to be carefully and meticulously chipped away using the chipping hammer which Clarke thoughtfully provide.
▼

W18
Then a full seam weld can be run from one end of the joint to the other.
▼

◄W19
The layer of slag should chip away smoothly and cleanly. Erratic rod movements will introduce slag into the weld and weaken the joint.

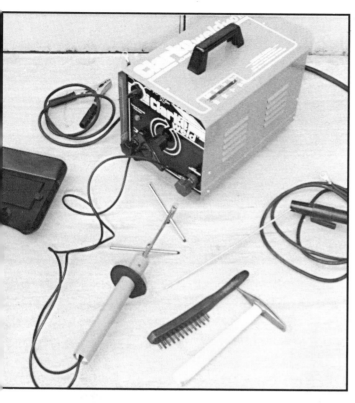

◄ W20
As already stated, all Clarke welders come with full instructions to assist you in getting started. This one is also equipped with a carbon-arc brazing kit, available as an optional extra.

W21
The carbon-arc rods create a heat-only arc which heats the metal and melts the brazing rod held in the hand. This enables the arc welder to successfully braze-weld thin sheet steel. It's not suitable for repairing major structural components however.
▼

Safety
Gloves should be worn when welding. The UV rays given off can be a health hazard and hot metal can burn! Sleeves should also be rolled down. It is vital that a full face mask is used at all times. Looking at a weld being made with the naked eye can cause an extremely painful eye condition short term; permanent eye damage long term. Keep children, onlookers and pets away. Looking through the safety glass provided rapidly becomes second nature. NEVER use an electric welder of any sort in wet conditions!

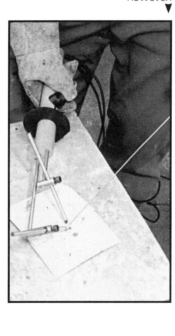

◄ W22
Repairing a thin sheet steel panel with carbon-arc brazing. Use of full head shield is essential because both hands are otherwise employed.

Power Tools

We are only concerned here with tools that will help you 'improve and modify' your MGB, but it's worth bearing in mind when selecting power tools that they can be put to other uses around the home. For instance, the Workmate 2 can be fitted with a circular saw and router table as an accessory, while the cordless tools shown, and the others in the huge Black and Decker range that we haven't considered here, are a boon for using all over the workshop, house or garden without having to worry about making the trailing lead reach far enough ...

The range of power tools available to the DIY enthusiast has expanded greatly in recent years while old favourites, such as electric drills and jigsaws, have a far wider range of features than was available in the old days. Black and Decker, probably the best known name in power tools the world over, are at the forefront in developments and we show several of their tools that relate to work carried out in this book.

PT3
The Black and Decker 'Proline' drill (left) is designed to operate under the toughest of conditions and will last the DIYer for many years, although the price reflects its 'professional' label. It's light and well balanced to use. The SR 910 RT, illustrated top-right, has a 2-speed gearbox, electronic speed adjuster, 1/2 inch chuck, hammer attachment and reverse. The torque control allows you to drive in, or remove, screws and there's a depth stop incorporated. Its sheer size might be a problem in some tight locations, but its capabilities are awesome! Finally, there's the Cordless reversible screwdriver drill which has power for any drilling application up to 5/16 inch. In the background are some of the twist drill sets available from Black and Decker.
▼

◄ **PT1**
Frankly, the Workmate is the sort of tool that, once you've got one, becomes the focal point for all your workshop activities. You can cover it in a cloth and respray small items, recondition engine components on it, varying the working height to suit yourself, or even use it as a vice when drilling or sawing. This Workmate is shown being spannered together, following the simple instructions enclosed, although the winding screw assembly caused a little hard thought!

PT4
The cordless jigsaw (left), shown with charging pack, gives more versatility. The multi-speed power jigsaw has a pendulum action blade, which means that the blade swings forwards on the upwards cutting stroke for extra cutting power. The dust extractor has adaptors which connect to your domestic vacuum cleaner. Black and Decker also produce a full range of blades.
▼

PT2
The rearmost part of the table clips on to the base in one of three alternative positions, allowing you to clamp various widths or to support quite wide work pieces

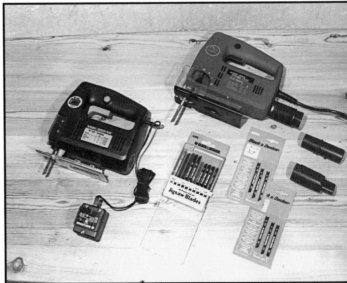

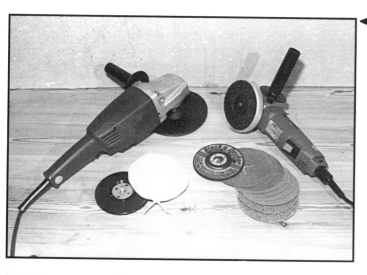

◄ PT5
Anyone tackling car bodywork repair or improvements really should consider investing in a mini-grinder. On the right is the Black and Decker PL80 4½ inch Sander/Grinder 'Proline' tool, made to work hard for long perids at cutting, grinding or sanding steel or filler. On the left is the Black and Decker LUM sander and polisher. This enables you to sand, or you can polish paintwork to professional standards of finish with the lambswool polishing mop fitted.

Tools that were once purely the province of the professional are now within the price range of the keen DIYer. New technology has meant that, as features offered are on the increase, prices in real terms have fallen. The use of professional-quality tools makes it possible for the home enthusiast to achieve professionsal standards, saving on the cost of paying someone else to do the job and more than offsetting the cost in tools and equipment.

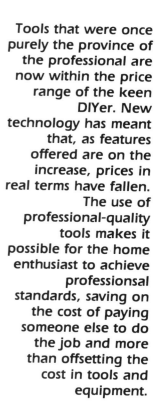

◄ PT6
The Black and Decker 180E Variable Speed Sander allows you to sand filler (or wood or plaster), at a rapid 11,000 orbits per minute, while slowing down to 6,500 orbits per minute for paintwork. '1/3 sheet' sanding papers are clipped to the front of the sander, after opening the paper clamp. Then, the clamp lever is returned to the 'closed' position ...

PT7 ►
... and the paper folded round the sanding bed and clamped in similar fashion at the rear.

PT8 ►
The punched holes enable the bulk of the dust created by the sander to be sucked out through the outlet on the rear of the sander body. The dust-extractor is connected to your domestic vacuum cleaner via the adaptor provided.

Power tools

Sanding dust in the air can create a health hazard. It may not be necessary to wear a face mask if an extractor system is fitted, especially if your domestic vacuum cleaner is powerful enough to take away the bulk of the dust, but if your sander is not equipped for dust extraction, or if the substance you are sanding, such as glass fibre, presents a health hazard in itself, you should then always wear a mask.

PT9 ►
The random orbit sander is wonderful for carrying out bodywork preparation! The sanding head spins in a normal way, but the spindle itself also rotates through a small circle. The highly beneficial effect is that scratch-free sanding can be carried out. If you try sanding filler or paintwork with an ordinary sanding pad, circular scuff marks would be certain to show through the paint finish. Sanding is carried out more quickly than by hand, to the extent that what would take days by elbow power, takes just a couple of hours using electric power.

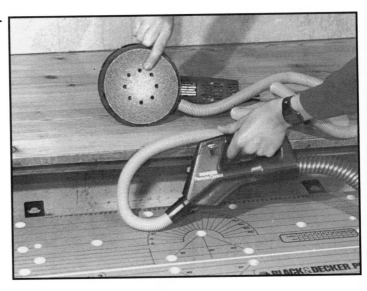

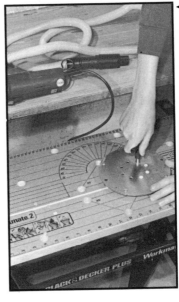

◄ PT10
In the background you can see the random orbit sander still connected to the dust extraction system. The sanding discs used are standard self-adhesive discs and, to allow the extraction system to operate, these have to be punched with holes. Black and Decker supply a pair of steel plates which locate against one another with the sanding disc popped between.

PT11
When you push through each hole in the plates with the cutter provided, using a slight twist of the wrist, a neat hole is punched in the sanding disc. It only takes a few moments, but it would probably encourage more people to use the excellent dust extraction system if Black and Decker were to make pre-punched discs available.
▼

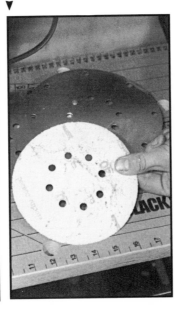

PT12 ►
Another Black and Decker sanding option is the Palm Grip Sander, a Proline tool designed for one-hand operation and very 'handy' (oh dear!) for smaller sanding jobs. The face mask is part of the Syke-Pickavant 'Safety' kit shown earlier and 'seals' around the mouth much more efficiently than those with an aluminium backing plate.

PT13 ▶
The Black and Decker Powerfile makes short work of materials as hard as wood and steel. Fitted with bench stand and grinding stop and clamped to the Workmate, Powerfile doubles up as an excellent tool sharpener.

On this page we start work on a project that cuts across several of the items in this section. Fitting a power bulge to a bonnet involves the use of power tools, glass fibre and filler, some hand tools and the use of a wide range of aerosol spray paints.

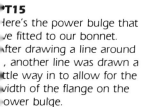

◀ PT14
This heat gun was shown in Chapter One helping to remove old styling stripes, but around the home its versatility extends to paint stripping, moulding plastics, soldering pipe joints or even lighting the barbecue!

PT16
After drilling a hole slightly wider than the blade the Black and Decker jigsaw was used to good effect. This isn't the scrolling saw, so on tight corners it was necessary to do a couple of 'three point turns' to get around without the blade binding in the sheet steel.
▼

PT15
Here's the power bulge that we fitted to our bonnet. After drawing a line around, another line was drawn a little way in to allow for the width of the flange on the power bulge.

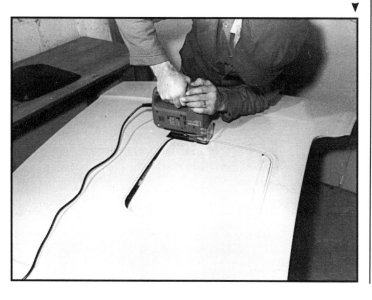

Fitting a power bulge to a bonnet may be necessary if you fit a taller carburettor - or even a tall engine! It can assist heat extraction when a highly-tuned engine produces excessive heat, or you might find that the power bulge is an interesting visual modification in itself.

Power tools

Workmate 2 makes a ideal workbench for this sort of project. The jaws can be opened wide giving a stable support with enough room between them for the saw blade to pass with ease.

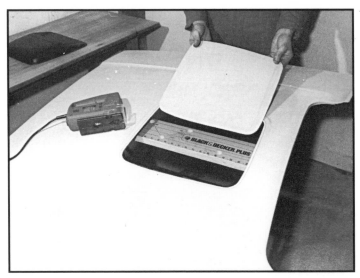

◄ PT17
Cutting out sheet steel with the jigsaw demands the use of the correct blade but gives one of the cleanest types of cut.

PT18 ►
The Black and Decker sanding disc attachment and medium grit sandpaper were fitted to the drill and used to clean paint from an area all the way around the hole.

PT19
The bonnet was turned over and after drilling pilot holes, the bulge was screwed down using self-tapping screws. The Black and Decker cordless screwdriver SC450 provided an incredibly quick and easy way of driving the self-tapping screws fully home.
▼

PT2◄
We wanted to protect th◄ edges of the power bulge s◄ put a strip of masking tap◄ all the way around i◄

Working with filler and glass fibre

Blending in with resin, mat and filler

We chose Plastic Padding products for this part of the work, partly because they are readily available from just about every auto accessory shop and in quantities which are just sufficient for projects of this size, and also because Plastic Padding Elastic Filler is noted for its ability to flex and to withstand shock and vibration without cracking or coming adrift.

Weight for weight, glass fibre is stronger than steel and yet is far easier to work with. It can be persuaded to adopt any shape that you wish and yet bonds with great tenacity. Its close cousin, body filler, is the perfect medium for filling gaps and smoothing out imperfections to give a perfect finish.

FF1▶
This is part of the large Plastic Padding range and it's worth mentioning that they also sell aerosol cans of Stonechip Protect for spraying onto sills, valances and other vulnerable areas.

FF2
You won't get in too much of a mess if you carry out work in the right order. Cut strips of glass fibre mat to the width and length required before mixing the resin.

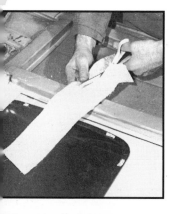

FF3 ▶
Add the recommended amount of hardener with the resin in a suitable container (this is the lid from the tin of Plastic Padding filler), and stir thoroughly until the hardener is well mixed.

◀ FF4
Brush resin generously onto the areas to receive the glass fibre mat. Don't brush it out like paint; leave enough to soak up into the mat.

207

Blending in with resin, mat and filler

Resin can be removed from hands after a generous application of hand cleaner, although it's best to use a barrier cream first as well. Alternatively, use disposable plastic gloves or even plastic bags tied around the wrists.

◄ FF5
Place the mat in place and add more resin. You're now at stage one, where you need to add a fairly generous amount of resin to break down the bonding agent in the mat, allowing it to go floppy.

◄ FF6
After you've 'wetted out' all of the mat, go back and stipple it vigourously with a brush. It will then follow the contours of the panel beneath, taking on its shape and the removal of any air bubbles will add strength.

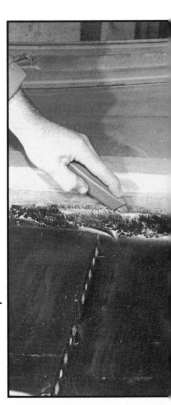

FF7 ►
The SP craft knife comes in handy for removing any excess glass fibre but only if you catch the glass fibre **after** it has ceased to be 'wet', but **before** it sets hard.

FF8 ►
When the glass fibre has gone hard, the Black and Decker angle grinder comes into its own, but be careful not to go right through! You will see on page 210 that the Plastic Padding hardener is yellow in colour. If the resin and the glass fibre are yellow all through, that shows that you've mixed the resin thoroughly.

FF9 ▶
All glass fibre dust can be harmful if inhaled while being sanded, therefore you should always wear goggles and a face mask during grinding or sanding operations. This is the SP kit featured earlier.

If you find that you need more resin or more hardener separately (although you shouldn't if you use it in the proportions recommended by Plastic Padding), there are individual cans of resin available in various sizes from your auto accessory shop.

◀ FF10
Being determined to obtain a good finish underneath the bonnet as well as on top, we spread a layer of Plastic Padding Elastic Filler over the glass fibre and then sanded it smooth later before painting it.

FF11 ▶
On the top side, the protruding self-tapping screws were trimmed down by fitting a cutting wheel to the Black and Decker angle grinder. Plastic Padding recommend cutting off any resin that may have oozed through with a craft knife before it goes too hard. Later you'd have to grind it away.

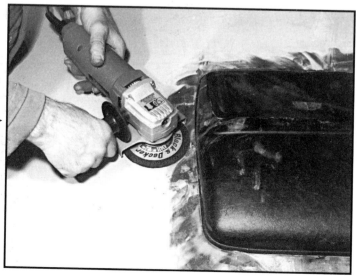

Filler 'goes off' (sets) by chemical reaction. The warmer the weather, the quicker the reaction and the less hardener you need; the colder the weather the more hardener you need.

◄ FF12
Plastic Padding Elastic Filler comes in a tube or tin with its own spreader and sufficient hardener for the filler in that particular pack.

FF13 ►
Take a piece of clean card, scoop out sufficient filler and squeeze on top as much hardener as you will need. Don't get hardener into the open tin nor, if you can help it, on your fingers, since it can be toxic. Later, wash hands thoroughly before eating or smoking.

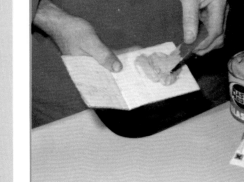

◄ FF14
Again, the Plastic Padding trick of including a strongly coloured hardener pays off because you can see clearly when the pigmented hardener has been mixed thoroughly with the filler.

Plastic Padding also produce aerosol Stonechip Protect for protecting sills, spoilers and the undersides of panels vulnerable to stone chipping.

FF15 ►
Carefully spread filler into the joint, leaving it very slightly proud but not so high that you have an enormous amount of sanding to do. Plastic Padding filler has the great advantage that it sands particularly easily giving a smooth finish. After sanding, you will invariably find a few dips and hollows which have to be filled with a further application of filler.

◄ PP1
As well as the aerosol paint itself, Spectra produce a whole range of ancillaries such as abrasive paper for rubbing down.

Aerosol paint is the ideal way of spraying anything up to a single panel at a time. After all, you don't need to buy any expensive equipment, only the can that the paint comes in.

◄ PP2
The Spectra 'wet-or-dry' paper was used with water to feather out the Plastic Padding filler, leaving no trace of a hard edge.

PP3 ►
Before starting to spray, the Spectra primer was taken outside, shaken vigorously, and the nozzle cleared.

PP4 ►
The can was held about six inches away and red oxide primer sprayed onto the bare metal.

Spraying with aerosol

Illustration PP9 shows why it's essential to shake an aerosol paint can for several minutes before using it. The agitator ball has the job of mixing the paint pigment, which may be quite thick at the bottom, thoroughly with the solvent. In very cold weather you may also have to immerse the can in warm (not boiling), water for several minutes before use. Never puncture an aerosol can nor expose it to direct heat.

◄PP5
This was magical (or at least, the results of sanding it later, were). Spectra High Build Spray Putty was sprayed onto the whole area ...

PP6
... and then, extending a little wider than the area of the original red oxide primer, a second coat of spray putty was applied after the first had dried.
▼

PP7
It's best to practise your spraying on a spare scrap of sheet steel. Hold the can too close and the paint will run; too far away and you'll have a 'dry' looking finish.
▼

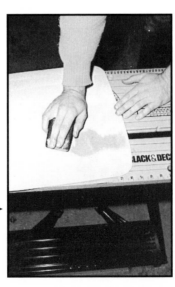

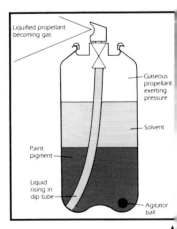

▲ PP9
How an aerosol works. If you tip the can upside down, the paint flow ceases. At the end of spraying, use this technique to clear the nozzle.

PP8 ►
Very slight runs may be polished out but most will have to be sanded out when the paint is dry using fine wet-or-dry paper.

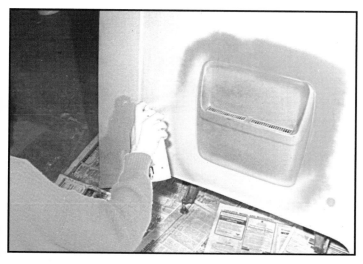

◄ PP10
Provided that the filler work was carried out properly, the use of High Build Spray Putty will allow you to remove every last blemish when you sand it out with fine wet-or-dry supported on a flat rubbing block.

When choosing your primer colour, go for red for dark shades of top coat, grey for lighter coats and grey or preferably white for white top coats and metallics.

PP11 ►
By now, and for no apparent reason, we were working with the bonnet laid horizontally. We chose to spray on grey primer paint as a barrier colour between the yellow and the white top coat to follow. Red and yellow have a nasty habit of 'grinning through' white surface coats above them.

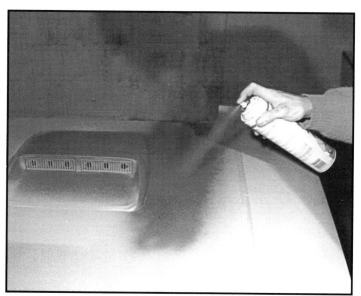

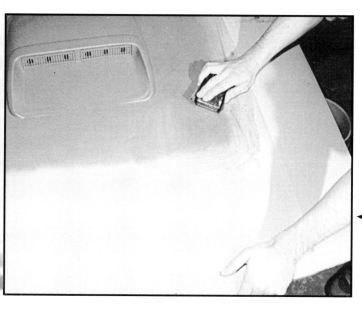

◄ PP12
Plenty of water, a few spots of washing up liquid, and the finest grade of Spectra wet-or-dry and the final primer coat was prepared for finish painting.

One of the main reasons we chose Spectra for this part of the book was because their aerosol paint containers are specially designed not to clog and not to spit blobs of paint onto the work. There's nothing more frustrating!

◄ PP13
To digress for a moment, the preparation of a large flat area can take quite a long time by hand. This is where the Black and Decker random orbit sander (see earlier item), was particularly useful.

PP14 ►
Now here's a tip from the experts. Holding a tin of black spray paint about a foot or more away from the job, a light coat was dusted onto the work.

PP15 ►
The idea is not to change the colour of the panel but just to put an even sprinkling of paint over the whole panel.

◄ PP16
Sand the entire panel all over once more with the finest grade of paper and the guide coat, as it is called, will be sanded off in all but the low areas. After you wipe off with a dry rag, any low spots and blemishes will stand out like a sore thumb!

◄ PP17
It might look uncomfortable but you should always hold the nozzle down with the very tip of your finger.

PP18 ►
If you do what comes naturally, the part of your finger sticking forwards catches the edge of the spray which builds up into a drip which is then shot forwards as a blob onto your lovely handiwork. Most annoying!

You can spray the first two finish coats on in fairly quick succession, just leaving a few minutes between them for the first coat to 'flash off'. The second coat should be at right angles to the first. (Drawing courtesy of Spectra.

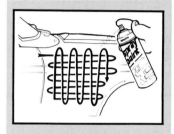

◄ PP19
The first coat was applied in regular strips up and down the bonnet, concentrating on obtaining an even coat without trying to blanket out the colour underneath. That's the way to achieve runs!

PP20 ►
The second coat, as already suggested, followed in a pattern which criss-crossed the first (see margin note), and this time the colour beneath did disappear from view. Ideally, you may want to give another one or two coats. If any little bits of dust landed in the surface, you may be able to polish them out with fine cutting compound, but be most careful not to go right through the paint and don't try it until the paint has had several days to dry really hard.

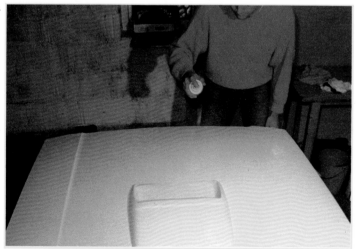

Using special paints

As well as the paint types already shown, Spectra also produce Extra High Gloss chrome or gold paint for customising, black heat dispersant paint for cylinder blocks, engines and exhaust systems to aid cooling and improve efficiency, and clear acrylic lacquer called 'Wheel Protector', for preventing corrosion on alloy wheels. Spectra recommend that you don't use heat dispersant paint on manifolds, the extra heat found there being just too much for it.

◄ SP1
Some people rave over Spectra's aerosol hammer finish paint. It gives an even hammer finish coat from an aerosol can without needing any primer beneath it. It also has good rust protection and easy-clean qualities.

SP2
Only the plastic components shown earlier would need plastic primer (see page 223). A second coat, sprayed at right angles to the first, gives a full, even coat. Do it within a few minutes of spraying the first coat but after the first coat's solvent has 'flashed off'

◄ SP3
Spectra clear lacquer is a cellulose-based lacquered top seal for sealing styling stripes or for keeping the gloss on cellulose paint finishes.

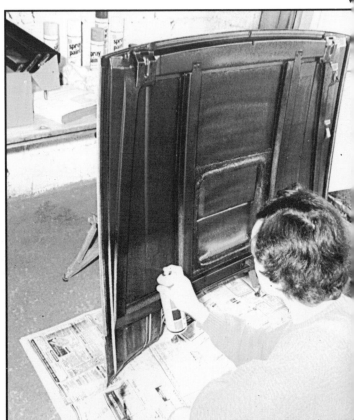

▲
SP4
Spectra Wheel paint comes in white, black, gold, silver and steel. You could mask off the tyre with masking tape and newspaper as shown in the drawing, or you could spread hand cleaner in a heavy layer onto the tyre before spraying the wheel. As soon as the wheel paint is dry, the hand cleaner can be washed off leaving the tyre good as new. For a final finish, paint the tyre with wall black.

Cellulose paint is not as durable as the 2-pack paint which DIY enthusiasts must never use without the proper facilities (see manufacturer's instructions), but it has the virtue of being able to be sprayed on a DIY basis and it can also be polished to give the best shine of any paint.

DYP1 ▶
If many coats of paint have previously been applied, they will have to be stripped back to bare metal before being repainted. Sanding of any sort is far quicker with a random orbit sander, such as the Black and Decker electric unit shown here. This has the distinct advantage of not creating scratches which will show through the finished paintwork.

◀ DYP2
Very minor blemishes such as pin holes or scratches in the paint should be filled with a thin scrape of Valentine G112 stopper which can be sanded down after drying thoroughly.

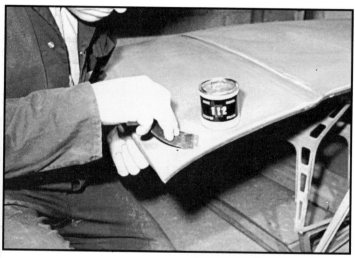

DYP3 ▶
Hand sanding should always be carried out with the aid of a rubbing block, other than in the corners of fluted panels such as that shown here, where your fingers make an ideally shaped tool.

Safety
All filler contains skin irritants, so you should wear gloves when handling it. When sanding paint or filler, particularly with a power sander, you must always wear an efficient particle mask otherwise the inhalation of sanding dust could damage your health. Nitro-cellulose paints, those made by Valentine for instance and shown here, are eminently suitable for DIY work. However, take full note of Valentine's own safety precautions and in particular, never spray in other than a well-ventilated work area. Also, bear in mind that paint, thinners and spray vapour are all highly flammable. Do not use near flames, sparks (including those created by central heating boilers and self-igniting gas cookers, etc), or any naked flames.

PREPARATION
Tools required:
Grinder, sander, P120 and P240 grit discs, P600 wet-or-dry paper, dust particle mask.
Materials required:
197-1005 degreasing fluid (this is esential for removing silicones which will most certainly ruin the finished paint surface if allowed to remain on the work), G112 stopper.

Before using primer check the existing paint to find out whether it is compatible with cellulose. Rub a small area of paint with cellulose thinner. If the paint film dissolves go ahead; if the paint wrinkles it is affected by cellulose and will have to be sprayed all over with isolating primer 200-6 to seal it.

◄ **DYP4**
With no attachment on the end of the hose, you can use the Clarke Air compressor to blow any remaining sanding dust off the panel (use of a Clarke Blowgun would have been useful here).

DYP5
The Valentine degreasing fluid should have been used before you started and should now be used again to remove any traces of silicones or other grease contamination

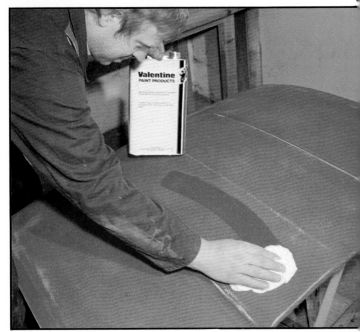

DYP6
The cordless drill was used with a paint stirrer in the chuck to stir the Valentine primer filler to an even consistency. Note the steel rule placed in the pot to aid accurate measurement when thinning the paint. Go initially for 50/50 thinning, but be prepared to readjust to suit the requirements of the Clarke spray gun.
▼

DYP7 ►
The Clarke gun has two adjustment screws at the rear; the top one is for the shape of the spray pattern, while the lower one adjusts the quantity of paint which comes out of the gun.

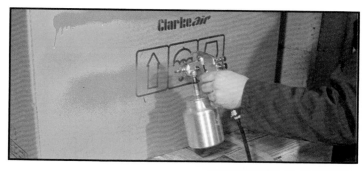

◄ DYP8
Adjust the two spray gun screws so that the spray pattern and spray density are as you require. Test it out thoroughly upon a piece of scrap board or a cardboard box.

DYP9 ►
The edge of this panel dipped away from the user so that part, the curved edge, was sprayed first. The Clarke gun has a light trigger action and is easy to use.

◄ DYP10
The whole panel was painted in consistent, even bands, each one half overlapping the one that had gone before.

DYP11 ►
The next day, after the two full coats of primer had thoroughly dried, a very light, heavily thinned coat of black paint was sprayed on with the Clarke gun.

PRIMING
Tools required:
Masking tape, masking paper (such as newspaper), paint strainer, Clarke spray gun, Clarke compressor, spray mask, tack rag.
Materials required:
As well as those shown earlier and on these pages: cellulose thinner 199-207 for any additional thinning above 50/50 (don't use 199-6 thinner for more than 50/50), Valentine red oxide primer 200-6.

Do-it-yourself spraying

TOP COAT

Tools required:
The same Clarke equipment and other 'hardware' as was used previously. Top coat paint must be strained. Add P1200 wet-or-dry paper and polishing compound for polishing out any dirt particles that may get into the final coat.

Materials required:
Spragloss 178 solid colour paint; Spragloss thinner 199-18 (mix 50/50). For further thinning, add more 199-18 thinner.

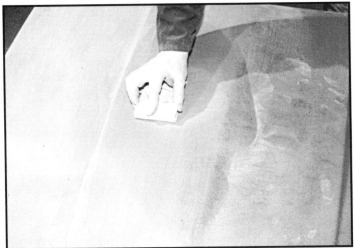

◄DYP12
When the primer is 'blocked' down with medium grit paper, the thin 'guide' coat which was sprayed on with the Clarke gun (although you could have used aerosol for greater speed), is sanded off as the primer filler coat is made smooth. It remains visible in the low spots, however, picking them out.

DYP13 ►
Before spraying the top coat, wet the floor to lay the dust but take care to avoid electrical connections.

◄DYP14
Use an air line to blow any dust from around the top of the tin. Clarke produce a trigger operated 'Blowgun', if you prefer.

DYP15 ►
The cordless drill is again used for several minutes to mix the entire contents of the Spragloss paint.

◄DYP16
Use a steel rule, if you haven't got the correct painter's measuring stick, to measure the correct amount of Spragloss paint and thinners.

DYP17
Pour in an equal amount of Spragloss thinner. Note: the supply of copious amounts of newspaper is essential!
▼

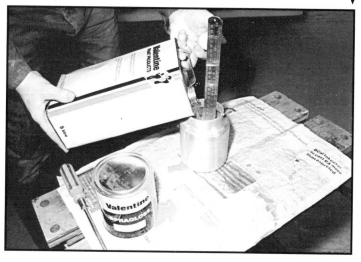

Keep your wrists stiff and avoid swinging the gun in an arc from your elbow, to ensure even spraying. Always spray at a steady, even pace.

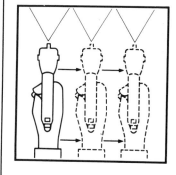

◄DYP18
After using the Clarke Air air line to blow off the panel once more, wipe it down yet again with Valentine spirit wipe ...

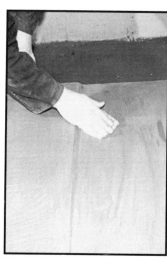

DYP19▶
... followed by wiping down with a tack rag to remove every trace of dust or dirt.

DYP20 ▶
An accepted way of checking that the Clarke gun is held the correct distance away (see margin note), is to use a hand span as a measure.

Do-it-yourself spraying

Always hold the spray gun at right angles to the surface you are painting, keeping it between six and eight inches from the car. (Diagram courtesy of Valentine)

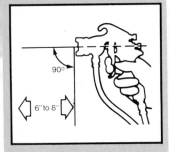

◄ DYP21
Robert started off by spraying a 'half coat' - a thin coat to aid adhesion without causing runs - sprayed in vertical, overlapping bands.

DYP22 ►
After this had 'flashed off' (ie, the thinners had evaporated), he sprayed a full coat in overlapping horizontal bands. The suspended panel reduces dirt contamination and an open door aids ventilation.

◄ DYP23
Valentine paints, shown here in their new livery, are professional paints perfectly suitable for both the DIY enthusiast and the professional bodyshop to use. **Follow the safety regulations printed on every can.**

DYP24
Robert surveys the wonderful depth of gloss which four coats of Valentine Spragloss solid colour had given, and proves that the 'DIY' Clarke equipment can give fully professional results.

▼

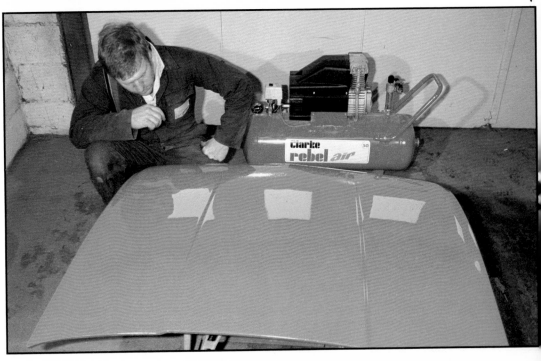

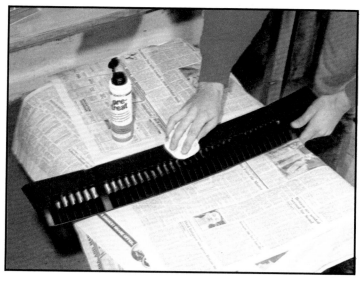

◄ PL1
We used a Richard Grant air intake cover for the VW Golf for this section, but the same would apply to an MGB plastic front spoiler, such as that sold by Richard Grant. Plastic primer treatment works just as well on any other plastic components, of course. Start by wiping over every nook and cranny with 'Pre-treat fluid' on a clean rag.

If you try spraying aerosol spray paint onto a plastic component without preparing it properly, the paint will simply peel off again very soon afterwards. Spectra produce a special plastic primer with a pre-treat solvent all in one pack.

PL2
Shake, shake, shake, shake, shake ... Thorough mixing is absolutely essential.
▼

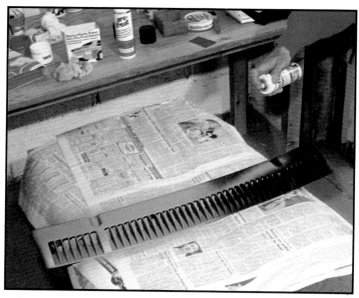

▲ PL3
The plastic primer can now be sprayed over the whole air intake cover.

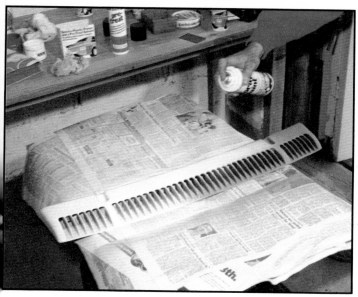

◄ PL4
Once the primer is dry, your car's body colour or any finish colour you choose can be sprayed on without fear of paint flaking off.

Bodywork preservation

Injecting rust proofing fluids

Although MGBs are more soundly built than most other cars on the roads, there is still plenty there for rust to get its teeth into. Now that all MGBs, except those re-built with a new Heritage bodyshell are of a 'certain age', most are afflicted to at least some degree by the dreaded rust bug. Corroless Rust Stabilising Cavity Wax is undoubtedly the best material available for preserving your MGB because, not only does it prevent more rust from starting, it also contains a rust inhibitor which tackles the existing rust and is said to stop it in its tracks.

◄ BPR1
For enclosed bodywork sections and seams, Corroless produce their highly efficient Rust Stabilising Cavity Wax, while for exposed areas and for paint chips there are other specially produced Corroless products such as Rust Stabilizing Body Primer, High Performance Finish and Stone Chip Primer.

BPR2
Each Corroless can comes with two spray nozzles. One for injecting the fluid into enclosed sections while the other is for use as a conventional spray can.
▼

BPR3
Taking the easiest areas first, inject Corroless fluid beneath the chrome plated trim strip along the bottom of GT rear windows. Rust always seems to be a problem in that area.
▼

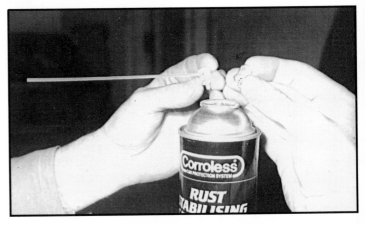

BPR4 ►
Another easy-to-get-at rust trap is the 'ledge' that you can feel by running your hand inside the front wings with the inner vertical liner removed. The inside of this rust trap can be treated through the engine bay as shown.

◄ BPR5
The tailgate door on a GT and the boot lid on a Roadster can both corrode. The tailgate suffers most along its bottom edge and around the glass. Remove trim panels as shown, and use the injector lance to squirt plenty of Corroless into the box section.

BPR6 ►
Spraying the insides of the doors will also involve removing the trim panel but door replacement is a very expensive business, so rustproofing this area thoroughly is well worthwhile. Ensure that drain channels in the bottom of the door are clear.

Corroless Wax has two crucially important plus-points in its favour, it 'creeps' particularly well, getting into spot welded seams where corrosion likes to take a hold. Second, it has unique rust **killing** qualities. Other rust proofers don't necessarily stop rusting that may have already taken a hold.

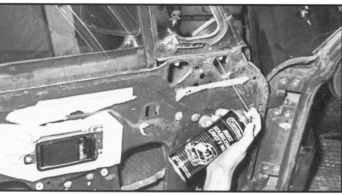

◄ BPR7
Don't forget the area beneath the quarter lights at the top of the door. Efficient rubber seals on door glasses will also help prevent rusting.

◄ BPR8
Corroless can be injected through the bonnet via existing holes at the front. As you do so, you'll see mist come out from all parts of the bonnnet support rails, indicating that no further hole drilling should be necessary.

BPR9 ►
After scraping all dirt encrustation from the inside of the wings or using something like a KEW-Hobby pressure washer (see page 59), inject Cavity Wax around the insides of the front wings, not forgetting the rearmost part of the wings which are best accessed after removing the mud trap.

Injecting rust proofing fluids

All rust preventatives evaporate over a period of time and 'topping them up' should be regarded as body maintenance. After all, bodywork is far more valuable than mechanical components, yet we think nothing of spending time and money maintaining **them.** Even existing bitumen-based protections harden in time, yet Corroless will creep into and seal any rust-inducing cracks or cavities and not need re-applying annually unless it is exposed to abrasion from stone chippings, etc. Thus your MGB could go on and on, especially if it's in good condition to start off with.

◄ BPR10
An alternative to removing the mud trap is to drill a couple of neat holes through it and to plug them later with a rubber grommet. You may also be able to insert the lance between the rubber seal at the edge of the mud trap and the wing itself.

BPR11 ►
Here the Black & Decker Cordless drill is being used to drill through the outer part of the sill ...

▲ BPR12
... but it's important to note that the sill consists of an inner and an outer section and that another hole will need to be drilled through the inner sill to give proper protection.

BPR13
One more favourite rust spot is the area where the rear inner wing joins the rear outer wing. This will have to be tackled from inside the boot, having covered or removed any trim from that area

◄ BPR14
Still at the rear of the car, it's time to start on the main chassis rails. The rear chassis rail has a conveniently placed hole already in its rearmost end.

BPR15 ▶
Beneath the centre of the car, main chassis rails run the full length, front to back. It's worth injecting a lot of Corroless Cavity Wax into these sections ...

◀ **BPR16**
... and into the much smaller but, in fact, much more rust-prone, 'castle' sections which run front to back beneath the sills. You will find pre-existing holes already in place.

BPR17 ▶
Joining the two, at the centre of the car, is a cross member which runs right the way across the car. More Corroless here please! Work in a logical fashion forwards until all of the box sections have been thoroughly treated.

◀ **BPR18**
One seam which is rather rust-prone is the support for the rear spring shackle where it fits against the body at its frontmost end. Scrape off any dirt, then spray on Corroless which will seep right into the seam.

MGBs were constructed with many box sections in order to give the 'top car' exceptional rigidity. Many of these box sections have existing holes through which the Corroless can be injected. If you have to drill more holes, be sure to have a supply of grommets on hand to plug them after drilling through. If nothing else, it leaves a much neater appearance. **Never** crawl beneath a car supported only by a jack. Use axle stands and chock the wheels remaining on the ground carefully.

Using rust proofing primers and paints

Corroless Rust Stabilising Body Primer contains the same amazingly effective rust killer as the Cavity Wax already described. By painting Corroless High Performance Finish on top, you'll give superb protection! This paint actually contains tiny glass flakes which provide it with far more resilience than any conventional paint. Stones and hard objects simply bounce off.

◄ BPR19
Rust Stabilising Body Primer is simply sprayed on in the conventional way. If there's any risk of overspray getting onto the car's bodywork, make sure that you have masked off thoroughly.

BPR20 ►
High Performance Finish give the incredibly tough surface already described which makes it quite suitable for sills and other potentially stone damaged areas, provided that you are happy to have a black or white finish.

◄ BPR21
Stone Chip Primer comes complete with a tiny wire brush in the lid. Use it for cleaning loose rust out of a stone chip ...

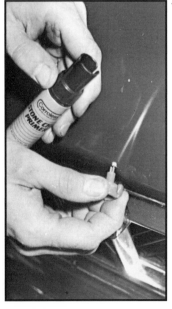

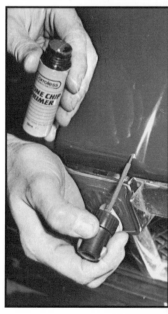

All MGB body colours can be bought in cellulose aerosol cans produced by Classic Car Colours, available from most MG specialist outlets.

BPR22 ►
... before touching-in the Corroless Primer with the fine brush provided. When dry, body colour can be touched-in over the top.

Mechanical preservation

Using the Slick 50 treatment

MP1 ▶
Adding Slick 50 to an engine oil is straightforward. Drain the engine oil when warm and fit a new oil filter. Shake the bottle of Slick 50 vigourously, immersing it in warm water beforehand if the weather is cool. Refill the engine using a high quality oil such as Duckhams, leaving enough room to add the Slick 50. **Do not overfill.** The manufacturers recommend an immediate journey of around thirty miles or leaving the engine on tickover for thirty minutes. By then, the engine will have received its permanent coating of PTFE. Slick 50 only has to be added once and does not ever have to be topped up when the oil is changed.

Slick 50 is a product with a very high specification which, despite its appearance, is not an additive. It uses the oil in the engine, gearbox or back axle as a means of reaching the metal surfaces there. Effectively, the PTFE in the product 'sticks' to the metal surfaces and forms a protective coating approximately two microns thick. The makers claim that once the initial thin coating has been applied, it will get no thicker while the only way to get it off is to grind it! Because of the reduction in drag and friction, the engine should run cooler and quieter, need less maintenance and there should be an improvement in mpg. PTFE is frequently billed as the slipperiest stuff known to man ...

◀ MP2
This V8 engine is benefitting from Slick 50 aerosol treatment on the throttle linkages. It's also ideal for things like window and sliding sunroof runners, door mechanisms and anything else that slides and touches.

MP3
Slick 50 is not a cheap product but is proven to give excellent results both inside and outside the engine. It is so efficient in fact, that it shouldn't be used on a new engine or gearbox until the components are run in. Otherwise, the Slick 50 will prevent bearing surfaces from bedding in properly!
▼

Gearboxes and differentials can also benefit from the Slick 50 treatment but it's important to note that a different pack is required. You can even buy Slick 50 grease for other bearing surfaces.

Chapter Six
On the track

Clubman racing
by Roche Bentley

Club Secretary, MG Owners' Club

Don't do it for money - you won't make any! Don't do it because you're the hottest driver in your High Street - you'll soon learn otherwise. Don't do it to become a World Champion - unless you are loaded, very skilful and extremely lucky, you won't be - but if you love MGs and like the thrill of competition, then try it - but do it for fun - it's the only way.

Ever had to visit the loo ten times in ten minutes before the start of a motor race? Start MG racing at Club level and you'll experience all sorts of new and unexpected sensations just like this. Your medical, too, won't necessarily mean that you need your head examined, though a cursory inspection of the matter between your ears may indicate that one or two nuts and bolts are loose. The fun, the fear and a brand new set of friends more than makes up for the alternative meaning to the letters MG. Forget about "Morris Garages", MG in some racing circles can mean "Money Gobbler", though if one sticks to Standard Class racing, the costs aren't really that bad at all and as the MG Owner' Club contributes towards your expenses buy giving away Start Money, the project can even look encouraging.

"Ectuelly I'm a Racing Driver!": the words roll off the tongue in any bar or restaurant as eager ears wait for heroic drives, triple spins on hairpin corners and accounts of how you started from the back and, a la Mansell, fought your way to a memorable victory which had the grand prix crowd rising to its feet.

It's no great deal to become a racing driver; you just need plenty of time, all your spare cash and of course your beloved MG, which, if you are careful and wise, will last you the season and be ready to be driven home as well.

By the fact that you are reading this book it's a safe bet that you are not in possession of an historic Bugatti, a D-type Jaguar or a Formula One racing Team. If you were, this book would be nicely on its shelf and all your problems would be big ones. As you are reading this book though, and as your attention has been attracted by the thought of actually competing in a race with your MG, a few hints on how to go about doing this might be of a little help.

Forget about rallying, grasstrack and stock car racing. There are one or two brave souls competing in classic MGs, but the former involves MG Maestros, MG Metro 6R4s and any cash that you can procure by any fair or foul means. The MGOC's MG Maestro does well in rallying; it won its class in the Cork rally and won the 1987 Mobil MG Maestro Challenge outright. It competed in the RAC Lombard Rally and was excluded after electrical problems took too long to cure and in all it cost thousands of pounds, countless man hours and much personal sacrifice. Unless you can be classed as completely bonkers and with far more money than sense, at this stage at least, stick to circuit racing and line up with fellow club members on grids at Brands Hatch, Silverstone, Donington and other top circuits.

So far I haven't put you off - and you are reaching for the telephone or note pad. A quick call to the Club Office will bring you a list of the things you need, details of how to get your RAC licence and famous medical and, of course, a set of the rules and regulations of the championship you'd like to compete in.

Yes, there's red tape; anything involving fun and excitement involves red tape. However, Club racing red tape is not that bad. You'll need an RAC competition licence and it arrives with a copy of the RAC bible, the "Blue Book". You will have hours of fun reading this just as Jackie Stewart, James Hunt and Nigel Mansell had to. You'll need to be a member of an RAC affiliated Club, but that has its own benefits too and will open the doors to other championships and perhaps other types of racing. The dreaded medical is a necessary expense as well and no NHS to bail you out here either. The prods, aaahs and just a small sample please are there to protect you, just like everyone else.

You've got your licence, you have been pronounced fit and the doctor was even polite about your extra stone or two. You now have to think about entering your first championship. Choose well - success, not failure, will quickly elude you and as the whole purpose is to have "fun", it's important to listen to advice.

Clubman racing

Yes, we all know that after a few laps practice, in "the right car", you would quickly equal and break the lap record - but just hold on and slow yourself down to a gallop. Start with a Standard Championship. It's cheaper, safer and you will learn so much more without making a total twit of yourself. Sure the MG Owners' Club has open championships and the MG Car Club has for years run excellent MG championships for standard, modified and ultra-quick MGs. Begin your racing career in one of these though and you'll be on your sixth or seventh lap as the leaders complete their tenth and the end of their and your race.

If you want to avoid the first major pitfall, do not build or convert your MG until you have carefully read the rules and regulations of the championship you have chosen. If you have wisely started with a Standard Championship, your MG will not be dramatically different to a standard road car and, more important, neither will your competitors. Thus you will have closer and more competitive racing with similar MGs and not be the last or near to the last of a lonely race.

On arrival at a race meeting you'll be wearing the right flame-proof clothes and will have a properly certified helmet. Your other carefully read information has advised you of the tome of your first practice and approximately the time of your first race. As your car sports a yellow square with an X, that's a racing 'L' plate to you, others will know that you are a virgin of the circuit and must be treated with love and care. One mistake by you and their MGs, championship points and self-preservation are in jeopardy. You are therefore granted complete consideration and given lots of helpful advice - free.

One thing you will find in MG racing, whether it be in the MG Owners' Club or MG Car Club Championships, is the total friendship and support of everyone involved. You won't win any championships in your first year; don't try to. Just go out and have fun; that's what MG racing is all about.

For more details write to MG Owners' Club Racing, 2/4 Station Road, Swavesey, Cambridgeshire and/or MG Car Club, Castle Road, Studley, Warks.

What we have aimed to do in this section is to give an overview of what racing preparation, especially for those interested in racing in the 'unmodified class', might involve. MGB racing afficionado and expert, Rae Davis of Moto-Build gives his advice.

Rae Davis, one of the three Davis brothers behind Moto-Build and one of the most knowledgeable and effective exponents of the art of racing MGBs, points out that MGBs that go out to **win** in the unmodified 'Standard Championship' class might look standard, but that appearance belies the enormous amount of hard work and some expense that has gone on beneath the skin. For a start, the cars that are competitive have been brought right down to the lower weight limit allowed. This involves fitting GRP front wings (this is allowed in the regs), the heater is removed, as is some of the trim and a GRP front spoiler is fitted. Invariably, the engine will have been 'looked at', not in a way that contravenes the rules, but in a way that ensures that everything that could possibly be done, whilst staying strictly within the regulations, will have been done. Some such modifications call for considerable ingenuity and, naturally enough, every driver who wants to be a winner will strive to gain some legal advantage over his competitors; that's the name of the game! What **no** winner will tell you, of course, is just what little 'wrinkles' he has come across, but the sorts of advantages that such changes can possibly make will be small indeed, and in the main, modifications carried out to 'unmodified' cars' engines will be common knowledge.

For instance, it is essential that an engine will have been 'blueprinted' if it is to be competitive and for most people, unless they are mechanical wizards, this involves a trip to one of the small number of tuning specialists (among which Moto-Build are one of the most prominent), to have the work carried out. Blueprinting, by the way, means completely stripping an engine and rebuilding it to exacting tolerances, ensuring that carburettors, manifolds and ports align just as they should, and that all of the inevitable compromises that have gone into producing a mass-produced engine have been ironed out. The rules allow an increase in compression ratio and reboring up to 60 thou. This is carried out as a matter of course and is, in itself, expensive! The engine will have cost £1,500 plus to build and after a season or season-and-a-half, the block will be worn and so, having already been bored out to its limit, will have to be scrapped. It is theoretically possible to fit liners to the cylinder block and start again, but Ray recommends strongly against it. The only way, if you want to stay competitive, is to start again with a new or second-hand block. Nevertheless, one very major consolation is that an expenditure of £1,500 on a full engine rebuild say, every season, is a very low price indeed to pay, relative to most other forms of motor sport where costs are simply beyond the reach of most ordinary folk.

Not surprisigly, under the circumstances, most drivers of competitive cars, those with blueprinted engines, elect not to drive their cars to and from the circuits, preferring to trailer them instead. In addition to having rather expensive engines, which the owner doesn't want to wear unnecessarily, the cars are invariably devoid of a power-sapping cooling fan and the suspension is rock hard, so the journey would not be without its complications!

But don't think that every car that runs in the 'unmodified' class is packaged in this way; it certainly isn't! There are still cars that owners use for driving to the meeting, where after a minimal amount of preparation, the car is raced and then used as transport home again. These cars, basically standard, although mostly with some of the modifications allowed and with everything set up and working correctly, will still be fun to race. According to Rae, they'll be about 10bhp down, on average, compared with those cars competing for first place, but running costs will be a lot less. They are driven by those who go racing on a limited budget and just for the fun of it, in a true spirit of amateurism which is rare in sport today, and also by those who are new to MGB racing and who want to enter the water slowly rather than diving in head first. In other words, this is a perfect way to have a go at MGB racing without having to make a major commitment, although Rae says that those who become hooked rarely are content to stay at the back of every grid and, after a season or two, are looking at more and more ways of making their cars competitive ...

However, having started by looking at what drivers do in order to make their cars go faster, it is important to remember one of the most important tips of all. It is summed up by Rae in saying that, 'In order to gain one extra second per lap through increased bhp, you will have to spend thousands of pounds; but the same extra second gained through suspension modifications will only cost you hundreds. So, it becomes obvious where the newcomer should start paying attention first.' The point Rae is making is that it is all very well being able to howl down the straight fractionally quicker and considerably poorer than you were before, but if you can't get round the twisty bits any faster when you reach them, you're never going to be a contender for the first three places. And improvements to handling come **far** cheaper than those to the engine's power output.

So what, then, is the least that you could hope to do to suspension and brakes in order to go racing? For a start, Rae claims that standard friction linings are inadequate for racing and must be replaced, front and rear, with harder, more efficent materials, the best of which, he claims, is Mintex Don M171. The standard friction materials will overheat after just a couple of laps and the driver will find the car going places it didn't oughta when the brakes fail. Then, the tyro racer must drain out all the old brake fluid and use racing brake fluid. Silicon fluid is better than the standard stuff, but for racing, use of the correct fluid is essential, otherwise the standard fluid will boil under the heavy and repeated strains demanded of it, a vapour lock will probably form in the brake line causing partial or complete brake failure and there will, once again, be an 'orf', as those who race Frazer-Nashs are prone to say. Next, the brake hoses

should be swapped for the braided 'Aeroquip' type. Standard hoses expand slightly even under normal circumstances, although on the road, it's not enough to cause any problems. When racing however, as the fluid gets hotter, the hoses become softer and expansion becomes more pronounced and the result is that the brake pedal feels spongy. Incidentally, Rae reassures that the basics of the good old 'B' braking system are more than adequate in all fundamental respects - a strong testament to a braking system designed over a quarter of a century ago! The only quibble he has concerns the tendency of the rear brakes to lock the wheels first under race track conditions. Moto-Build fit smaller wheel cylinders from one of the Mini-Coopers to overcome the problem. However, those parts of the system that remain in place, both in the braking and in the suspension department, need to be absolutely 100 per cent, for safety's sake. Similarly, it would be the height of folly to go racing in an MGB that was not totally sound and uncorroded, inside as well as out. It might well pay to make a visit to one of the specialists in order to have the car checked over **before** lavishing large quantities of hard-earned shekels upon it.

You don't **have** to do anything to the suspension in order to race but, as said before, everything in that department must be in tip-top order. The suspension modifications described in Chapter Four are generally 'de rigeur', or at least those that are allow you to retain the existing lever arms, since regulations don't permit the use of telescopic units. Rae's racing MGB has the stiffer anti-roll bar and solid bushes described in Chapter Four, 50 per cent uprated shockers and stiffer coil and leaf springs that conspire to lower the car by a dramatic two inches. In this form, the MGB goes round bends as though on rails, but it is so spine jarringly hard, that to drive it on our increasingly run down and neglected roads (we used to scoff at the French road system!), would be to invite a visit to a chiropracter!

One of the most elementary areas in which improvements can be made comes in the four small patches where the theory of the faster car makes contact with the reality of the road beneath - the tyres. Most race organisers allow the 'B' to run on the maximum of a 175 section tyre width, while MG Car Club events allow 185 rubber. However, Rae reckons that there is no contest because 185 tyres on standard rims distort, allowing excessive sidewall flexing and tyre roll. 175 section tyre stay more rigid and thus, againing according to Rae, gives better grip.

Only certain types of tyre are permitted by the sport's ruling body, the RAC (of which more anon), but the cost need not be anywhere near as great as you might think. But first a digression into what would be the ideal tyre if regulations only allowed it. In dry weather, completely bald tyres would be perfect; that's why racing cars use slicks, so that the maximum amount of rubber can be leaching itself down to the tarmac at any one time. But in the wet, oh Lordy! If you've ever seen Formula One cars caught in a sudden downpour, scrabbling around pathetically for grip and direction, like so many Bambis on ice, you'll know the importance of tyre treads in cutting through water, allowing the tyre to contact the road beneath.

So, why need not MGB race tyres cost too much? Well, if you were to to out on the race track with a brand new set of fully treaded Yamadunlops, you'd be in for an expensive surprise! New treads grip, twist and come out in handfuls, quickly wrecking the tyre. In any case, their lack of tread rigidity means that lap times will be slower than if the car was properly shod, to the tune of two to two and a half seconds per lap, Rae calculates. The serious people go to the trouble of buying new covers, then have them scrubbed so that only around 4mm of tread remains. Cost conscious drivers simply buy part-worn tyres, at low prices, to start off with. Whichever you use, it is important to remember that tyres, when racing, should be inflated to a much higher figure than would be used on the road; start with 40lb/in² and experiment from there.

Most elementary of all in the quest for the competitive 'unmodified' MGB are some of the simplest and cheapest steps of all; steps that many drivers simply forget to take. For example, the car should have its track checked and re-set after every half-a-dozen races at most, and after every race where it may have clobbered the kerb. Incorrectly set track causes tyre scrubbing and loses precious energy and thus speed/time. Even more important is the need to ensure that wheel bearings are not set too tight, that front brake calipers are backing off freely and rapidly when the brakes are released, and that the rear brake shoes are not adjusted so that they bind. Rae has shown, on the rolling road, that binding rear brakes can lose you the equivalent of three to four precious bhp before you start! As a rule of thumb, Rae advises that you should be able to push your car easily and smoothly on the flat. Just hope that you don't have to do it too often!

Having looked at some of the things you can or should do, what about some of the things you absolutely must do. First of all, you are required to have a competition licence, issued by the RAC, and secondly, satisfactorily pass a medical. Conveniently, the RAC publish the 'Blue Book', which sets out these requirements, and more; such as the types of tyres you may use, referred to earlier, and it also stipulates that your car be fitted with an approved FIA-approved roll cage, such as those made by John Aley Racing, a full harness-type seat belt and you must wear an approved crash helmet and flame-proof clothing of the correct type. Rae says that it isn't obligatory to equip your car with a fire extinguisher, but that you'd be mad not to do so. After all, you could find yourself with a small fire which you could easily put out by yourself, but the same fire **sans** fire extinguisher could lose you your car. Which brings up the question of car insurance. There isn't any, at least not while the car is on the race track, so you always have to be mentally and financially prepared for the possibility of a total write-off. If you drive on the road a car which is modified, you must notify your insurers and face up to the higher premiums, or you could find yourself illegally uninsured.

MGB racing enthusiasts claim that it is the cheapest way of having pleasure, excitement and fun, at least in public, that they know of. There are those who get the bug and go on to race in the all-consuming (well, money consuming, mainly), 'modified' class. However, beginners find the 'unmodified' Standard Championship class a financially acceptable route into racing, while top-place men find the challenge and demands of making their cars and their driving skills more competitive than the next driver's, an all absorbing one. If you are interested, you could start by writing to the MG Owners' Club and the MG Car Club at the addresses shown at the end of the article by Roche Bentley on Clubman Racing, and to the RAC Motorsport Association, Motorsport House, Riverside Park, Colnbrook, Slough SL3 0HG. **More power through your differential!**

Chapter Seven
Specialists

MG Specialists

We asked one MG specialist from the North and one from the South of England to contribute to this book. Each is among the very best in the MG world and both produce high standards of workmanship, some of which can be seen in the pages of this book, and an excellent spares supply service to boot. In addition, Moto-Build have considerable race experience and a first-class trim shop, while Murray Scott-Nelson also import rust-free MGs from the United States for sale in Europe and the UK. Both companies are run by a close-knit team; Moto-Build by brothers Ray, Graham and Darryl Davies, while Clive Murray and John Scott-Nelson have worked together since their schooldays.

Moto-Build Ltd, 328 Bath Road, Hounslow, Middlesex TW7 4HW
01-570 5342, 01-572 5437, (Mail order) 01-577 0074, (Car sales) 01-572 8733
  MG sales, parts service, restoration, racing and trim specialists

---

Murray Scott-Nelson, 16 Greenfield Road, Scarborough, North Yorkshire YO11 2LP   0723 361227
  Cars located to order, commission sales, MG parts, sales, service and restoration

---

Specialists and manufacturers

Acoustikit, Unit 2, Lowfield Road, Shaw Heath, Stockport SK3 8JS   061-480 3791
  Ready-to-fit sound deadening kits

Aeroquip, Think Automotive Ltd, 292 Worton Road, Isleworth, Middlesex TW7 6EL   01-568 1172
  High performance brake hose components

A&I (Peco) Acoustics Ltd, Sandford Street, Birkenhead, Merseyside L41 1AZ   051-647 6041
  High performance exhaust systems, and air filters

Aldon Automotive Ltd, Breener Industrial Estate, Station Drive, Brierley Hill, West Midlands   0384 78508
  Engine tuning specialists, two-litre MGB engine, new ignition distributors, rolling road

---

John Aley Racing Ltd, 7 Lime Tree Close, Hessett, Bury St. Edmunds IP30 9AY   0359 70954
  'Aleybars', competition and road-use roll cages

Automec Equipment and Parts Ltd., Stanbridge Road, Leighton Buzzard, Bedfordshire LU7 8QP
  Copper brake lines and Silicone Brake Fluid   0525 376608 & 375775

Autoplas, 90 Main Road, Hawkwell, Essex SS5 4JH   0702 202795
  Suppliers of body kits and interior accessories

Black and Decker, Westpoint, The Grove, Slough, Berkshire SL1 1QQ   0753 74277
  Manufacturers of a huge range of professional and DIY tools

---

Blaupunkt, Robert Bosch Ltd., PO Box 98, Broadwater Park, Denham, Uxbridge UB9 5HJ   0895 833633
  Full range of in-car entertainment components and systems

Branyl Ltd., Unit 17, Kimberley Way, Redbrook Lane Trading Estate, Brereton, Rugeley WS15 1RE088 94 76528/9
  Self-adhesive car stripes, badges and decals

Britax-Excelsior Ltd., Chertsey Road, Byfleet, Weybridge, Surrey KT14 7AW   09323 41121
  Child safety seats and front and rear seat belts

Burlen Fuel Systems, Spitfire House, Castle Road, Salisbury, Wiltshire SP1 3SA   0722 21777
  'Original' SU carburettors, manifolds and fuel pumps

Carflow Products (UK) Ltd., Leighton Road, Leighton Buzzard, Bedfordshire LU7 7LA   0525 383543
  Wheel clean discs and locking wheel nuts

Clarke Group, Lower Clapton Road, London E5 0RN
01-986 8231
Huge range of workshop equipment, including welders, compressors, jacks, hoists, etc.

Comma Oil & Chemicals Ltd., Comma Works, Denton Industrial Area, Lower Range Road, Gravesend, Kent DA12 2QX
0474 64311
A full range of valeting products for the private and commercial market

Duckhams Oils, Duckhams House, 157/159 Masons Hill, Bromley, Kent BR2 9HU
01-290 0600
Producers of high performance oils and lubricants for high performance engines

Cruise U.K. Ltd, Sherborne Garage, Town Lane, Idle, Bradford
0274 618756
UK distributor for 'after market' Cruise Control

Artur Fischer (UK) Ltd., Hithercroft Road, Wallingford, Oxon OX10 9AT
0491 33000
C-Box range of quality cassette holders

Glasurit Valentine, Automotive Refinish, BASF Coatings + Inks Ltd., Coldham Mill Road, West Drayton, Middlesex UB7 7AS
0895 442233
Specialists in Automotive finish paints for the DIY (Valentine) and professional (Glasurit) markets

Hella Ltd., Daventry Road Industrial Estate, Banbury, Oxon OX16 7JU
0295 272233
A wide range of general parts and accessories

Kenlowe Ltd., Burchetts Green, Maidenhead, Berkshire SL6 6QU
062 882 3303
Electrically-driven engine cooling fans. The 'Hotstart' engine pre-heater

K.E.W. Industry Ltd., K.E.W. House, Gilwilly Industrial Estate, Penrith, Cumbria CA11 9BN
0768 65777
K.E.W. Hobby Washer and accessories

Kimble Engineering, 33 Highfield Road, Hall Green, Birmingham B28 0EV
021-777 2011
MGB aluminium rocker covers

Lenham Motor Company, 47 West Street, Harrietsham, Kent
0622 859570
Top quality MGB hardtops

Link-Sedan Ltd., Bone Lane, Newbury, Berkshire RG14 5TD
0635 44796
Wide range of automotive accessories for the DIY enthusiast, customiser and family motorist

Mitchell Marketing, 140 Leicester Road, Wigston, Leicester LE8 1DS
0533 881522
Corroless products, full range of unique rust proofing fluids and paints. Also Slick 50, Protectalines and Backflashes

Mintex Don Ltd., P.O. Box 18, Cleckheaton, West Yorkshire BD19 3UJ
0274 875711
High-performance brake and clutch lining manufacturers

Moto-Lita Ltd, Thruxton Racing Circuit, Thruxton Airport, Nr Andover, Hants SP11 8PW
026477 2811
Manufacturers and distributors of Moto-Lita steering wheels

Harry Moss International Ltd., 2a Lancaster Road, Wimbledon Village, London SW19 5DP
01-946 366301
Moss Professional Series accessories including central door locking

Pacet Products and Co. Ltd., Wyebridge House, Cores End Road, Bourne End, Buckinghamshire SL8 5HH
06285 26754
Oil coolers

Piranha Ignition Systems Ltd., Unit 5, Carlisle Street, Lower Audley Industrial Estate, Blackburn, Lancs BB1 1BN
0254 680187
Optical electronic ignition systems

Pirelli Limited, Derby Road, Burton on Trent, Staffordshire DE13 0BH
0283 66301
Car, truck and motorcycle tyres and tubes

Plastic Padding Ltd., Wooburn Industrial Park, Wooburn Green, High Wycombe, Buckinghamshire HP10 0PE
06285 27912
Full range of glass fibre and fillers for bodywork

Richard Grant Motor Accessories Ltd., Moor End, Eaton Bray, Nr. Dunstable, Bedfordshire LU6 2JQ
0525 220342
Wide range of body accessories

Robert Bosch Ltd., P.O. Box 98, Broadwater Park, Denham, Uxbridge UB9 5HJ
0895 833633
Wide range of spark plugs and car electrical accessories

Specialists

Rokee Limited, Unit 18, Central Trading Estate, Staines, Middlesex TW18 4XE Wooden dash and door trims, in various woods	0784 62588
Spax Ltd, Telford Road, Bicester, Oxon Standard and uprated lever-arm shock absorbers, telescopic kits, suspension tuning kits	0869 244771
Spectra Automotive and Engineering Products plc, Treloggan Industrial Estate, Newqay, Cornwall TR7 2SX Aerosol spray paint	0637 871171
Sykes-Pickavant Ltd., Kilnhouse Lane, Lytham St. Annes, Lancashire FY8 3DU Manufacturers of DIY automotive and industrial service tools and Speedline hand tools	0253 721291
V8 Conversion Company, Oak Farm, Green Street Green, Orpington, Kent MGB conversions to Rover/Buick V8. Conversion kits supplied	0689 58716

Clubs and Magazines

American MGB Association, PO Box 11401, Chicago, Illinois 60611, USA	
American MGC Register, PO Box 2816, Setauket, New York 11733, USA	
Central Ohio MGB Association, Mike & Lisa Schon, 318 Reber Avenue, Lancaster, Ohio 43130, USA	
Cleo Walton & Rudi Landrum, 16416 Oak Creek, Lane 6, Bedford, Texas 76022, USA	
Ken Bottini, Treasurer & Membership Chairman, 12835 North East 36th, Bellevue, Washington 98005, USA	
MG Car Club Newcastle Inc, Mrs Fran Hodgson (Secretary), PO Box 62A, Newcastle 2300, USA	
MG Car Club, PO Box 251, Studley, Warwicks B80 7AT	052785 3666
MG Enthusiast Magazine, PO Box 11, Dewsbury, West Yorkshire WF12 7UZ	0924 499261
MG, MG, MG. Milwaukee & Great Lakes, MG Motorcar Group, 9832N Range Line Road, Mequon, Wisconsin 53092, USA	
MG Owners' Club, 2-4 Station Road, Swavesey, Cambs CB4 5QZ General Club business: **0954 31125**. Special offers: **0954 31318**. Insurance: **0480 300023/3000717**	
MGCC DE Centro, Larry Berger, 19600 Crystal Rock Drive, 24 Germantown, Maryland 20874, USA	
Philadelphia MG Club, Steve Harding, 1913-D Darby Road, Havertown, Philadelphia 19083, USA	
Rocky Mountain MGCC, PO Box 152, Denver, Colorado 80201, USA	
San Diego MG Club, PO Box 112111, San Diego, California 92111, USA	
Tom Le Blanc, 190 Lyric Lane, Santa Barbara, California 93110, USA	